For the first time ever, Bruce A. Paster and Albert J. Viscio, the founding par of the Strategic Leadership Practic Booz•Allen & Hamilton, one of the w top management and technology consulting firms, offer a comprehensive strategy for business survival and success. At the heart of this landmark work is a new model for the 21st-century corporation that will bring growth and prosperity. *The Centerless Corporation* goes beyond the lines and boxes of today's rigid organizations. It defines new relationships which make traditional corporate center, command-and-control models obsolete.

Pasternack and Viscio, two of the most respected and gifted thinkers in today's business world, believe that the principles and organizational models used in most companies, which have evolved for well over one hundred years, are now outmoded. In today's double-speed, highly complex world the conventional model does not deliver. Technology is tying the world more closely together; markets are becoming more global, competition is based more and more on capabilities and knowledge, and demographics are altering the composition and preferences of the work force.

The upheaval in the corporate world is costly in both human and financial terms as firms try to cope with change. In response to greater complexity, many of the world's most prominent companies, such as AT&T and Westinghouse, have streamlined their portfolios, and most have undergone significant downsizing and restructuring programs. Increasingly, disappointing company performance results in a highly publicized replacement of the CEO. The basic corporate model needs an overhaul.

*The Centerless Corporation* is a compelling model that presents practical solutions for how to build a more effective global organization, develop capabilities for growth, formulate a New People Partnership with employees, implement a learning organization, and cultivate leaders at every level in the organization. The foundation of many of this book's concepts was developed by a Booz•Allen & Hamilton task force charged with studying emerging trends and alternatives for large corporations to cope with the new business environment.

*(continued on back flap)*

# THE CENTERLESS CORPORATION

## A NEW MODEL FOR TRANSFORMING YOUR ORGANIZATION FOR GROWTH AND PROSPERITY

# BRUCE A. PASTERNACK
## AND ALBERT J. VISCIO

SIMON & SCHUSTER

SIMON & SCHUSTER
Rockefeller Center
1230 Avenue of the Americas
New York, NY 10020

SIMON & SCHUSTER and colophon are registered trademarks
of Simon & Schuster Inc.
Designed by Irving Perkins Associates, Inc.

Manufactured in the United States of America

1   3   5   7   9   10   8   6   4   2

Library of Congress Cataloging-in-Publication Data
Pasternack, Bruce A.
The centerless corporation: a new model for transforming your
organization for growth and prosperity / Bruce A. Pasternack
and Albert J. Viscio.
p.   cm.
Includes bibliographical references.
1. Organizational change. 2. Management. I. Viscio, Albert J.  II. Title.
HD58.8.P368   1998
658.4'063—dc21      97-32984   CIP
ISBN 0-684-83835-4

# ACKNOWLEDGMENTS

**WE** are deeply grateful to the many people who provided inspiration, support, guidance, and ideas for this book. It is a special privilege to work with an extraordinary group of partners and staff at Booz•Allen & Hamilton. We learn from them every day and enjoy our professional affiliation and personal relationships. Our support from our colleagues at Booz•Allen & Hamilton was essential to this book. We would like to thank all of them. In particular, our Chairman and CEO, Bill Stasior, and our President, Brian Dickie, were enthusiastic and steadfast in their encouragement. The firm's Worldwide Commercial Leadership Team endorsed the concepts and funding of Booz•Allen's Strategic Leadership Practice which is the new organizational home within our company for many of the topics covered in this book.

Our innovation team, devoted to the concept of a Global Core, helped pioneer many of the concepts of the new corporate center. These include Deanne Aguirre, Heidi Amponsem, Barrie Berg, Hugh Dickinson, Jorge Forteza, David Howe, Daniel Jaouiche, Gigi Jorissen, Shelley Keller, Klaus Mattern, Luiz Maurer, John McCarter, Carlos Payan, Deven Sharma, Karen Van Nuys, and Martin Waldenstrom. Shelley Keller was especially helpful in developing the ideas and cases for Chapter Three, The Triumph of People Power. Chuck Lucier, Jan Torsilieri, and Terry Thygessen were instrumental in helping to develop many of the concepts discussed in chapter four, Mining the Riches in Knowledge. Martin Waldenstrom deserves special recognition for his originality in developing many of the Global Core concepts, and his willingness to test these ideas with his clients.

We would also like to recognize the contribution of those partners who were instrumental in sharing their experiences, providing a good sounding board, and helping test many of the concepts in real client work. Among them are Paul Anderson, Paul Branstad, Chris Dallas-Feeney, Etienne Deffarges, Brian Dickie, Cyrus Freidheim, John Harbison, Walter Jewett, Paul Kocourek, Dan Lewis, Chuck Lucier, Joe Mallory, Jay Marshall, John McCarter, Helmut Meier, Gary Neilson, and Joe Nemec. Jim O'Toole, Managing Director of Booz•Allen & Hamilton's Strategic Leadership Center and former Executive Vice President of the Aspen Institute, provided important critiques and suggestions.

We owe a special debt of gratitude to Booz•Allen's professional staff who worked long and hard on providing research and analyses for the book's contents—Gerard Cunningham, Peter McWilliams, Lisa Sellards, Terry Thygesen, and Jan Torsilieri. Our support staff—Anna Barker, Ardiss Ekroth, Brenda Keegan, Lori Patrick, Amy Pratt, Amy Matthews, Josee Fonseca, and Robin Swanson—assembled the text and graphics, verified the facts and sources.

There are many others who provided guidance along the way. Booz•Allen & Hamilton's Advisory Board reviewed and critiqued many ideas in early form—we received considerable help from Bob Bauman, Chairman, British Aerospace PLC; Oscar Bernardes, CEO, Bunge International Ltd.; Jürgen Dormann, Chairman, Hoechst AG; Larry Fuller, Chairman and CEO, Amoco Corporation; Henry Kissinger, Chairman and CEO of Kissinger and Associates; Yoh Kurosawa, President, The Industrial Bank of Japan Ltd.; Drew Lewis, retired Chairman and CEO, Union Pacific Corporation; Yoshio Okawara, Executive Adviser, Keidanren; Didier Pineau-Valencienne, President Directeur General, Schneider SA; John Prescott, CEO, Broken Hill Proprietary Company Ltd.; Dick Rosenberg, retired Chairman and CEO of BankAmerica; Bob Shapiro, Chairman and CEO, Monsanto; The Rt. Hon. Lord Young of Graffham PC, Chairman, Young Associates Ltd.

Many of our friends and colleagues in the academic community provided helpful suggestions, including Professors Sumantra Ghoshal and Costas Markides of the London Business School; Professors Jeff Pfeffer, John Roberts, and Charles O'Reilly, and Dean Mike Spence of the Stanford Business School; and Professor Nitin Nohria from the Harvard Business School.

Sonny Kleinfield was a joy to work with as he provided lively, informative, timely, and wise counsel and support in the development of the book. His creativity, insight, and ability to mesh our two writing styles were especially helpful. Joel Kurtzman, editor of the *Journal of Strategy and Business,* lit the fire to have us play in the marketplace of ideas. We owe special thanks to our editor at Simon & Schuster, Dominick Anfuso, his capable and personable assistant Ana DeBevoise, and our agent, Richard Pine.

All of this help and guidance would not have meant anything without the support of our clients, who make management consulting such a challenging, exciting, and rewarding profession. Our clients provide us with the opportunity to tackle demanding problems, to anticipate the future, to stretch our imagination, and to innovate new approaches to management in these difficult times. They question, respond, enlighten, test, and make going to work fun. The hundreds of clients we have served are truly an exceptional group of business leaders.

Finally, and most importantly, our families allowed us to intrude on their time and gave us the inspiration to do our best work. We take special pride in our children: Joanne, Laura, and Dan Pasternack, and Jamie and Peter Viscio. We encourage them to strive to be the very best at whatever they do in life and to make a difference to those whose lives they touch.

*To our families, Joanne, Laura, and Dan Pasternack, and Adrienne, Jamie, and Peter Viscio; friends; colleagues at Booz•Allen; and our clients who made this book possible.*

# CONTENTS

# PREFACE

**THIS** book was born out of upheaval. It is rooted in our experiences working with top executives at large corporations around the world trying to grapple with the turmoil in their business environments. In our interactions we noticed a decided change in what executives wanted. While still mightily concerned with cost structure, business process reengineering, and maximizing operational effectiveness, they had shifted their focus to issues of how to be more effective global organizations, how to build capabilities for faster growth, how to attract and retain the very best people, how to become a true learning organization, and how to develop leaders at all levels in the company.

The heightened interest in these sweeping issues was coming at a time of very specific changes in the business climate, changes that question the fundamentals of how companies have been constructed and managed for most of this century. Technology, especially in terms of computing and communications, has radically altered the requirements for building and managing a successful business. Distance is becoming a shrinking barrier. Geographic proximity is no longer essential for people to work together. At times, in fact, it may be an inhibitor to getting the best work done.

Competition is now based more on capabilities than assets. Firms compete, not by acquiring market share, but by doing things consistently better than the competition, driving the marketplace, and creating more business space for themselves. Knowledge and learning are now critical elements of success. As a result, companies are becoming more aware of processes for building and using knowledge.

Stepped-up emphasis on knowledge and capabilities means that people become even more important, and the relationship between the company and its people is changing rapidly. Firms need access to explicit skills, which in today's fast-moving world become obsolete so much quicker. What should firms do to ensure access to skills? What should they do with people whose skills no longer match the needs? And how does one address evolving demographics? Dual career couples are the norm. Family values and personal time are at a premium. Old-style employee loyalty is dead.

Booz•Allen & Hamilton is a global technology and management consulting firm. Through our encounters with our clients, we recognized a common thread across these types of issues. This prompted us to create a firm-wide task force to understand the issues better, to assess the implications to our clients, and to develop a perspective on what companies should do. This activity was part of our own knowledge program. The task force included partners and staff from the United States, Europe, Asia, and Latin America, and represented a cross section of industry practices. The team was given a full-time staff. The research lasted for over a year. It was a major investment of the firm.

The initial charter of the task force was to look at the evolving role of the corporate center. Early in the process, it became obvious to us that we had to broaden the scope to include the other elements of the corporation—its business units, governance, and services. We drew from case studies of client engagements and from desktop research. The work was refined by constant testing in the marketplace of ideas.

What resulted from the massive foundation of knowledge assembled by the task force were the outlines of a radically different corporate model. We came to call it the Centerless Corporation.

In the course of our research, we examined a landscape of organizational experiments where companies pioneered novel approaches to deal with the increasing speed and complexity of both their external business environment and their internal workings. It was out of that experimentation that we saw the emergence of this new organizational model. However, we did not find the new model. Rather we saw indications of pieces of it across a growing number of companies. We stitched this mosaic together and in that way defined the Centerless Corporation.

We found that large firms, in particular, have been facing almost insurmountable challenges to transform. Many have suffered through repeated reengineerings and downsizings, and yet failed to thrive. The failure of many of these improvement efforts has been the topic of recent studies which have shown that, for the most part, much of the pain of downsizing was either ineffective or insufficient to revive performance over a sustained period. Something important was missing from the solutions.

The biggest target of restructuring has been the corporate center. Some of the efforts resulted in thousands of people being moved out. Staff reductions of 50 percent and more have become the norm. In fact, now we see a backlash against removing capabilities of corporate groups.

Wave after wave of downsizings have been accompanied by significant restructuring of corporate portfolios. Current conventional wisdom dictates that firms should streamline and simplify their portfolios. Today we are witnessing a dismantling of the corporate world. The volume of spin-offs from large corporations more than doubled during the period 1994 to 1996, when it exceeded $50 billion.

As we delved deeper into the subject, it became clear to us that complexity is really the critical factor. While the size of today's corporation is approaching staggering proportions, the ability of management to achieve their desired results is weakening. Again and again, we hear the question, "Can a large company grow at a fast pace?" The solution being promulgated by many gurus is to get smaller. Shed businesses and focus. But guess what? We see many focused businesses struggling at the same time that some highly diversified ones are flourishing.

It seemed to us that the limiting factor in successfully growing and globalizing is not complexity itself. Rather, it is the tools businesses have to deal with it. The current paradigm under which businesses are built and run is a century old. Modified, yes, but still old. While there is value in something that is tried and true, there is no value in something that is obsolete. The next generation of leading firms will be the ones best able to deal with complexity. They will step outside the endless debate of centralization or decentralization and will do both at the same time.

Leading firms will infuse the means to unleash the potential of their organizations by changing the roles within the organization. We hope we can help show them the way. In this book, we will introduce new terminology like "key enablers" and the "Global Core" to help explain our new model. We will describe new organizational roles, how to develop the leaders acquired to bring these companies the practical guidance they need, and the steps to be taken to transform a company into the Centerless Corporation. To be sure, all of this will require a fresh mind-set, but we believe there is little choice. From all that we see, we expect that those that become a Centerless Corporation will be the winners and the leaders in the coming decades.

# CHAPTER ONE

# A MODEL FOR TOMORROW

**OUR** favorite company these days is GloCorp. In almost every sense, it's a pretty remarkable place. Among its many noteworthy achievements, it is the first corporation to reach a stunning $500 billion in annual revenues. In an age when so many companies are shredding their work forces and pruning their business portfolios, GloCorp has been doing the exact opposite. It can't hire people fast enough. Through steady diversification, it has achieved double-digit growth in revenues and return to shareholders for ten consecutive years.

Its strategy is not unique, and some would chastise it for pursuing approaches that run counter to the focused, asset-shedding habits of the 1990s. GloCorp is already engaged in seven major lines of business, and there are constant rumors that it is contemplating others. As it is, the company makes everything from car parts to consumer electronics, computers, fabricated metals, and paper plates. The portfolio may seem absurdly broad, but in truth all of the businesses are based on only a few key capabilities in microelectronics and process control.

GloCorp's strategy has been to expand primarily through a vast array of alliances and joint ventures. Nearly three-quarters of its revenues flow from two hundred alliances. Many of these unions have been essential to the company's diversification. For example, the alliance with Sunny Corp stands as the world's leader in hand-held video players using optical cartridges; the venture with Boxco is the foremost producer of recyclable cardboard in Latin America.

GloCorp is one of the first genuinely global companies. Its headquarters has changed continents three times in the past fifteen years, gravitating from Atlanta to Hong Kong to London. Each new chief executive has understandably chosen to operate out of his primary country of residence. For GloCorp, this has not meant much adjustment. When you visit GloCorp, don't ask for directions to the corporate center. There is none. Instead of relying on one of those plump corporate centers heavy in cumbersome bureaucracy, GloCorp has its chief executive and his senior executives work out of something known as the Global Core. That's a lean, nimble entity that does only the things that the individual businesses themselves cannot. It delegates and distributes everything else.

The Global Core consists of little more than the CEO and his immediate team. Corporate-level activities are performed by just two hundred people, and they have been dispersed to more than twenty countries for the past decade. This distributed Core gives GloCorp a decided edge over its competitors. Just recently, GloCorp managed to get the inside track on an equipment deal with a Latin American water purification system because it was already a household name through its local presence in electronics.

Why is GloCorp so special? It has recognized that success is really driven by people, knowledge-sharing processes, and a coherent business model. It's quite clear that the company is an immensely pleasurable place to work—it has palpable energy and we see more smiling faces than anywhere else we go—and it's not hard to understand why. GloCorp gives dignity and meaning to work. It has empowered its line managers all over the world, deemphasized corporate headquarters, yet provided a firm foundation of people and resource allocation, knowledge transfer, financial controls, and a business system that operates independently from organization charts and hierarchy. One could describe it as being a centerless, though hardly a leaderless or headless, enterprise. It is driven by its core values.

If we didn't already have good jobs, we'd be thinking of applying to GloCorp ourselves.

There is one problem. GloCorp doesn't exist. We just wish it did. For it is exactly the sort of organization that we envision as the company of tomorrow. In every respect, it exemplifies a radical new business model that we have devised over the past few years. We call it the Centerless Corporation. This model revises old verities and creates a company that thinks and behaves much differently from anything that we now know.

Elements of everything described in our hypothetical GloCorp exist in some corporation right now. We have seen these elements at work in one company or another, but not operating together, completely and seamlessly, in any one organization. But we know that they can and that the corporations that successfully adopt this model can gain a virtually impregnable competitive position. We very much feel that the Centerless Corporation is the prescription for the successful, growing, motivated, and energized business of the next millennium.

Before we get into further details of our new model, let's consider the current state of things. If you take a hard look at how your business works, you'll see that it's arranged in the same old tightly bound command-and-control model that has endured since the mills of Britain more than a century ago. Sure, technology may have made it flatter and larger, but there's still that creaky nineteenth-century notion of a headquarters staff barking orders from the top.

Guess what? That model is dead.

Even though students in business schools have been cautioned for years to forswear the command-and-control mentality, they aren't really taught what to substitute for it. And so while most chief executives will insist that they believe in an open and sharing leadership philosophy, one need only look at the organizational chart to see how emphatically vertical it is. And if it's vertical, then it's command-and-control. The problem is, executives fall back on this trusty and familiar approach because they lack a viable alternative.

In today's complicated, double-speed world, however, the conventional model simply doesn't deliver, leaving companies bruised, weary, and grasping for alternatives. It reminds us of one of those carnival fun houses, so convoluted and layered that you wind up wandering around endlessly, bumping help-lessly into mirrors and being blown about by sudden gusts of compressed air, all the while getting nowhere. The evidence is everywhere in the acute crisis of confidence and self-consciousness being experienced by the leaders of many of the world's biggest and best corporations. Business executives are being assailed from every direction for downsizing their work forces and for supposedly deciding that the only way to make money is to sell divisions and shuck people. And the reason for this disarray is much deeper and more fundamental than al-most anyone realizes.

It doesn't have to go on. This book introduces a dynamic new beginning for corporations—a new model, new language, new concepts, new rules, and new expectations for growth, value creation, and profit-making. Quite frankly, our hope is that its principles will change the way executives think and run their businesses and will dictate who the winners and losers will be in the new world. Properly applied, it should build companies that won't need to condense their work forces, but will be forced to hire more people.

Granted, that is promising quite a lot. But as part of the research program at Booz•Allen & Hamilton, one of the most elaborate investigations of corporate behavior, we have stud-ied hundreds of the premier companies in the world and how they are structured, function, and perform. We have inter-viewed at length many of the world's foremost and most in-ventive chief executives. This multilevel research effort is based both on case studies of individual companies and on empirical research. It is informed by academic inquiry and our own links to a stellar international network of universities and scholars.

This exhaustive reservoir of work and experience has en-abled us to recognize startling things about the challenges that lie before us and the ways to meet them—given us a new divining rod for growth and dominance. It boldly demon-strates that the classic business model that has dictated the structure of every company from General Motors to Microsoft is so at odds with contemporary economic currents that it must and will disappear. Its life engines have ebbed. In our view, corporations are overstructured, overcontrolled, and overmanaged—but underled in terms of the people at the top concentrating on that handful of real leadership tasks that will bring success in the future.

So where does that leave us? Our research has led us to an entirely new model, a model where most of the key missions of the organization are distributed to the myriad individual pieces and unity comes from the vigor of people and the free flow of knowledge, not a burdensome central headquarters. Executives fear that if they shed their command mentality, they will lose control. In our model, we believe they can relinquish a good portion of that command and actually achieve more control. The Centerless Corporation reinvents the corporation, with youthful panache.

We have been sharing this new information with our clients and assiduously guiding them through a fundamental transformation of the ways their companies work.

## THE ANSWER TO TURBULENCE

Clearly, there is a new world upon us, an all-out, cutthroat battle for territory, winner take all. It is a world of greater complexity, one that is more global and in which the pace of change is swifter. It is a world in which corporations are becoming open networks or systems of specialized parts, more reliant on knowledge and alliances. Through our daily contact with chief executives of the world's most prosperous companies, we hear again and again how they are confused and are vainly looking for a business configuration better suited to the vagaries of these turbulent times. John Browne, the chief executive of British Petroleum, one of the world's largest and most diversified oil companies and a company with which we work, has asked, "How do I and my top management team create value in managing such a global enterprise?"

Meanwhile, John Prescott, the managing director of BHP, Australia's largest company, asked us to help him determine how to "equip the company for growth." These questions, simple though they may sound, represent a rethinking of the concept of the corporation. For some companies, they have become questions of life or death. What they disclose is the degree to which senior management, even at successful companies, is searching for something substantial and new.

Many CEOs have told us of their discomfort with the downsizings of the last decades, with their human and resource costs and negative impact on morale. They are searching for answers to questions such as how they should respond to legitimate concerns about their reductions in work force in times of record profits and soaring stock prices. How do they reconcile the economic responsibility of creating wealth with social responsibility? How do they justify the decline in real wages with record incentive payouts for executives? How do they attract and motivate employees when the promise of long-term employment is gone forever? How do they accomplish globalization when it means reducing commitments to traditional markets and uprooting families? How do they approach a business environment in which new products and competitors are emerging with blinding speed?

All the barbecuing of corporations because of downsizing misses an important point. We see this reengineering as graphic evidence that the old principles no longer work in the new age. It is an emergency-room procedure for a patient that should never have become ill. While it is certainly true that many people have had their lives disrupted because of the upheaval in the economy, the real problem is a ruinously dysfunctional mismatch between today's business environment and the classic business model. We believe the failure that caused these societal disruptions—disruptions that are far from over—is a conceptual one. Businesses have reached the old model's limits with respect to complexity. Although total employment may continue to grow, without the correct business model in place we will find more boom and bust in employment of individual companies.

In the coming years, new business models won't be exceptional. Indeed, we feel it is vitally important that corporations convert to a new model early, intelligently, and compassionately, or else pay a huge price in a fiercely and relentlessly competitive marketplace. Quite simply, the wrong model may transform a company into the vehicle of its own death.

The big question is, What is the right model for today's environment? How do you implement it? How do you lead it?

## A LUG NUT IN AN INNER TUBE

Imagine a corporation that has a core but not a center. Imagine a corporation that is built around resources (people, knowledge, capabilities) rather than the assets lined up on financial balance sheets. Imagine a corporation that is characterized by the interdependence rather than the independence of its parts. Imagine a corporation that manages its people with a relationship that we call the New People Partnership rather than downsizing lists. Imagine a corporation with a Knowledge Department and a Chief Knowledge Officer. This is the Centerless Corporation.

In the Centerless Corporation, roles rather than organization get revamped. The real answer to today's daunting challenges lies in a model based on the same building blocks of the traditional corporation but with fresh functions for those building blocks. It lies in new ways of treating people, forging linkages, and deploying knowledge. Accustomed ideas are replaced by unaccustomed ones. It is our belief that this new model imparts propulsive energy previously untapped and permits the process of growth to start up once again.

If you were to draw a simple sketch of the Centerless Corporation, it would look like a lug nut surrounded by an inner tube (see Exhibit 1). The four corners of the lug nut are the Global Core, the Business Units, Governance, and Services. The inner tube represents a sort of free-flowing glue that contains People, Knowledge, and Coherence.

## EXHIBIT 1: CENTERLESS CORPORATION

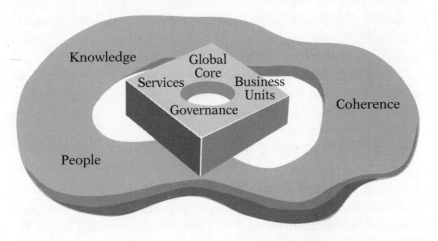

The traditional corporate model focuses on linear chains of command to govern independent and relatively isolated entities. The structure is hierarchical, with a large corporate and division staff, centralized functions, and self-sufficient divisions. It is multidimensional along major product lines.

The Centerless Corporation is pancake flat with a network of interdependent business units and strategic alliances managed by group executives. It is not horizontal per se, but rather nonlinear, meaning that rather than everything flowing up and down it flows in whatever direction it is most effective for it to go. There are different structures for different products and geographies in line with specific needs. There is an absolute minimal staff at the corporate and group level. Staff functions are placed in the business units, a services unit, or outsourced. This arrangement allows firms to compete with their full set of capabilities no matter where these are housed in the organization. What's more, these capabilities come together without the hub-and-spoke process found in most corporations today. Best practices and knowledge flow freely, finding their most productive use. The result is a more open and interdependent corporation.

The most striking thing about this model is, as its name implies, there is no center. In our concept of the corporation, there is no longer a need for a center in the familiar sense.

Instead, the real center of the Centerless Corporation is an extended leadership team. The model is leadership driven, because management is not enough anymore. The world moves too rapidly for any company to rely heavily on what to do and how to do it. In the Centerless Corporation, leadership is spread throughout the pieces of the company to match the way the company works.

The heart of the Centerless Corporation is what we call the Global Core, which is a revolutionary overhaul of the old corporate center or headquarters. It is global in the sense that it is responsible for key missions across the entire corporation. It is a core because it is meant to impart value to all of the other elements of the model, and not simply add excessive and needless overhead. It is not a center because the execution of its missions is distributed across the innumerable pieces of the corporation. The global nature of business makes it imperative that companies perform many Core activities close to where they are needed. Technology enables this to happen. The Core's role is to add value where the business cannot, with the "burden of proof" for what activities it performs resting entirely on the Core.

The Global Core is a bare bones operation. It consists solely of the CEO, his team, and only those services necessary to add value to the corporation. There are no centralized services. For instance, there is a human resources component in the Global Core, but it deals strictly with high-level strategy, leadership development, and allocation of key people, while things like payroll and benefits administration are carried out in the Business Units. It has a public affairs component, but it deals just with corporate identity, not with brand management. But while the Core is far smaller than the old corporate center, it has high leverage in the things it does. Its members work cooperatively as a team rather than hunkering in functional silos.

To a large extent, the Centerless Corporation represents a

mind-set change as much as anything else. It does not so much look radically different as it acts radically different.

## FROM WOOLEN MILLS TO MICROSOFT

Some perspective.

The current business model was created in the woolen mills and iron founderies of Britain more than two centuries ago. It was refined in the United States as the railroads grew to span the continent and, finally, defined precisely by GM's Alfred Sloan in the 1920s. This model, described vividly by Harvard historian Alfred Chandler and by management theorist Peter Drucker, was essentially a rigid, mechanical model designed to cope with simple mass-market businesses—in many cases single-line businesses. In the era of dirt roads, protected markets, nonexistent regulations, centralized financial markets, and closely held stock, the command-and-control model worked quite well. A few men at the top of the organization could control huge sectors of the economy and mobilize resources on a massive scale. In its embryonic days, the command-and-control model was sufficiently robust to open the country and much of the world, to new—albeit almost identical—products. As such, it was able to lift almost half the world out of abject poverty and into the middle class by the beginning of the 1960s.

Traditionally, debate over the "center" revolved around the matter of centralization or decentralization. It was a case of individual independence at the level of one or of many. The concept of the center connotes interdependence and connectivity. We feel that the flip-flopping between more and less centralization is a fruitless effort and is based on a flawed concept of how each piece of the corporation adds value.

Over the years, the basic model has evolved in a number of crucial aspects—it is flatter, larger, and appreciably more far-flung than before. But in many respects these changes have been a matter of cosmetics. The essential functions are unchanged. Responsibility for corporate strategy, finance, human resources, and policy is centralized in headquarters of varying sizes. Operations—whether mining, manufacturing, or services—are usually located in business units with various levels of autonomy. Business units—and sometimes even the headquarters itself—are often subdivided by region, country, or continent with differing rules, regulations, and sometimes laws dictating the way business is conducted in each of these areas. Sitting on top of this is a board of directors and a chairman who are responsible for making certain that the interests of the shareholder are served. This is the very model that P&G adopted at the outset in the 1830s, and it is the same model that helped Bill Gates when he cofounded Microsoft a little more than two decades ago.

The world, of course, looks much different than it did when the basic business model came into being. Consumers insist on ever greater variety in the goods and services they buy. (Henry Ford's black Model T would be nothing more than a specialty item today, not the mass-market product it once was.) Trade barriers and regulations are less of a market inhibitor today than in the past. Shareholders are more restless and vocal. Industries are restructuring at a breakneck pace.

Although the basic business model has survived, even thrived, for generations, such changes in the economic environment have significantly chipped away at its effectiveness. But two changes in particular have recently conspired to assure its demise. These are globalization, which has stretched the model to the limits of control, and the telecommunication revolution, which has called into question the notion of command.

These two changes in the way business is conducted go hand in hand. E-mail, Lotus Notes, Internet, intranet, various types of centralized and distributed computing, and video and telephone conferencing were supposed to help headquarters keep track of what was happening anywhere in the global field. No activity, however slight, would go unknown. That was what the theory promised. Using this technology, so the story went, savvy CEOs would be able to keep an eye on all the disparate elements of the company and be ready to lend a hand when it was needed, or sort out a thorny problem when it occurred. Using this technology, a CEO and the top team back at headquarters would be able to spot when a business unit was off strategy, and gently nudge it back on course. The CEO, in this model, would become a kind of electronic helmsman glued to readouts and dials as the business was piloted past the shoals and into the wind. The world would grow bigger, but no matter. Technology would make it manageable. Centralized command-and-control would continue unabated, the superior way to run a company.

## THE OLD BUSINESS MODEL CONFRONTS REALITY

Reality did not quite play out that way. Today, instead of a helmsman piloting a craft, the CEO of global companies occupies a place that is more like a node on a decentralized electronic network. This network is supposed to link a complex field of coordinated—and often uncoordinated—activities. Companies, in the real world, resemble that old engineer's joke about helicopters: thousands of well-designed, highly machined parts flying in formation—hopefully.

Each of the company's activities—manufacturing, marketing, finance, human resources, and so on—interacts with other parts of the network, often on its own, as well as with the world and the market outside the company. Barriers between companies, which were once solid and absolute, are now permeable. And risk is rampant. Companies today must thread their way through the growing volatility of the stock, bond, and currency markets, as well as through the manifold perils associated with product liability, the environment, and political turbulence.

In addition, the market—which was steady and constantly expanding when the old model came into being—is now rife with change. Product development times are shorter and new markets leap into being overnight. For example, Ken Lay, the chairman and CEO of Enron Corporation, a diversified natural gas and power generation company, recently calculated that a full 40 percent of his firm's income emanates from businesses that did not even exist little more than a decade ago.

No business leader of forty or fifty years ago imagined the multifold shape of the world and economy that has unfolded at breathtaking speed in recent years. Companies today operate in a testing environment of monumental and continuous fluctuation. Changes on a massive scale, which once occurred sporadically, are now everyday parts of the landscape. And it is unlikely that we will ever be able to retreat to the simpler ways of the past.

Ponder the following:

- The pace of business is appreciably faster with ever-rising customer expectations. New products burst into the market at a record clip. Astoundingly enough, Rubbermaid aims to develop a new product every day of the year. Today there are twice as many products cramming supermarket shelves as there were a decade ago. Computer chip makers estimate that a new chip is reduced to a commodity in a scant three months.
- Information is becoming readily available around the world at an unprecedented pace. The ever-expanding information highway affords customers and competitors instant access to each other. During the past twenty-five years, the cost to process one instruction per second has fallen by half each year. In the United States, the number of households subscribing to on-line services or using the Internet grew approximately 120 percent in 1995 alone. Technological change has delivered the Information Age and converted it to the Knowledge Age.
- Markets are globalizing, as are the companies that compete in them. About half of the sales of the fifty biggest companies come from outside the headquarters country.
- Competitive pressure has been intensifying and it is becoming harder to achieve leadership and to stay on top.

Consider that 116 companies on the Fortune 500 list in 1983 were off it by 1993. The dropout rate continues at this feverish pace. In another sobering sign, in the 1990s, the rate at which chief executives of Fortune 500 companies were heaved out by their boards has increased drastically.

- Industry structures continue to evolve. In some cases, the definition of industry is changing. Witness the dizzying convolutions in telecommunications and media. Between 1989 and 1994, there were more than 1,500 mergers just in the United States banking industry. These changes mean new dynamics and totally new barometers of success.

- The regulatory environment is becoming stricter, and penalties are far harsher. For instance, more stringent environmental codes have been reinforced in the United States by 1991 Federal sentencing guidelines, which provide for jail sentences and stiff fines for executives of companies that violate environmental laws.

- Capital markets have evolved significantly. Investors are more activist and informed, and have themselves become agents of change by demanding superior performance. In the United States, institutional investors currently own 44 percent of all stocks, compared with just 6.1 percent in 1950. In 1990, more shareholder proposals passed than in the entire history of shareholder proposals.

- Much snide and sneering cynicism is being directed toward business motives and values, exacerbated by press reports on the immense downsizing scythe being wielded by corporations. Witness the huge response to a seven-part series in *The New York Times* and the "Corporate Killers" cover story in *Newsweek*. Mistrust of business has returned to the forefront of the public mind, with people once again asking what corporations owe society. Business has often been under attack. There was the student movement of the late 1960s, the environmental wave in the 1970s, and the disenchantment in the wake of the 1987 stock market crash. But now we are seeing broad-based, global, and unyielding criticism. Companies are being castigated for trying to achieve their fundamental mission—creating value for their shareholders.

This new world, where barriers are porous and competitors in one market may establish alliances in another, is highly complex. Too complex for most companies to manage even with the latest technology. And so many companies are opting out. They are desperately shedding businesses and laying off workers in a concerted effort to simplify what they do. Or they are engaging in corporate fusion to try to keep in step, twisting themselves into all manner of new shapes and sizes.

Some companies are simplifying, focusing more on their core businesses, and getting smaller. Other companies, listening to a conflicting siren call, are getting bigger by tacking on new capabilities through acquisitions and alliances, seemingly swapping what from the outside may look like greater complexity for enhanced capabilities that they hope will gain them a competitive edge.

Percy Barnevik has taken ABB, the diversified Switzerland-based company involved in things like making power-generation equipment, building locomotives, insurance, investment management, and industrial robots, and smashed its old business model to smithereens. The company's headquarters staff was reduced to 140 people. At the same time, the number of business units throughout the world soared to an astounding 1,400. Most of the people once working at headquarters are now toiling in the business units, which are linked to headquarters through a complicated electronic matrix that fuses the company's operational and financial functions with its overall performance goals. To anyone who does not dream in higher math, it is hard to find a stress-free moment at ABB. Barnevik himself calls it a sometimes-loose, sometimes-tight federation of businesses that must continually be reminded of their links.

Downtrodden companies seem most likely to pursue simplification. Kmart, for instance, has been selling its specialty businesses. As Floyd Hall, the retailer's chief executive, put it, "The sale takes us out of a business that we perhaps didn't know as well as we should." AT&T's historic deintegration into three companies was ostensibly both for focus and to allow Western Electric, the manufacturing arm now called Lucent, to sell to rivals of AT&T. In 1988, Sun Oil (Sunoco) carved up the big oil corporation into an upstream company concerned with exploration and production and a downstream company that performs refining and marketing. The head of Oryx, the upstream sibling, said that the benefits and synergies of being one company failed to outweigh the costs of management attention, bureaucracy, competition for investment, and the like.

Which is not to say that other business leaders aren't avowedly channeling their energies into integration. News Corp., Time Warner, Disney, and other media giants are scrambling to integrate so they can offer a package of services and content, as well as to redefine the very soul of their industries. And while Ma Bell is getting divorced, the Baby Bells like Pacific Telesis and Southwestern Bell are getting married.

The miscellaneous actions of these companies—and many others—suggest that infatuation with structure in a bewildering world has become a dominant concern on the agenda of corporate managers, and an issue that has sown much confusion.

When we consider the great shifts that have been shaping the economy in recent decades, and the deep, persisting evidence of disarray, we are pondering a genuine and radical transformation. Indeed, it is a transformation that will challenge the very core of our psyche. These changes have enormous implications for what a company has to do and how it has to think to be successful. Profit opportunities have become more fleeting as an onslaught of products has flooded the market. At the same time, products must be increasingly differentiated from each other, not just in highly fragmented home markets but also when companies enter global markets and bump into national differences and preferences. Thus a company must become adept—not to mention catlike quick—in its ability to adjust to changing times. It must also become much more precise in targeting windows of opportunity, more creative in how it competes, and more customized in what it delivers.

Unfortunately, most large companies, no matter how eminent, have proven themselves particularly inept in responding to the steady heat from these demands.

## THE CENTERLESS CORPORATION REVOLVES AROUND THREE AXES

The answer, we believe, is the Centerless Corporation. As we imagine it, it directly addresses all of these concerns. For while the old business model is structured around individual businesses, the Centerless Corporation is built along three axes: people, knowledge, and coherence. They are what allow the corporation to breathe and function. While we will discuss each of these concepts at length in separate chapters, here's what we think is unique about them:

**PEOPLE.** Though it may sound like a truism, it bears repeating that people are a firm's most underutilized resource. People are the firm's repository of knowledge and they are central to the company's competitive advantage. Well-trained, highly motivated people are crucial to the development and execution of strategies, especially in today's faster-paced, more perplexing world, where top management alone can no longer assure the firm's competitiveness.

In the future, corporations will have to rely more on committed and entrepreneurial workers to ensure their competitive position. The complexity of identifying opportunities, creating new products, and working across the organization requires more and better people. As a result, people are a significant investment in the future performance of the corporation. Motorola, for example, spends almost $100 million annually on education and training and calculates a return of $3 in sales for every education dollar spent.

To attract and protect this resource, we suggest that companies adopt a "New People Partnership." Recognizing that lifetime employment is no longer feasible, this "partnership" involves a mutual commitment to establishing the environment for learning and for ongoing employability as part of the overall package offered to the work force.

**KNOWLEDGE.** Never before has knowledge been as critical as it is today, and yet many companies are at a loss in knowing how to tap and manage this vital resource. In the Centerless Corporation, the management of knowledge is one of the highest priorities. Quite simply, knowledge enables growth and productivity.

We think of knowledge in the broadest possible sense. Though knowledge is often derived from information, it is much more than data. We define it as a set of understandings used by people to do work or make decisions. It is amassed from experience and constitutes the primary building block of the company's capabilities. It is strategic and focused on adding to the company's prowess by enabling the firm to do something significantly better than others. And so real knowledge creates real value for shareholders.

Managing knowledge involves, among other things, managing interactions and exchanges across organizational boundaries. The external boundaries to knowledge are coming down at a rapid rate. Knowledge must be gathered and made available to ensure access to such crucial factors as best practices and customer intelligence. The very best companies today are building networks of knowledge (the so-called intranet), are transferring best practices seamlessly around the world, and are erecting the infrastructure to make this work. The Centerless Corporation has a formal Core Knowledge Team to drive the knowledge through the corporation. Booz•Allen & Hamilton is among a growing number of companies that now have actual chief knowledge officers.

**COHERENCE.** This refers to the linkages that hold a company together. Indeed, they have never been more important in a global marketplace. They are the connectors among the many pieces of the firm, such as the global network of offices and systems, which allow the firm to globalize yet work as one, management processes which enable the firm to function smoothly, and a whole range of other factors which bind together the value-adding horsepower of the corporation and create value greater than the sum of the parts.

These linkages range from the vision and values of the firm to specific management processes like budgeting and compensation. For example, IKEA's top management abolished its budgeting system altogether. Instead, they have introduced a set of simple financial ratios that act more as benchmarks for carefully managed internal competition. Chaparral Steel has introduced a bonus salary system for all employees; what's more, 93 percent of all staff members own company shares.

Information linkages through systems have proven to be power tools of strategy implementation. For instance, Banc One has installed a Management Information and Control System which posts and ranks each of its 100 banks' monthly performance. All bank managers have access to the system. This allows managers to identify high performing units and actively seek out best practice information from them. Kao, Japan's leading soap and detergent company and now the second-largest cosmetics company, has perfected an information network called a "Value Added Network" (VAN) that gives front-line managers access to information throughout the organization. Kao has even shared information advantage with its retailers to help them build volume and profits on Kao's products.

This new model perforce has to have a different style of leadership. Rather than managing the activities of the corporation, the CEO creates the context for growth with a heavy emphasis on the three enablers of growth. The context provides direction in terms of vision and culture. The enablers actually make growth happen.

Refocusing the business model on people, knowledge, and coherence means radically different roles for the four basic elements of the Centerless Corporation: the Global Core, Business Units, Services, and Governance. Let's briefly look at the new responsibilities of these components before returning to them in individual chapters.

## THE GLOBAL CORE CARRIES OUT ITS MISSIONS WHERE NEEDED

The Global Core has five key missions. These are value-adding functions that cannot be provided by the Business Units. The Global Core must provide strategic leadership, help distribute and provide access to capabilities, create an appropriate identity, ensure access to low-cost capital, and exert control over the enterprise as a whole.

In carrying out these tasks, the Global Core should never be confused with the old central or corporate core, which is at the heart of the traditional business model. The differences have a major impact on management and leadership, as well as on the way business is conducted. They not only affect the bottom line, but also directly affect the top line.

In our work on the Global Core, we have pioneered the concept of a distributed core so that the five basic missions can be carried out where they are needed. That means locally. Make no mistake, this is different from the concept of a decentralized core, an artifact from the days of telegraphs and railroads that is now making its way through businesses and business books.

Decentralization, as a concept, implies a more limited degree of decision-making autonomy than occurs in the Centerless Corporation. When the core is distributed, the distributed parts can make real decisions. Charles Handy, the British management writer, calls this subsidiarity.

But when the core is decentralized, the decentralized parts can make decisions—but only up to a point. Thus, in our concept of the corporation, there is no longer a need for a center. This hastens decision-making, unburdens high-level staff, and keeps information flowing to where it is needed, rather than drowning people in a flood of data that is often, as is so commonly lamented, content-free. In our work, we have found the distributed model to be very well suited to companies that are globalizing and to firms that are attacking emerging markets.

Let's be clear, leading a distributed organization requires a different set of skills from leading a decentralized one. It requires different reporting systems, management targets, and technology. It requires a new type of CEO and new type of governance.

Managing and leading the distributed organization requires a blend of science and art. The art comes in the ongoing, self-critical, strategic questioning that must take place within the Global Core. For example, in the Centerless Corporation, the top team must continually ask itself why the corporation has the set of Business Units that it does. It must also be bold enough to ask whether the Business Units would do better set free to function on their own or staying with the corporation. The top team must also ask whether the corporation should acquire or build a business in a certain segment of the market. And it must determine the fundamental questions of whether the corporation itself—the Global Core—is creating sufficient value to justify itself.

While asking these questions is the art, answering them is the science. The science comes in the analysis of these answers and in the measurement of their results. The Global Core, whose main purpose is to create value, must track how much improvement it has made with respect to each of its five missions. And, at the same time, it must track the value creation of the Business Units.

## BUSINESS UNITS MUST ADD VALUE

Not only must the Global Core contribute to the well-being and creation of value in the Business Units, but the Business Units must also be able to contribute to each other's ability to create value. In our formulation, the value created by the whole must greatly and measurably exceed the value created by the sum of the parts. When that fails to be the case, the Business Units are probably better off on their own.

This enhanced value may come from one or more sources. The business may benefit more from a number of sources, including the Core. It may also benefit from interactions with other Business Units in activities like best-practice exchanges, knowledge sharing, and capabilities transfers.

To capture some of their potential value, Business Units will have to be managed differently. Greater interaction between units will have to become the standard. The boundaries separating the units must be permeable and flexible. Thus the predominant measures for the corporation will be performance of the whole, not the sum of the parts. The challenge is that the clear accountability that has been established over the years now has some ambiguity. Unfortunately, that is the cost of greater growth.

Some companies have been very good at creating significantly more value by flying in formation rather than by breaking up. Hewlett-Packard and Canon, to name two notable cases, have managed to combine capabilities from several Business Units to create new products and new business lines with significant leveraging effects.

Volvo's structure is an ambitious attempt to provide superior customer service through a lateral customer-driven organization. The functional dealer is replaced with self-managing teams of mechanics who are dedicated to groups of frequent customers (they always get the same team). Nike has opted for a network integration model. The company provides its marketing function and strategic management for a network of independent firms. Nike designs the information and logistic systems for the network's benefits. In a similar vein, Procter & Gamble reorganized its product supply system into a superfunctions unit by combining formerly independent functions of purchasing, engineering, and distribution. A product supply manager was created for each division and the functions report to him. This reduces flow time and inventories, and it increases on-time delivery and quality.

## SHARING SERVICES

As businesses find themselves integrating larger numbers of specialized parts, services are becoming more specialized as well. Services perform functions like payroll, accounts payable, benefits administration, and data processing. More and more, it makes sense to separate these services from the businesses to achieve greater advantage from specialization. After all, businesses do not create value by performing and delivering services to themselves. They create value by developing, making, and selling products.

To fully realize the advantage of separating the services from the businesses, it is necessary to develop new means to tie them together. Since many services are not key parts of the value creation process, they can be done outside the corporation. Often, however, the market for such services is rudimentary. The prices are too high and the level of service too low. The solution is to create a market within the corporation by establishing a separate unit to supply these services and forcing the unit to be market-efficient. This is the concept of shared services.

Ideally, a shared-services organization operates as if it were an independent business entity. The important thing is that service delivery in the Centerless Corporation can flow from several sources, but central services out of the corporate center should not be one of them.

Among the best examples of companies gravitating to this approach are Mobil, Amoco, and Rhone-Poulenc. Each of these corporations has created its own effective version of a shared-services unit.

## THE RISE OF GOVERNANCE

Governance takes on an appreciably larger and more sophisticated role in the Centerless Corporation. Governance, as we think of it, has three facets—the governance of the entire corporation by the board of directors, the governance of intercorporate entities like alliances and joint ventures, and the governance of intracorporate entities like shared services.

Several forces are driving this need for a bigger role. A push for performance is creating more active boards with greater CEO accountability. Expansion of capital markets and the need to access new capital are especially important as family-owned businesses look to obtain financing or companies seek out capital in emerging markets like China. Regulatory actions are forcing boards to become more proactive to deal with everything from privatization issues to taxes on "excessive" CEO compensation. And alliances, especially international and cross-cultural ones, are requiring adjustments in how ventures are governed.

The new governance model involves a closer relationship between the board and the shareholder base. Instead of playing its familiar passive role of guardian, the board is transformed into an active supporter of the business imperative. It continues to perform its fundamental responsibility of guarding the interests of shareholders. But it does so in a more complex manner. Under the new model, the board does things like bring insights on customers from a cross section of industries and services. It challenges the effectiveness of the CEO and senior management, as well as the role of the Global Core. It makes sure the company is developing key business capabilities. In every sense, it becomes an advisory as well as a control body.

No company has yet achieved the Centerless Corporation in its entirety, but a number are striving for Centerlessness.

Bob Shapiro, who became chief executive of Monsanto in 1995, has been moving inexorably toward Centerlessness. Contemplating the company, he saw an organization burdened by too much bureaucracy and hierarchy, with multiple layers of staff at corporate headquarters and in the divisions. So he simply blew up the group structure. In its place, he established a number of strategic business units and then shed part of the company that no longer fit. He built his vision on knowledge and people and has doggedly focused the company on three objectives: achieving operational excellence, staying small and connected, and releasing the potential of Monsanto's 30,000 people. It is small wonder that Monsanto's stock has soared.

E. John Browne is a compact, animated, cigar-smoking businessman who holds a physics degree from Cambridge University. As the head of British Petroleum, one of the world's great oil companies, he has been a whirligig of change. In 1992, when he was made the CEO of BP Exploration, the upstream exploration and production business, he was aghast at what he saw: the archetypal evils of excessive bureaucracy, steep costs, lackluster success rates in exploration, and a decidedly moribund operation.

Moving with impressive dispatch, Browne set new and high goals, developed and accentuated a fresh strategy, and revolutionized the organizational structure. He put into effect more than forty empowered business units, sharply shrank the role and size of the corporate center, and turned to technology to help reduce the number of management layers to help aggregate business results.

In short order, results improved markedly. Browne was elevated to CEO of the entire company. In his new capacity, he has continued his bold and restless ways. Not long ago, he assembled his top team and directly asked them what each of them was doing to impart value to the company, why did their jobs need to exist, and why did they even need a corporate center. In short, he is challenging the essential beliefs by which they run the business.

In March 1996, BP announced that it was merging its marketing business in Europe with that of Mobil Oil in a move that will change the competitive landscape of the industry. And so this young, remarkable man is swiftly putting his imprint on not only a company but an entire industry.

## THE PARADOX OF SUCCESS

To sum up, we are faced with a paradox. As we embark on a new and bewildering business era, our major corporations have available to them unprecedented opportunities to capture rich new territory. Yet the archaic model they are organized in continues to hamper their performance and thwart their efforts to win that territory. A counterweight is needed.

This book will be our transition guide to getting out of a state of confusion and darkness and into the light of the Centerless Corporation, so that we can get what we want for our corporations, our employees, our shareholders, and ourselves.

We have studied attempts to move toward a new model at companies in Argentina, Australia, Brazil, the United States, and Switzerland, as well as in parts of Asia. But, so far, no company has done it all. While the paradigm is shifting, it has yet to reach another stable state.

We do not rely on intellectual abstraction but use real businesses led by real people to illustrate ideas for the blueprint of the company of the future. There will be plenty of positive examples in the following chapters of Centerless heroes who are making a difference. They are rooted in old-line businesses like manufacturing as well as hypermodern ones operating in cyberspace. This book will not develop the new model as pie-in-the-sky. We think of this book as a friendly excursion into our, and our firm's, latest thinking on how to build, structure, grow, and measure companies. To thrive amid the formidable complexities of the new business environment, an entirely new type of corporation is called for, one that is distanced from the excessive levels of command that companies have become comfortable with. That corporation must have a much stronger focus on the basics of what ultimately creates value—knowledge and people and coherence. It must evolve toward a new business model that fosters the creation of value and ensures that each piece of the business contributes to system-wide value. And it must take account of the fact that the milieu of success today necessarily extends beyond the workplace and the interface between government and business into the social climate itself. Without such changes, businesses face a sad and unsatisfying future. The primary direction for large corporations will be toward becoming smaller and weaker in an ever-fruitless and desperate effort to counter the complexities of size and diversity. What the picture of the future will look like for our major corporations depends on the choices that business leaders have still to make.

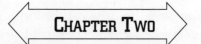

# CHAPTER TWO

# BUSINESS SPACE IN THE AGE OF GLOBAL SPECIALIZATION

**AS** the twenty-first century advances at fast-forward speed, the sacred thing that everyone relishes is success. But what will constitute true success in the new world? Great products? High profits? A hot stock? If you ask us, the ability to adapt to different conditions is the most telling measure of success for any organization. We respect survival, but we really admire long-term prosperity. In sports, the triumphal teams that lay claim to championship after championship (the calibration of success in that stressful, ruthlessly competitive world) are celebrated as dynasties. Witness the fabled New York Yankees and the Boston Celtics of years gone by, and perhaps the Chicago Bulls of today, all of which evoke an almost unfathomable and yet elemental superiority.

In deciphering enduring success in business, we use rather different measures. For the most part, we look at size and the creation of shareholder value. General Electric has had a protracted run as one of the world's largest corporations. It cracked the initial Fortune 100, and never deserted the list. With amazing regularity, Microsoft has been minting millionaires out of many of the people who work there (not to mention the billions it has showered on Bill Gates). These are the stunning success stories of today's business world. Wouldn't everyone love to join their like.

Far more companies, however, fail or at least never live up to their potential. The dropout rate of companies on the Fortune 500 has doubled since the 1970s, as company after company loses its moorings and drifts off into list-less space. It seems that it is harder than ever to become a business dynasty, or to even come close.

But why?

This book hopes to show what a firm must do in a much more challenging and confounding world to be successful, what it must do to become a GE or a Microsoft, and not one of those candidates for replacement on the Fortune 500 list. But before we dissect our new business model and reveal its inner workings, it is important to understand the context that demands the Centerless Corporation.

To begin with, you must be mindful that firms have a choice about how they compete for value. That choice is extremely relevant to how they should adopt elements of the Centerless Corporation as well as to which elements are most crucial to their success.

Indeed, not all companies even play the same game. In fact, some participants are grappling on entirely different playing fields.

There are numerous ways to calibrate the success of a company, but one of the surest ones is, in effect, by tracking real estate. How much territory in the competitive landscape does it control and what kind of territory is it? Much like the topography of the world, some areas are notably more advantageous and lucrative than others. They can generate more wealth. A high escarpment or overhanging cliff may be the preferred position for a battle, a fertile valley the wisest place to grow crops. History is replete with roily confrontations over space—for the fertile valleys of the Tigris and Euphrates, for the gold in the Black Hills, for oil in the Middle East. To occupy that space, you have to either win it or defend it from someone else. Many cultures have been erased in the course of bitter and bloody struggles for territory.

In business, battles for space, if less bloody, are also often a matter of life or death. Companies have perished fighting for supremacy, or at least a foothold, in the computer business, just as they have jousting for wealth in five-and-dime-style discount merchandise and in pursuit of profits in steel. So clearly the choice of what playing field to occupy is the single most important decision a firm must make. We call the playing field Business Space. How much shareholder wealth a company creates is determined by how much of that Business Space the organization occupies and how valuable its position is.

## WHAT IS BUSINESS SPACE AND WHERE DOES IT COME FROM

The term "Business Space" derives from the notion that firms occupy positions that can be delineated by a set of dimensions. A cube can be represented on a graph using three dimensions, the standard $x$, $y$, $z$ coordinates we all learned in school. These days, any decent computer graphics package can whip one up in a flash.

Business Space, however, needs more than three dimensions. Innumerable factors define the boundaries of the competitive landscape. Mathematicians refer to areas demanding multiple dimensions as $n$-space. That, in essence, is what Business Space is. There is no way to put an exact number to its dimensions.

Conceptually, we can divide Business Space into new and old varieties. This is a critical distinction for companies when they plot their strategies. Old occupied Business Space is likely to be congested with competitors not well-disposed toward interlopers. It can be a treacherous environment, albeit one that has a well-established order to it. New and unoccupied Business Space is like a frontier: wild, unprotected, lots of opportunity, and lots of risk.

Where does Business Space come from? Its origin is analogous to what happens in cosmology. The Big Bang exploded matter into existence and thrust it into space. But what space? Nothing was there before the Big Bang. In essence, momentum from the Big Bang created its own space, and that momentum continues to cause the universe to expand. Hence space creates itself. There is nothing out there into which space expands, but once it expands, it has created its own space.

Business Space gets created as well. Forces like economic growth, market evolution, shifts in customer tastes, technological breakthroughs, social changes, and political events can expand (and sometimes shrink) Business Space. For the most part, preexisting space expands. For example, people drive more each year and so the market for gasoline grows, giving rise to more space for gas stations as well as a bit of space for the makers of electric cars.

Governor Pete Wilson of California signed a bill on September 23, 1996, that restructured the electric utility industry by ending the monopoly of the California utilities. Because of this new law, electricity providers will be facing a competitive environment in California by the year 2000. Thus new Business Space will open up. If, as some predict, electricity costs plunge as much as 30 percent for some large industrial users, then increased usage will generate still more space.

Every time Business Space grows, fresh and lush opportunities sprout up for firms to prosper. It is small wonder that most large firms today have some plan, if not a real footprint, in the world's emerging markets. Places like China, Eastern Europe, and Latin America are lands of immense potential growth and of tremendous appeal to those trapped in slow-growing, mature economic sectors in the United States and Europe. Many of the world's mightiest industrial and consumer product companies are searching for ways to establish themselves in these manic growth regions and ride the bubble of expansion. If nothing else, this interest has meant good business for the airlines ferrying people across oceans.

Companies very much set their own destinies. For one thing, every corporation chooses the space in which it competes. But as existing space continues to expand, so, too, do new dimensions in Business Space get created. This unoccupied territory represents a land of opportunity for the technological and strategic innovators who can create it. Anyone who can invent a better mousetrap will have for himself virgin Business Space. Throughout history, great inventors like the indefatigable Thomas Edison created vast tracts of new Business Space all to themselves.

Sony is a prime example of a company that has created a lot of Business Space, some for itself and some for others. The Walkman is a perfect case of an idea brought to life without a market in clear sight. Left to the marketing gurus, the Walkman would have never risen from the drawing board. After all, who would want to stroll around with ear plugs hooked to a tape machine? Sony also created tremendous amounts of Business Space with the VCR. In fact, its Betamax format was undeniably the better mousetrap. Alas, once VHS seized enough of the space, there was not enough room left for the Beta format to breathe.

Technological advances like the electric arc furnace can actually rewrite Business Space. This is akin to the universe going back in time and redefining part of the space. The electric arc furnace completely recalculated the economics of the steel business. Companies such as Nucor were able to grow rapidly and seize a large share of the business value by expanding the production technology dimension of space. Large integrated steel companies are still playing the game, but they have had to redefine themselves in order to vie for a more dominant position.

Strategic innovators create their own space as well. In these instances, nothing has to be invented except a concept. Wal-Mart, for example, found a way to reign over underserved retail markets and put in place a business system that made it one of the most dynamically successful companies for more than two decades. Wal-Mart has been able to define its relationships with suppliers and customers, and to improve their logistics network of getting inventory on the shelf. For an extended time, it reveled in the luxury of having its Business Space all to itself. Other firms now vie in the space created by Wal-Mart, but they started from a distinctly disadvantaged position.

It's fair to say that the preponderance of firms compete in very crowded space. While they can do quite well in such congested territory, it is difficult for anyone to get solid enough footing to become dominant and to capture large chunks of space. In order to deal with these circumstances, we see a lot of firms lining up into a value chain alliance—e.g., suppliers to the auto industry or the many companies tied to Microsoft as they develop new platforms for Microsoft's products. It is perhaps the surest way to survive when Business Space gets heavily populated.

## A NEW ERA MEANS NEW BUSINESS SPACE

The strategic selection of the best competitive positioning in Business Space is complicated by the fact that the characteristics of Business Space change over time. The world is a vastly different place than it was a hundred years ago. It is different than ten years ago, five years ago, last year, last week! At certain points, the difference becomes material. Successful firms recognize change. Very successful ones anticipate it.

At times throughout history, confluent developments have accelerated change so rapidly that a new era or phase of business bursts into being, a busily enterprising milieu containing huge expanses of Business Space. This new Business Space is often unoccupied territory just waiting for fast movers to enter and grow rapidly. The Industrial Age brought on big oil, big steel, and big railroads. Giants in their day, some of these companies have passed the test of time.

The "phase transition" periods between new eras are also highly significant. They are invariably rocked by economic dislocations as previously dominant firms are displaced among the "who's who" of business. New competitive dynamics lead to greater instability in the profitability of companies, and new skill requirements foster changes in the relationships between employers and employees.

As new dimensions to Business Space are added, the old ones do not really disappear. The former competitive landscape remains. There is still opportunity to be had there, it is just not as rich and robust. A start-up company like Vermont Castings became highly successful in the manufacture of wood-burning stoves, a staple of the nineteenth century in a very attractive niche market. But the added space affords the most tantalizing opportunity for dominance.

Thus Business Space becomes more complex. That is because characteristics are added frequently, but subtracted infrequently. Complexity increases because there is no other direction to go.

One sees this same progression from the simple to the complex in nature. At the time of the Big Bang, the universe was all energy and subatomic particles. The simplest of elements—hydrogen and helium—formed first. Heavy elements composed of more particles, protons, electrons, and neutrons are basically second-generation elements. All elements heavier than iron were formed from exploding stars, which means a star had to have been born and then die before this level of complexity could be reached. We deal with this complexity in fields like physics and chemistry. It is not necessary to refer each time to the quantum behavior of things. Instead we work at a higher order of aggregation, at a higher system level.

Likewise with life itself. The first life-forms were the simplest, nothing more than single cells. We actually still have single-cell life today. In fact, it represents the largest form of life in terms of numbers, and by some estimates represents the greatest mass of life. Quite a few of these simple life-forms can literally kill us. But since the first life-forms emerged from the primordial soup, life has become notably more complex. Again, it had to happen. There was no other way for it to go.

How does one deal with ever-increasing complexity? Life-forms resort to a higher-order system to simplify things. True, it might be nice for us to talk to our cells, but we delegate that communication to different parts of our body. In fact, we outsource quite a bit to single-cell forms. For instance, bacteria help our digestion in a sort of strategic alliance. Meanwhile, we worry about the big picture. We make sure that we get sufficient nourishment, rest, and exercise, our enablers of success. Our "partners" and "subordinates" handle the day-to-day, or second-to-second, business of getting the benefits to our cells.

We see the same graduated shift to higher complexity in business. And over time, businesses have dealt with increasing complexity by moving to a higher order to manage their affairs. That is not to say that the basics are ignored, but they are just not enough to get the job done anymore.

At their most elementary level, businesses revolve around providing a good or service. They arise from knowing how to make or do something. What is the formula for making canned soup? How do you connect the wires in a radio? What are the steps to make a tire? Early on in history, businesses were simply craftsmen plying their trades. Competition arose over who made the best pottery, the best cloth, and the sharpest knives.

Today it is not enough just to know how things are made. Perhaps knowing the ins and outs of how pipes work is adequate to run a local plumbing business with some success. But operating a multibillion-dollar global corporation demands far more than craft skills. It sure helps to know what you sell, but that's only the beginning of what a big-league CEO has to do.

The transition from the simple craft business to today's highly complex, often diversified, evermore global enterprises was not accomplished in one step. It occurred in myriad steps across centuries. And the change continues. At times, the pace of change becomes so rapid that a threshold is crossed and it takes a different type of firm to be dominant. These periods of great change mark entirely new eras of business.

Companies that chose to capitalize on the opportunites had to transform themselves as well. They had to break out from the pack and discover new forms and new ways of doing things. The leaders defined the dominant business model of their era.

What do we mean by a new era? History is replete with ages. We've all heard about the Stone Age, the Bronze Age, the Iron Age, the Information Age. When a new era comes along, does this mean that all the rules have changed? Is there a complete turnaround in the winners and losers of the world? Yes and no. It depends on how you keep score and what area of Business Space you do the measuring in.

We like to think about a "new age" as a period during which vast amounts of new Business Space is created. Indeed, so vast an area can come into being that it changes perspectives. We see the world working in a different way. Those who are visionary enough to detect the change early enough are often able to benefit immensely. It's not that all others suffer. But there is a new order and a new set of dominant players.

## NEW ERAS DEMAND NEW LEVERS OF PERFORMANCE

In our own studies of corporate behavior over the years, we have paid special attention to how companies have responded to some of the big changes in Business Space. And we've noticed some interesting things. The companies that have attempted to fill the new space and achieve the permanence afforded large growing companies have consistently constructed new business models to manage the greater complexity. This very complexity forms a competitive barrier and enables the leaders to have a running start on the rest of the pack.

What we find is that complexity is most effectively managed by creating higher-order levers. Certainly, the focus of management must include all the nuts and bolts of how products are made and services delivered. But it must also include certain higher-order levers, because most companies' products are too numerous and changing too fast for the CEO to make every last decision.

Perhaps the best way to think of these levers is as levers or enablers of performance. In fact, the higher the order of the lever, the greater the overall impact on the company.

Let's look at a few episodes in the evolution of business to demonstrate how large new changes in Business Space are by necessity more complex and how simplification is achieved by introducing enablers to manage that complexity.

The market economy has been with us since the dawn of mankind. It seems to be part of our nature to trade. We like to buy and sell. Recent discoveries have shown how widely our ancient ancestors traveled to trade. The remains of Ice Age men clutching goods from trade have been found buried in remote mountain passes in the Alps. Europeans were discovered buried along the Great Silk Road, part of an extensive expatriate community for trade during the Dark Ages. Globalization is not new, it's just more pervasive.

Historians debate the evolution of capitalism. It's been with us a long time. Certainly it was part of early man's daily life, for small amounts of capital accumulation were needed to plant crops and to manufacture. To grow to big businesses, it was necessary to accumulate and move sizable sums of money. But it took innovations in commercial vehicles like letters of credit and joint stock companies to really have the Age of Capitalism take off.

Moving large sums of money has always been a risky task, a market niche for pirates and highway robbers. But out of Renaissance Europe came a different way—the creation of large banks and trading companies. We almost take for granted today the ease with which very large companies, like Exxon can operate across the globe, handling over $100 billion in revenues. It wasn't always so easy, and Exxon could not be Exxon as we know it without that nimble capacity to maneuver large sums of money over great distances.

Without getting into the historian's debate on the when, how, or why of capitalism, these innovations in commercial vehicles injected a new success factor into businesses. Although the world has always been ruled by *caveat emptor*, buyers are aware of difference and are able to vote with their dollars. So being efficient in making quality goods has always been with us. The dominant businesses were always those that produced the best value in the marketplace. Often these were the best craftsmen.

The Age of Capitalism did not change competition at the most basic level. Rather it added a new dimension to manage in order to be dominant. A new enabler of success was created. In order to be a dominant company, it was important to raise capital and transact larger sums over vaster distances than ever before. Immense trading companies like the East India Company developed networks of agents to facilitate global trade. Large banks like Rothschilds' emerged to provide credit and clearing for financial transactions.

But businesses needed more than capital to grow. The Industrial Age, circa 1750 in Great Britain, witnessed the confluence of several factors that enabled businesses to swell to immense sizes. Steam power (which was actually first introduced to the world by Hero of Alexandria in A.D. 100 to open temple doors) found its way into locomotives, ships, and factories. Improved distribution through better roads and the arrival of railroads enabled goods to reach markets faster and farther away (read cheaper). And a whole host of other key inventions came along: coke smelting to reduce the cost of iron making, mechanical looms, and the cotton gin, among others.

Now that companies found themselves blessed with the means to produce large volumes and move them to "distant" markets at reasonable costs, scale became important. It was only through scale that a business could fully use the new capacity of the inventions of the day. Scale was also important to capture the Business Space that was now available. This new space was huge untapped territory. It fostered the creation of industrial giants, and it did so quickly. By 1900, the roots of some well-known companies were already well established: du Pont, Anheuser-Busch, R.J. Reynolds, Eastman Kodak, Exxon, AT&T, Johnson & Johnson, Procter & Gamble, Coca-Cola, and General Electric, among many other household names.

Large-scale business demanded greater specialization. Elaborate functional departments were required to oversee key areas. Thus the emergence of production, marketing, accounting, sales, and research. Big firms like Standard Oil and du Pont were run as functional organizations. It was the functional departments that oversaw the day-to-day operations in their areas. Management was given the role of coordination.

To coordinate, managers needed information, and hence the growth of elaborate corporate staffs.

The complexity created by scale—by 1900 Western Union was one of the largest firms in the United States, with a capitalization exceeding $97 million and revenues of approximately $25 million—was overcome by simplifying the management oversight function of senior executives. A hierarchical business model of management put in place the ability to oversee many different types of activities by reporting results at a more summary level and using the chain of command to execute orders.

By the first quarter of this century, the science of management, which was just budding at the time, originated a widely used management model. The ability to manage one step removed helped spawn the Age of Diversification. Change was percolating in corporate America. Large companies were seeing the advantage of controlling more of the value chain. Vertical integration led the way for the more general diversification that followed on its heels. Now that the barrier of managing had been breached, the limits to diversification tumbled quickly.

Diversification, both related and unrelated, added yet another dimension of complexity to managing a firm. The response was the development of multidivision firms, essentially the collections of fairly autonomous business units that most big companies are today, as well as holding companies, which apart from their common ownership and funding, are basically independent companies. If we look at today's list of Fortune 100 companies, every last one is diversified to some extent.

The complexity of these firms is managed through the creation of "virtual" small companies within the larger company. Corporate management focuses on the performance of these "virtual companies" as wholes, while business unit managment tends to everyday matters. In fact, the way the system really operates is that it is not until you get several levels down within a business unit that you catch sight of a hands-on manager.

In Alfred Chandler's seminal book, *Strategy and Structure,* he demonstrated that companies in the oil industry that adopted the then new multidivision business model had a significant performance advantage over those that remained in the older functional model. And that advantage evaporated when all competitors had adopted the newer form.

In summary, we have seen that the dimensions of Business Space increase over time, adding complexity and furnishing attractive new opportunities for those who can successfully navigate the new environment. Further, the creation of enablers is the surest vehicle to overcome complexity. Higher-order levers of performance subsume the others.

## INTO THE AGE OF GLOBAL SPECIALIZATION

What about today?

We are in the midst of one of the most profound transitions in the history of business. That says a lot. It also means a lot if you are trying to compete. We are witnessing the end of an era that began over two centuries ago with the Industrial Revolution. Right now, we are in a tumultuous transition period to a new age defined by global competition and faster communications, an age in which complexity now inhibits greater size and greater value creation.

Complex systems have their own peculiar makeup. When we look at a business today, we see a collection of very specially trained individuals working together in teams or small organizations. These units, in turn, are connected across organizational boundaries within the company. The very specialized clusters are then attached to specialized clusters of other firms (often in different specialties) through alliances, supplier relationships, customer interactions, and other means. This constellation of specialization is greater than the sum of its parts. It must be managed in a way consistent with its complex nature. And since most companies are either competing on a global basis or influenced by global forces, we call this new period the Age of Global Specialization.

The concepts of how to construct a business model originated in the early days of the Industrial Revolution in the textile mills of England. Although the business model has evolved quite a bit, it is still geared to a rigid structure and command-and-control mentality. This model was well tailored to an environment where change was evolutionary rather than revolutionary. It helped foster a sense of accountability, of order. It has discipline. What it sorely lacks is flexibility.

A major driver of the shape of businesses has been the need to know: for management to know the state of the company in sufficient detail to make decisions and for employees to know what management wants them to do. Larger, more complex organizations have had to develop elaborate channels of information flows to accomplish this. The need for a hierarchy of information has made for a command-and-control approach to business and the need for very formal structures.

On paper, these types of organization may seem like paragons of efficiency. If measured on a stand-alone basis, that is, by looking at themselves in a mirror and judging flows of information both up and down the organization, they may be marvelously efficient. However, no company is an island. The need to interact with customers, with suppliers, and with the markets in general make this very inefficient and much too slow to keep pace with today's highly networked world.

The biggest changes have been due to the impact of communication and information technology. The ability to communicate across vast distances at ever lower costs and improving quality is transforming the way people and companies interact. It is also transforming our notions of where to locate. The world's fastest planes are no match for the speed of a video conference.

The new environment is characterized by faster change, more far-reaching technological advances, and a consumer who has adjusted to this quicker pace and whose fickle preferences are revised with the speed of a television commercial. The old tried and true approaches no longer work as well. Strange things are afoot. Nimble competitors can quickly establish a beachhead and outduel firms with fifty years in the game. A paper company like Smurfit can easily overtake the major integrated firms with a recycling strategy. The space wars going on in this age are more pronounced than any we have yet seen. The opportunities are great, but so are the competition and the chance of failure. You can rise higher but you can also fall farther.

Strategies for the new millennium must reflect the shifts in Business Space that characterize our times. The business model that is required to develop and implement those strategies must also reflect the new conditions. Needless to say, the transition from the standard business model is significant. It is a change less of structure than of roles, less of form and more of function.

The factors that brought success in the past, while still necessary, are no longer sufficient. The new business model for this new era, the Centerless Corporation, requires more, not less, of what we have in today's model.

## A More Free-Flowing and Distributed Model

Responsiveness requires connectedness. Thus, the future suggests that there will have to be greater networking among companies and greater networking within companies. In such a world, each piece of the business must add value, or it is dropped from the network. The network itself must add value or it ceases to exist. Responsiveness is needed to change, to adapt to conditions, to make bold strokes.

And, alas, responsiveness is lessened by hierarchy and controls. By the same token, neither does it thrive in anarchy. Thus we see a need for a new definition of order. By design, it must be more chaotic than the traditional business model, but it must still have certain rules and a distinct governance process.

What we are talking about is a more free-flowing organization than has been the norm, one that can act as required by the conditions. In a large company, this means smaller pieces of the firm taking on greater responsibility for making the right decisions. Companies that cannot make the transition to this more distributed model will surely become the dinosaurs of the twenty-first century. Make no mistake, speed and responsiveness require distributed actions.

What exactly do we mean by "distributed"? We mean that the center of decision-making is dispersed organizationally and geographically: "geographically" in the sense that any part of the organization, for example, the Global Core that replaces the former corporate center, can be physically distributed to meet the geographic distribution of the business. Its activities are still the responsibility of the Core, but the people may be in more than one location.

Distributed also means across the organization and its boundaries. Within a company, organizational lines will be much less rigid. Jack Welch uses the term "boundarylessness" to describe working across organizational lines within GE. Distributed responsibility means that there is a greater ability for various pieces of the company to act, and they have the power to act on behalf of other parts of the organization. For example, businesses may share support services across business units as they enter new countries.

Distributed models also go beyond a firm's borders. Strategic alliances, partnerships, and outsourcing are all vehicles that allow something of importance to a firm to be done outside the firm. Why? Others may do it better, cheaper, or in a more appropriate location. Self-sufficiency is now too high a cost. Comparative advantage, which economists define as a relative advantage among countries, accounts for international trade even though there may be absolute disadvantages. Now both within and among companies there is an emerging sense of comparative advantage. Firms or parts of firms focus on what they do well, and they link with others to overcome any comparative disadvantages.

The big question is how does one manage a business where more and more is distributed? Does the need to act quickly, to be more responsive to the external world reduce the importance of executive management? Must we lessen the complexity within the organization by refocusing the business on core activities so that senior management can maintain control? Have firms reached a natural limit to size and complexity? Is it still possible to control an organization that requires greater distributed responsibility? Or must we manage chaos?

## FOCUS ON THREE KEY BUSINESS ENABLERS

The answer is that we have reached a limit to what can be accomplished using today's management approaches. There is little doubt that the traditional hierarchical organizations cannot get bigger without cracking and running the risk that they will be unable to respond to the competitive challenges of the day. But by changing the way we manage, that constraint can be removed.

As we have pointed out, companies have always adapted to larger and more complex forms by having management focus on higher-order levers of performance. Today's transition requires the same focus.

We have coined a new term to describe those levers—"business enablers." They "enable" the firm to become more distributed yet act as one. They put the capabilities in place for the right actions to occur. They enable decisions that are in the interest of the corporation as a whole. They ensure that the right resources and skills exist for the company to compete and grow.

Remember, managing the business enablers does not replace managing the business. It is something that must be done on top of normal duties, and thus it represents a significant shift of focus.

To manage the Centerless Corporation, we have concluded that you must pay attention to three key business enablers:

- People
- Knowledge
- Coherence

We briefly discussed these in the last chapter, but they are important enough to run through quickly again. People as an enabler is almost a cliche, but a cliche on paper more than in reality. To get to the right decisions quickly, to distribute responsibility, to be at the leading edge of competitive performance require that the firm has access to the right set of people. We need both more business skills and more people skills. We also need a relationship with the employees that forms the bonds of an understanding of how they benefit as the firm benefits. There are many variations on this theme, but a motivated and committed set of employees is critical to success.

Knowledge: what the firm knows. Companies today deliver value often by being able to provide something to the market that others cannot, or cannot at a lower cost. Knowledge includes the know-how of creating value. It includes the processes of how the firm works. Best practices are very much a form of knowledge, and they must be shared more rapidly to stay competitive. Customer intelligence, new business concepts, R&D, and competitive intelligence are all forms of knowledge. In the Centerless Corporation, companies will have to be more structured in learning, capturing, and disseminating knowledge. Senior management must guarantee that knowledge processes are in place and working well.

Coherence is what holds the firm together. It is the glue that binds the various pieces, enabling them to act as one. It includes a broad range of processes. It begins with a shared vision and shared set of values, and expands to include numerous linkages across the company. Firms are tied together with communications, management processes like planning, human resource management, and knowledge management. Coherence also includes the more structured information technology of the firm, the hard-wiring of the businesses through which the various parts communicate.

Business enablers represent a higher-order set of levers than the financial performance of the business units in the corporate portfolio. While that financial performance is extremely important, the ability of corporate management to influence that performance is greatly enhanced through the three enablers of people, knowledge, and coherence. This shift of focus goes well beyond the standard debate of long-term versus short-term focus of management. Management must make sure that all three of these enablers are in place and are working well. In that respect, this is a short-term focus. They must be there now. If they are, both short-term and long-term performance are enhanced tremendously.

To sum up, we are embarking on a breathtaking new age full of promise and packed with pitfalls, but quite frankly managers lack the organizing principles to confront it. A new model is imperative. It is our contention that the Centerless Corporation, with its focus on three business enablers and its new roles for the basic building blocks of a business, is uniquely tailored to win the Business Space Wars of today and tomorrow.

In the following chapters, we will take you through the distinct pieces of the Centerless Corporation so that you will fully understand how each of them works and fits into the whole. We will begin with separate chapters on each of the three business enablers, for they are the essential elements that propel the model.

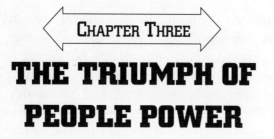

# CHAPTER THREE

# THE TRIUMPH OF PEOPLE POWER

**PRODUCTS** can be copied. Technology and training can be duplicated. No one, however, can match highly charged, motivated people who care. For that reason alone, people are one of the three key enablers of the new business model. At all levels, companies need people who can deliver at the frontier of performance. They must understand where the company is going and be able to influence its path. They must share in its fortunes and be motivated to push for greater achievements. They are the ones ultimately entrusted with the competitiveness of the corporation. They are the repository of much of the knowledge and skill base that makes the firm competitive. No company can be successful with a detached and unmotivated work force.

## THE CHANGING RELATIONSHIP

Of the radical shifts that result in the Centerless Corporation, none is more significant than the new relationship it requires between the company and its people. While we talk about how fast the business environment has changed, probably no dimension is changing faster than the dynamics between employer and employee.

The epitome of the traditional model was the "company man" of the 1950s and 1960s. When Charles Handy, the prominent European management guru, first joined Royal Dutch Shell about forty years ago, he recognized that Shell, at its whim, could repeatedly shuttle him and his family anywhere in the world. His first loyalty had to be to the company if he was to advance in his career. But in that process, he knew the company would take care of him and his family's needs over both the short and the long term.

In the days of the "company man," employers offered job security and a stable work environment with rising responsibilities and pay in return for loyalty and acceptable performance. This kind of relationship is exceedingly rare today. Today, companies must continually reinvent and restructure themselves to gain competitive advantage. The consolidation of industries, global markets, and activist investors have exacerbated competitive pressures. This demands doing more with less.

Jack Welch, the CEO of GE, argued that lifetime employment produced a paternal loyalty that left workers shielded from the real world. That cocoon idea has been replaced at GE by a new psychological contract, where loyalty is an affinity among people who want to win and who believe that GE's jobs are the best in the world for those who want to compete.

Technological innovation, the rise of customer-driven markets, and regulatory actions are dictating new skills to be successful. This poses significant challenges for companies in recruiting, developing, and retaining skilled staff. In a 1996 study by the Conference Board, 43 percent of companies reported that they had problems recruiting and keeping high-quality workers. Global markets are forcing companies to redeploy resources across geographic boundaries. Indeed, in many companies the bulk of the work force resides at corporate headquarters and manufacturing plants in areas where the company has traditionally had operations. As these companies become more and more global, they are looking outside traditional areas to emerging frontiers in places like China and India. In some cases, they are finding that the bulk of their growth opportunities exists in these new areas and they do not have the people with skills, suitable cultural sensitivities, language ability, and willingness to relocate to these areas.

From the employee's perspective, the world is also changing rapidly. Companies have repeatedly demonstrated that there are no guarantees when it comes to employment and people do not expect any. Yet, downsizing or right sizings have cut deeply and affected the psyche of the average person on the street. Many workers see little benefit in doing anything that requires "going the extra mile." On the other hand, employees realize that their greatest security is their skills and that there is a very attractive market for talent.

Demographics and cultural aspects are also changing the composition and preferences of the work force. More women are entering the work force, and more households than ever are composed of two-income earners. Life-style issues are more important in general as the "New Age" work force seeks some kind of balance. People are becoming highly trained and mobile, if not geographically, at least across companies. This has dampened the willingness of many people to relocate just because the company feels they should.

Furthermore, the changing relationship between companies and employees is reflected in our communities. From the perspective of many communities, an era of corporate social responsibility has largely passed. Relationships between companies and communities are increasingly strained. In an era of continuous restructuring to achieve and maintain competitive advantage, it can be hard to come by stability, equity, and job growth in many communities.

Consider the case of Aaron Feuerstein, the owner of Malden Mills, a $400 million manufacturer of Polartec fabric based in Massachusetts. When fire destroyed the company's plant facilities, Feuerstein was hailed as a hero in the press around the country. Why? For what was perceived as his unusually high commitment to the community and to employees by keeping people on the payroll for months after the fire as the company worked to rebuild operations. The reality today is that Malden Mills is a true exception. Wall Street often reinforces announcements of job cuts with significant stock price increases. Beyond the issues of economic stability, relationships between communities and companies have also been strained by recent press and court cases involving racial and gender equality in hiring and promotion at many companies. Community groups are placing increasing pressure on companies to make visible changes to what are considered unfair practices.

In many ways, these are worldwide issues as companies everywhere face the ongoing challenge of restructuring. In Latin America, issues surround fair treatment at times of restructuring and privatization in countries with little social safety net for the unemployed. In Germany and France, companies face the specter of significant restructuring balanced against their commitment to traditional industrial relationships policy. And even in Japan, lifetime employment is coming under some stress, as restructuring forces industry to rethink its commitment to workers.

The irony in all of this is that if you examine most corporate declarations of values, vision, or strategy, you will spot something like the following statement: People are our most important asset. It sounds awfully nice. Alas, the paradoxical fact is that the statement usually just sits there as little more than a mute reminder of what could be. If companies only behaved in a manner consistent with such endearing rhetoric, we would have a much more productive and contented society of workers, and much sturdier and successful corporations. But, loquacious as they are in touting the worth of workers, most companies fail at what matters most, and we are paying the consequences. Recognizing this, former U.S. Labor Secretary Robert Reich said, "American companies have got to be urged to treat their workers as assets to be developed, rather than costs to be cut."

In a Wirthlin report in January 1996, researchers found that nearly two-thirds of the people surveyed believe that today's employers are less loyal than they were a few years ago. In turn, 58 percent say that employees today are less loyal to their employers. Only half of employees feel especially secure in their jobs. Hardly the foundation for a successful enterprise.

The bottom line is that a successful corporation must be able to craft a new relationship with its employees—it must be able to live the ideals of people power, rather than merely talk about them. This "New People Partnership" must fulfill the business need to:

- continually improve performance and enhance value to shareholders
- enable the company to attract and retain top talent
- motivate all employees to work to their fullest potential
- develop the skills of white- and blue-collar workers
- balance the interests of all stakeholders, including shareholders, employees, unions, government, and society

Accomplishing these goals requires navigating a tricky road—reconciling the stated concern about people and the understanding that people are the key enablers of corporate success with the waves of downsizings, attacks on corporations, and rampant insecurity rippling through the work force.

## THE EMERGENCE OF A NEW PEOPLE PARTNERSHIP

What exactly is this New People Partnership? Reduced to its simplest terms, the partnership is the full implementation of the new realities that exist between the corporation and its employees. Specialized skills are increasingly required by firms, yet these skills are what make employees more mobile in the marketplace. Since companies can no longer guarantee lifetime job security, a new quid pro quo is needed. Thus, the New People Partnership. In essence, it is a fresh perspective that dictates that the company owns the work rather than the employee's career. The company assumes responsibility for investing in the employee and providing work that makes the individual "employable" in the marketplace. The employee owns his or her career and takes on the burden of building the capabilities that add value to the organization and ensure his or her own marketability. The employee and company work together to ensure that the organization meets market needs and is successful, since ongoing success provides the context for ongoing employment.

Competitive realities are already inducing companies in some industries to move toward the New People Partnership. High-tech companies have shared an accelerated urgency to forge a new relationship with their employees. Phenomenal growth has accentuated the need to come to different terms with employees. These companies provide some leading-edge examples of where ultimately all must go.

## INTEL

Intel was one of the first companies to move toward the concept of the New People Partnership, believing that maximizing job satisfaction and career opportunities for employees can bring higher productivity. The new concept is aptly explained by CEO Andy Grove, who says, "The only thing you can rely on is your ability to end up where the invisible hand of the economy wants you to be. Our phrase for it is 'owning your own employability.'"

Intel realized it had to rethink the traditional relationship when the decision to exit the dynamic random access memory (DRAM) business forced the company to cut its work force by 30 percent and shut down eight plants in 1985. While Intel had historically focused on individual ownership for career development and had never had a no-layoffs policy, the downsizing led to more significant changes in the employment relationship. Since that time, Intel has emphasized its "own your employability career" philosophy, believing that people development has to keep up with changes in business technology.

Innovative processes and programs have been designed

to meet business requirements, support the new philosophy, and establish a balanced relationship. First of all, the company committed to open communication. Employees receive an update on the state of the business every quarter. It commences with a video explanation of the most recent financial results, a pretty frank and detailed discussion of the market and challenges looking forward, and a summary of the marching orders for the next 180 days, presented in the context of changing skill requirements.

The CEO is involved in the delivery of the corporate part of the message. It then cascades down into the organization, rather than getting distributed centrally. To reinforce the importance of the communication process, a survey is sent out every quarter asking each employee to evaluate the video, the corporate part of the presentation, the length of the presentation, and the effectiveness of his own manager's presentation.

Intel also accelerated its investment in training, so that it now spends 6 percent of its annual payroll on programs that range from technology and management issues to corporate values and culture. A stunning 2,800 courses are provided, and senior managers get up before the blackboard and teach at its university at least once every quarter.

The company, which added some 9,000 people to its rolls in 1995, has an extremely active internal posting program to help employees evaluate career options. Almost all jobs are posted and accessed on computers. Employees can get their name in the hopper simply by sending an e-mail to the job owner. Guidelines have been established, and employees are encouraged to tell their manager that they are applying for a particular job. The current manager can overrule a move because of critical skill requirements, but this doesn't happen very often. Managers don't want to see good people leave the company, so they support the program voluntarily.

At Intel, each employee receives a formal annual review. During this review, individuals are told three things: (1) how they rate against expectations of the job—outstanding, successful, or improvement required; (2) how they rank against others performing similar work—top, middle, or lower third;

(3) how they are trending—faster, equal to, or slower than others. If there are sustained performance problems, a corrective action plan is developed with a three- to six-month timetable. Three-hundred-sixty-degree feedback is given to everyone, even the CEO. The employee then puts together and drives the process of preparing development plans. A career development center with a variety of counseling and career resources supports employees in preparing their development plans and determining longer-term career options.

Rewards are clearly linked to performance. About half of pay is tied to company and/or divisional performance, and more than 70 percent of employees have rights to purchase stock options. The way Intel management sums this up is, "The reward system reinforces the company's high expectations of its employees to grow, learn, and lead."

The company monitors changing skill requirements and shifts existing employees from declining into emerging areas whenever possible. When it becomes neccessary to downsize a business, Intel institutes its redeployment program. Under this program, managers effectively lay off people, and the head count of the business unit is moved off the payroll. These people enter a redeployment pool under the auspices of human resources. Once in the pool, employees generally have four to six months, and can do one of three things: (1) search for another job within Intel; (2) seek additional training that will enable them to pursue a new position; (3) take a temporary assignment that doesn't count against their time in the pool. By no means is the redeployment pool a dumping ground for performance problems. Poor performers leave the company rather than enter the pool. The company treats redeployment as a benefit, spending $6 million to $10 million a year on the program.

Two vignettes of actual Intel employees sheds some light on how the system actually works.

In the spring of 1992, after twelve years as a production specialist at an Intel semiconductor manufacturing plant in Folsom, California, Joe Silva and his colleagues were facing a departmental downsizing. Instead of viewing this as a career threat, Joe looked on the demise of his job as, of all things, a lucky break. As he put it, "I felt that I never had a chance to grow."

Silva knew he would have an opportunity to explore other options. About two years before, Intel had introduced its redeployment policy. While it calls upon workers to take the lead in identifying their own potential talents, learning new skills, and searching for opportunities, it also requires that Intel managers take chances on people like Silva.

Within three weeks, Silva found an opening, arranged an interview, and convinced the manager that he could learn the necessary skills, including phone installation, cable management, and setting up networks. He began his new job with the intent of studying other communications fields and potentially becoming a planner.

Several years ago, a maintenance technician at one Intel plant by the name of Roger had a heart attack. His cardiovascular condition prevented him from returning to strenuous maintenance work and required that he find less physically stressful work. Roger wanted to remain with Intel. "Even though he'd had no education beyond high school, Roger had an interest in computers," says Maureen Shiells, who at the time managed a group that dealt with Intel employees on disability leave. "We had him talk with different computer folks to see what he might like, and after that Roger went to a junior college to learn computer programming. The people at the plant found him an old surplus computer to use at home. Meanwhile, he'd work one day a week, so we could keep him on full benefits. In two years, after earning his AA degree, he started full time as a programmer."

## 3Com

3Com, one of the nation's leading global data networking companies, has moved aggressively toward establishing a people partnership based on the concept of employability. 3Com has been growing at an annual rate of 50 to 75 percent, and one of the key reasons is the company's handling of people. Half of its employees have less than one year of service, and there is an independent work force that accounts for 20 percent of employees. The company added nearly 1,200 jobs in 1996. Roughly 50 percent of the workers are nomadic, meaning they can and do work anywhere.

3Com stresses interdependence, not loyalty, as the basis of the employer-employee relationship. It seeks commitment from employees as part of an interdependent adult relationship where self-esteem and power come from within the individual. Debra Engel, the senior vice president of corporate services at 3Com, is careful to draw a distinction between loyalty and commitment. She cautions against "blind-faith loyalty," for she feels that in that kind of environment it is difficult to keep people shaken up and moving forward. Given the rapid pace of growth in its industry, speed is a critical requirement for 3Com. The "old *Silicon* Valley culture" produced sluggish, dependent organizations which move way too slow in an environment where half the revenue stems from new products.

At 3Com, this new employee relationship shows itself in a sense of urgency, high productivity, high commitment, collaborations, and adaptability/flexibility. Engel believes that people crave honesty, openness, meaningful work, learning support, recognition that they are whole people, and more control over their lives. The new employment relationship moves from dependency to interdependency, from paternalism to partnership, and from entitlement to earning what you get.

People systems are designed to drive commitment to results and productivity. At 3Com, for instance, all jobs are posted, no matter how high. For every job, searches are conducted on both the inside and the outside. This accomplishes two things: it keeps the tension on people and it lets people refer others they know who may be appropriate. At the end of the day, about one-third of the positions are filled internally.

3Com also provides easy access to services that enhance productivity. For example, 3Com offices are outfitted with such niceties as fitness centers, dry cleaners, shoe repair, video rental counters, car repair, car washes, Starbucks in the lobby, as well as other services that help make workers more productive. Unlike at other companies, however, these are not treated as entitlements. 3Com charges for all of them and requires that they at least break even, as well as stimulate productivity. 3Com will consider almost any proposal for a new service that makes business sense and can satisfy the break-even requirement.

## HEWLETT-PACKARD

Another good company to learn from is Hewlett–Packard. It was founded on two passions: the passion to make a unique technological contribution in any product area, and the passion to implement a unique approach to people management. The founders hoped to "create the kind of company we would like to work for." The objective was to bring about an environment to attract and retain top talent, allowing them to "become all they can be." Bill Hewlett described the HP way as follows: "I feel, in general terms, it is the policies and actions that flow from the belief that men and women want to do a good job, a creative job, and that if they are provided the right environment they will do so." The principles that underpin HP's relationships with its employees have always been:

- Entrepreneurial spirit
- Accountability for results—little tolerance for those who don't make a contribution
- Share in the company's success
- Free and open communications
- Informality
- Creativity and innovation
- Emphasis on teamwork
- Treating people with dignity and respect
- Trust and belief in people
- Not a hire-and-fire organization

HP's formal and informal people processes and programs have always reflected these principles. For example, HP pioneered profit-sharing type programs in the 1940s with its production bonus system. The company operates an open-door policy that guarantees the right of any employee to access any other for consultation and advice. The practice of "Management by Wandering Around" at all levels of the company reflects a commitment to keep up to date with individuals and activities through impromptu discussions, "coffee talks," communication lunches, and the like.

HP found itself at a critical juncture in 1985, when it reached the dire conclusion that it had the wrong skill mix and deployment of people. Job security had been a long-standing by-product of HP's philosophy and practices. To be sure, there had never been a no-layoffs policy at HP, but its set of beliefs was intended to guide the company to the kinds of businesses it would enter—for example, walking away from big military opportunities in the 1940s for fear of becoming a hire and fire company. As a result, it revamped its corporate objective from job security to one of providing employment security based on the performance of the individual, the business, and the company. HP felt it was critical to inject performance and accountability back into the company. Nevertheless, management will do all that it can to avoid layoffs if practical alternatives exist, and the company requires employees to be flexible, to take overtime, time off, and commit to continuous learning.

In contrast to a company like 3Com, HP wants to encourage loyalty. It feels that security helps attract and retain top people, and that it can be a differentiator. It doesn't like the word employability if it means that at the end of every paycheck the employer and employee are even and owe each other nothing. HP believes that the primary source of competitive advantage is attracting and retaining people.

Hewlett-Packard has introduced its own series of programs to support the changes in its people philosophy. When cuts in the work force have to take place, voluntary severance is offered to everyone, capped to the numbers that can be accepted. If more individuals apply, HP uses length of service as its gauge to accept applications (those around the longest leave first).

Second, HP offers enhanced early retirement to anyone in the work force. Since 1985, it has only been used three times for general downsizing.

Third, HP has a redeployment policy, which it uses to find the individuals required to achieve the target numbers. Businesses identify excess people and can protect critical skills. Those protected, however, cannot exceed 10 percent of the employee population. Individuals are given three months to find another job within HP. They are also given half a month's pay per year of service if they leave HP during the three months. After three months, if they have not made a choice HP will place them directly.

## OTHER EARLY ADOPTERS

High-tech companies are probably the farthest along in terms of developing and implementing the New People Partnership, but they are by no means the only companies that are moving in this direction.

The cover of Monsanto Company's 1995 annual report, quoting from an article in *Barron's,* says, "Say 'biotech' and chances are you'll think anything but 'Monsanto,' a lumbering, 94-year-old chemical maker in St. Louis." Founded in 1901 as a manufacturer of saccharin and long known as a chemical company, Monsanto is undergoing a transformation to prepare itself for the twenty-first century. Robert Shapiro, its CEO, set the company on a course to become a life sciences company, with strong bases in agriculture, food, and pharmaceuticals. With the spin-off of the company's remaining chemical businesses to shareholders in 1997, Monsanto has effectively completed that transition and become a $6 billion life sciences company, one focused on feeding the world, creating a sustainable environment, and helping people to live longer, healthier lives.

To fully achieve its vision, Monsanto must not only capture particular opportunities in each of its businesses, but also integrate capabilities across agriculture, food, and health by sharing knowledge and scale and by applying a range of skills across the interconnections among the businesses. As its assistant chief scientist and chief biotechnologist, Ganesh Kishore, says, "The opportunities in life sciences exist at the explosion of interfaces."

Exploiting those opportunities requires a fundamental change in how people work together. The company will require greater foresight, insight, and creativity, along with speed and the courage to move forward in a rapid and ever changing world. Success will depend on sharing and leveraging the knowledge inherent in people and exploiting diversity in thinking and people to enhance results.

One of the areas of early focus has been on communicating and building the desired culture and behaviors—through traditional means like videos and newsletters as well as day-to-day conversations. Bob Shapiro talks about the personalized conversations as perhaps being more important to the company's success than any other single factor. Through a series of formatted small group conversations (as opposed to traditional workshops), employees are encouraged to discuss the transformation into a life sciences company—the nature of the strategic business opportunities, what it requires for Monsanto to succeed, the desired culture, how to work together, the personal transitions required, and so forth. The idea is to address the issues at the personal level, and thus create the desired sense of passion in each employee. In addition to the "conversations," Monsanto has recently launched a quarterly videoconference, beamed by satellite around the world, in which a panel of people selected from throughout the company, engage in a dialogue with the CEO about where the company is going. All employees are invited to submit questions.

Managing resources and building an organization to deliver performance consistent with the vision is requiring a reassessment of Monsanto's people systems. Redefining the relationship between the company and its employees is one critical element. Monsanto recognizes it cannot offer job security—and that many of the types of people it desires don't plan to stay at one company for their entire career. The company wants to attract talented individuals who are passionately committed to making a difference for the company. To build that sense of passion and commitment, Monsanto wants to create a "fabulous place to work" by offering exciting opportunities for work and for growth and development, highly competitive rewards that will build a sense of ownership, and an environment that makes people feel loved and valued while helping them maximize their potential in their work and personal lives.

To that end, employees have been given greater accountability for their career development through an "open-market" staffing process. Personal Development Centers have been established to provide counseling and support to employees as they explore their development needs and opportunities. Leaders are being held accountable for facilitating the development of their people. The company is exploring a range of options (e.g., child care and concierge services) designed to help create a supportive environment that lets people manage their busy lives so they can be more productive when they are at work.

Reward systems are being redesigned to focus on growth and instill a sense of ownership in the company. Beginning in 1996, Monsanto granted stock options to the 95 percent of employees who previously did not participate in a stock-option program. In 1997, Economic Value Added (EVA) was adopted as the primary measure of financial performance. Incentive plans are tied to EVA, and employees eligible for management incentives have had a portion of their incentive converted into options.

Development of an overall learning strategy and the establishment of a Life Sciences University are also under way to meet the need to build relationships and leverage insight and knowledge across the organization.

At the Norwest Corporation, career development is very much a shared responsibility. Richard Kovacevich, the president and CEO of Norwest, says it all too well: "The primary responsibility of business managers is to influence the hearts and minds of our people, consistent with the culture of Norwest, so they care more about our business than competitors care about theirs." Norwest employees are expected to take charge of their own career development, understand the competencies required for their next job, and then enroll in Norwest training courses to build those competencies. The company invests in extensive training courses to increase knowledge, support continuing education, develop management and leadership skills, provide mentoring and coaching, and find challenging new assignments. More than 85 percent of Norwest employees are shareholders, thereby strengthening their bond with the company and their commitment to company performance.

Southwest Airlines has built an effective people system by tightly linking its people processes with an emphasis on customer service and cost management. The company stresses business priorities that make a difference: intense commitment to customer service and focus on maintaining low costs. Southwest puts great stock in a family culture with a high degree of loyalty. Heavy emphasis is placed on social interaction, creating a fun work environment, and facilitating sharing of information among employees.

Employees enjoy an informal communication style and complete access to all levels of management. The CEO, Herb Kelleher, is known to everyone as "Herb." He maintains an open-door policy that allows line workers to contact him, and he promises to respond to employee ideas or questions within five days.

The strength of Southwest's relationship with employees enables it to sustain a superior cost position and exceptional performance. Lack of work rules common in the airline industry enables Southwest employees to work longer hours and to perform multiple jobs. The longer hours mean higher wages for the workers, while the company enjoys competitive, if not lower, hourly labor costs. Southwest's dedicated work force delivers superior performance, measured by on-time performance, fewest lost bags, and fewest number of customer complaints, and produces higher aircraft utilization through faster airplane turnaround. At Southwest, turnover is among the lowest in the airline industry, and the company has never had an employee furlough or layoff.

Marriott's emerging relationship with its employees and its human resource strategies are yielding big returns in increased productivity and enhanced service levels. Marriott is finding creative ways to deliver gains with its staff of more than 130,000 hourly workers (e.g., housekeepers, laundry staff) that average only about $7 an hour in pay. These low-wage employees typically present a variety of management challenges: lack of education, little knowledge of English, poor attendance, culture conflicts, and so forth. Marriott has found that it cannot ignore the needs of this work force—in times of low unemployment, replacements are not as easy or as cost-effective to find—and has stepped up to the challenge of making the system work with these employees. Instead of raising wages, Marriott has focused on helping solve workers' problems, whether by having managers spend time counseling individual employees about child care, providing "English as a Second Language" courses on site, or setting up its Associate Resource Line that staff can call (in more than a hundred languages) to obtain the services of a social worker. Marriott estimates it will achieve a return savings of five times its $2 million investment for the resource line in reduced turnover, absenteeism, and tardiness.

## COMMON THEMES AND PRINCIPLES

Clearly, each of the companies we've mentioned is pursuing an employment relationship and set of human resource policies that makes the most sense for its unique situation, and they are at different stages of implementation. Keep in mind that the New People Partnership is not a rigid prescription but a flexible concept that must be adapted to the demands of each company. And clearly, the need for defining a New People Partnership will fluctuate by industry and certain company attributes. As we look across industries and companies, we find that a New People Partnership is becoming particularly important for companies:

- With high dependence on technology whose skill requirements change rapidly as technology advances, thus requiring a more highly skilled and flexible work force
- With a high degree of customer interface, where employee satisfaction is a critical driver of customer satisfaction
- In industries with significant competition where employee productivity is critical to market success
- In industries where people are the sole source of competitive advantage and where reliance on demonstration of individual skills makes it critical to attract, develop, and retain talent
- In markets where there are labor shortages and it is critical to attract and retain key talent
- Where there is a strong government or trade organization role and high expectations of the company's role in providing ongoing employment
- That are large and decentralized, in which isolation from other staff increases the importance of establishing clear common goals

What are the principles that define this New People Partnership? A successful people partnership is a coherent set of people systems and processes that reflect the business environment, individual company strategy, and organizational values. Each one will be unique to a company and its employees. But there are some common threads and lessons that can be learned from all the companies that are exploring the New People Partnership. Boiled down to its essentials, there are five key principles to this New People Partnership:

1. Both parties commit to *employee well-being* as a core value
2. *Open communication* forms the foundation for the day-to-day relationship
3. Employees manage their own *careers*
4. Employees gain "employable" security by *building critical skills*
5. *Accountability* for performance extends to all levels of the organization

Let's look at how each of these principles works and what it means to implement it.

## BOTH PARTIES COMMIT TO EMPLOYEE WELL-BEING AS A CORE VALUE

The first step toward a New People Partnership is a commitment to the well-being of employees. As Robert Saldich, the former CEO of Raychem, said, "Companies must shift from using and then harvesting employees to constantly renewing employees." Unless both the employer and the employee abandon any illusions and agree that employee well-being is a core value, the New People Partnership will surely disintegrate. This commitment has to originate at the highest level in the corporation and through more than sheer rhetoric. It must be embodied in everything the company does and everything it communicates internally and externally. And there must be a coherent link between the people strategy and vision and the business strategy and vision.

To begin to think about how to understand and implement this principle, a company must first articulate, and preferably quantify, how employee well-being affects organization performance. While the logic is reasonably straightforward, the real business case for sustaining and improving employee well-being can be hard to make. In the hospitality and airline industries one can define the link between front-line employee satisfaction and customer satisfaction. In many of these cases, the costs of high turnover can be readily quantified. In the high-tech arena, where companies have aggressive growth objectives and there is a shortage of the most highly skilled labor, the cost of turnover can be substantial. In other industries, the business case can be harder to develop. But without the business case, it can be difficult to instill employee well-being as a value if it has not been viewed as one in the past.

A company must also demonstrate that it is wedded to maintaining and furthering the well-being of its employees. This is not a one-time event, but an ongoing commitment. At the same time, the employees must make the business argument for programs designed to bolster their well-being, and they must appreciate the relationship between their well-being and the organization's performance. 3Com's ongoing commitment to evaluate and provide any service (whether a car wash or a dry cleaner) that improves productivity and meets the break-even requirement is a clear example of this practice at work.

At Monsanto, Donna Kindl, the vice president of human resources, talks about the company's need for "complete people." This is not intended as an altruistic statement, but rather a reflection of the fact that the company needs to tap into the full potential of its employees when they are at work. At the same time, it reflects the belief that if people are working incredibly long hours—not taking off weekends, skipping vacations, getting inadequate rest and exercise, not seeing their families—then they cannot be performing at their peak at the office. She encourages employees to take the lead in thinking about how to achieve "full-life integration," reaching maximum potential in all aspects of their lives, and solicits feedback from their families. Moreover, the company is looking into offering a variety of services that help people manage their busy lives so they can be more productive.

Motorola offers another example of this principle. It has developed a broad-based approach to identify, elevate, and resolve employee issues. In what is called the Individual Dignity Entitlement Program, employees are asked to answer the following questions every quarter and review them with their supervisors:

1. Do you have a substantive, meaningful job that contributes to the success of Motorola?
2. Do you know the on-the-job behaviors and have the knowledge base to be successful?
3. Has the training been identified and made available to continuously upgrade your skills?
4. Do you have a personal career plan, and is it exciting, achievable, and being acted upon?
5. Do you receive candid positive or negative feedback at least every thirty days which is helpful in improving or achieving your career plan?
6. Is there appropriate sensitivity to your personal circumstances, gender, and/or cultural heritage so that such issues do not detract from your success?

For any question to which the answer is "no," there is an established process for bringing the issue to the attention of the supervisor's supervisor. Unresolved issues bubble up all the way to the CEO.

## OPEN COMMUNICATION FORMS THE FOUNDATION FOR THE DAY-TO-DAY RELATIONSHIP

In this new approach, the burden is fully on the company to clearly communicate the basis of the employment relationship to all its employees and to keep employees abreast of issues facing the company and the implications for them as individuals. For companies that have typically been reluctant to communicate information until necessary or until the desired course of action becomes absolutely clear, this may constitute the most formidable challenge to breathing life into the New People Partnership. It requires new confidence, trust, and flexibility.

3Com has committed to an open communication process in which managers tell employees what is going on and what the implications are for individuals. Most departments hold weekly meetings to discuss the state of the business and the implications for employees. At Intel, every new employee participates in seven seminars during the first year of employment that cover the company's values, culture, and business, and spell out the employee behaviors that go along with living the Intel values. Every quarter, CEO Andy Grove provides a two-hour overview on the state of the business. HP communicates its operating results on a quarterly basis, along with measures of the business fundamentals and employee satisfaction.

## EMPLOYEES MANAGE THEIR OWN CAREERS

For employability to work effectively, employees must actively seek and create their own career opportunities. They need to communicate openly about personal and professional needs and expectations. And they must be afforded unrestricted access to alternative job opportunities in the company.

What does this mean for the company? For one thing, it must support employees in identifying and evaluating job opportunities inside and outside the company. It needs to communicate openly about the future of the business and the implications for the individual, allowing employees to build a customized career path. In this environment, there is no stigma attached to looking for a new job, there is limited ownership of people except in cases of critical skills, and there is a recognition that employability and managing careers are in the best interest of both the corporation and the individual. This is about a mutual investment which creates real barriers to separation, and it is about genuine trust in each other.

Many companies have formalized their job posting processes which enable people to identify and apply for job opportunities. They are also setting up career development centers which help workers identify their own talents, learn new skills, and search for opportunities both inside and outside the company.

Raychem provides additional insight into career management under the New People Partnership. At Raychem, all jobs are posted. Any employee can apply for and accept an assignment that is offered while giving just two weeks' notice to his or her current manager. As a result, Raychem is seeing appreciably more movement of people laterally and across functions. For example, an organization development person settled into his new position after stints as a controller and logistics manager.

Raychem has also placed significant emphasis on individual development planning. Everyone in the organization, including all operators in the plants, has a written development plan. Everyone is on "community feedback," a simplified version of three-sixty feedback in which three to five people are selected by the employee and his or her manager to provide feedback. Each employee has a quarterly update to determine how well he or she is doing against this development plan. One of the first and most visible steps Raychem took in promoting the new employment relationship and the concept of employability was to provide on-site career services. They now have several of these career development centers that give employees access to career counselors and other resources to assist in development and career planning.

## EMPLOYEES GAIN "EMPLOYABLE" SECURITY BY BUILDING CRITICAL SKILLS

The notion that employees must learn critical skills to ensure their employability rests at the very heart of the New People Partnership. Employees are furnished extensive opportunities to build skills that are desired in the marketplace, not just in their own company. Learning and people development are entwined in all aspects of the business.

But it is not a one-way street. Employees must also commit themselves to continuous learning to develop these critical skills. The days when someone is promoted because of who he knows and his exquisite understanding of the politics and processes of the company are numbered. What matters is what you know and how you get things done.

In an organization like Intel, employees must take personal accountability for learning and building their skills. Intel provides the resources to support learning through its training programs and career centers. Employees must understand their own performance reviews, as well as their own goals and objectives, and lay out a plan that addresses both.

Motorola was one of the first to truly integrate education with business targets. At Motorola, gaps between strategic objectives and skill levels set the stage for training and development goals. Comprehensive training systems have been developed to support strategies (e.g., Six Sigma Defect Reduction Program).

The company has committed the resources to make it happen. Motorola University, established in 1981 with a budget of $2 million, now has some two dozen sites worldwide and a $120 million annual budget. Every Motorola employee receives at least forty hours of training annually. Many training courses have been offered not only to employees but also to suppliers and customers. In its courses, Motorola favors apprenticeship or "embedded learning"—new employees learn tasks under a more experienced worker's guidance, in addition to formal training.

And Motorola has the dedication to stay the course. While it is difficult to measure the rewards of training, Motorola claims that each training dollar yields $30 in productivity gains over three years. Its commitment to lifelong learning extends beyond training current employees to improving students' preparation for the workplace and investing millions in a campaign to overhaul school curriculums. As Robert Galvin has said, "Today, we spend hundreds of millions of dollars on training. These items don't 'cost' us any money because they make each of us a little smarter, a little more competitive."

## Accountability for Performance Extends to All Levels of the Organization

An important tenet of the New People Partnership is that employees take personal responsibility for the company's competitiveness. They have to accept the reality that their personal future and the attractiveness of their job are directly tied to the company's performance. Accordingly, employees are held accountable for the organization's performance at all levels, and the performance of managers is measured against the New People Partnership.

Again this means some notable changes in the way a company evaluates and rewards its work force—linking pay with organization performance and offering employees the opportunity to share in both the risks and returns. At HP, all employees participate in a profit-sharing plan. And employees may be asked to accept a reduction in work schedule and pay if business performance suffers. Intel also links employee pay with company and/or divisional performance, and more than 70 percent of employees have rights to purchase stock options.

At Norwest, 85 percent of employees are also owners. As one employee puts it: "We think and act like owners because we are. With 85 percent of us owning stock in Norwest, we are aligned with the interests of shareholders, have a growing stake in the company, and are rewarded through a higher stock price for ideas that improve efficiency, enhance service to customers, and increase sales."

## Making the New People Partnership Happen

Make no mistake, implementing the New People Partnership is no easy assignment. The concepts are relatively straightforward, but executing it in a coherent and consistent manner that fits one's own company is very difficult. It requires a coherent link between the business strategy, the people strategy, and measures and rewards. This means a fundamental transformation in many companies. To accomplish it requires:

- Determining the business imperatives that demand a New People Partnership
- Developing a people strategy that is clearly linked to the business strategy
- Defining the principles that will guide the New People Partnership
- Designing or redesigning human resource processes
- Establishing quantifiable measures and a process for tracking implementation success

Understanding the business imperatives that require a New People Partnership is all about developing the business case for change. It is about understanding how employee well-being and employee satisfaction affect organization performance (the first principle of the New People Partnership). To underscore the point, it is worth repeating that an organization needs to be able to make a real and quantifiable business case for change. This forms the basis for everything that follows. In the absence of a well-understood case for change, the organization runs the risk that this is a "flavor of the month" initiative that will fade away before having any measurable impact.

Once the imperatives for change are understood, a well-developed people strategy is needed to meet the organization's long-term requirements for people resources. Companies need a structured, analytical approach to identify anticipated gaps and imbalances in people resources, staffing levels, skills, and anticipated movements. They need to drive the business plan down to specific human resource action plans as well as develop a corporate-wide agenda.

Business requirements in turn shape the desired type of organization and people. Once grounded in the business realities, the principles guiding a New People Partnership can be articulated in a way that meets the needs of the business, the needs of employees, and the needs of the communities. Specific principles around employee well-being, communication, career management, learning and skill-building, and performance accountability can be defined and tailored to meet the needs of the organization.

To make the New People Partnership a reality, companies will need new people processes. The disconnect between the stated value of people to the organization and the actions that result is most often a reflection of people systems and processes that are out of date and way out of sync with the needs of the business. The gaps can be significant. For example:

- Recruiting and staffing—an imbalance in internal movement, inadequate in some areas and excessive churn in others; the wrong skill mix against future needs; long hiring cycle times and high costs per hire; burdensome succession planning
- Employee development—process out of sync with current career paths; development planning a paper exercise with no accountability for implementation
- Performance management—too many objectives to keep employees focused on top priorities; objectives not linked to desired changes in behavior and skills; marginal performers continue to thrive
- Rewards—rewards tied to promotions that are increasingly unavailable; compensation not aligned with new organizations (e.g., team-based); compensation structure does not provide for true sharing of risks or returns
- Separation—best people leave; other employees not prepared for transitions; cost of packages spiraling upward

Addressing these gaps and making the New People Partnership really work means delving into the details of all these processes. If the day-to-day handling of people-related issues does not reflect and reinforce the New People Partnership fully, it is difficult to be successful. At the highest level, an organization must focus on five people-process imperatives to drive the New People Partnership:

- Create recruiting and staffing processes that place exceptional diversified talent at all levels and career stages, while allowing employees to pursue opportunities without restriction
- Place accountability for career development with the individual, while renewing commitment and resources devoted to training and development
- Establish continued development as a condition of employment and enforce a disciplined performance management process to continually enhance performance
- Redesign rewards to link them closely to performance
- Establish separation as a natural career stage and separate those who consistently underperform

While these are not the only people processes likely to require some degree of redesign to support the New People Partnership, they are usually the most critical areas to be addressed. At the same time, it is worth emphasizing the role that information technology plays in enabling many of the desired changes. Investments in information technology may be required to develop and deploy tools to support employees in identifying and pursuing job opportunities, developing career plans, and obtaining appropriate training.

The last critical step in implementing the New People Partnership is establishing quantifiable measures and a process for tracking implementation success so that everything is tied back to the business case. Many companies implement new people processes and programs without any good way to measure the impact they are having on the organization and the return on investment. We find that you get what you measure. To really make the New People Partnership work, it is critical to determine methods for tracking key components of the model. Based on the business case, there should be measures that can be tracked like unwanted attrition, shortages in key skill areas, and customer satisfaction.

Focus groups and employee feedback surveys can also be very helpful as vehicles to gauge employee satisfaction. Pete Peterson, formerly Hewlett-Packard's vice president for human resources, lauds the benefit of employee surveys. By looking at worker surveys over twenty years, HP has been able to understand how employee attitudes are changing, where problems are arising in various units of the company, where managers need to be consulted to address some of these concerns, and when things are veering off course.

## REALIZING THE BENEFITS

Early adopters of the New People Partnership have been universal in applauding its strategic, operational, and financial benefits. The strategic benefits include greater employee loyalty and commitment to business goals, a way to drive cultural and behavioral change, a stronger corporate image to key stakeholders, an advantaged access to labor markets, and improved customer relationships and customer satisfaction.

The operating benefits include a reduction in unwanted attrition by enabling companies to retain key talent and lowering absenteeism. And, not surprisingly, the financial benefits include higher revenue and profits, lower labor costs, and more efficient use of resources to enhance overall productivity. Companies like HP, Intel, 3Com, and Southwest Airlines all fundamentally believe that their relationship with employees and their integrated people strategies have been critical drivers of their success in the marketplace.

As organizations begin to move toward the vision of the Centerless Corporation, redefining the relationship between employer and employee will be central to the organization's ability to succeed in the marketplace. Success in the Centerless Corporation will be driven by the people out in the marketplace, not by those at the top. That means having a skilled, knowledgeable, and motivated work force at all levels. Without defining a New People Partnership, we don't believe it will be possible to get there.

We feel it is important for any company hoping to compete in the twenty-first century to incorporate the ideas of the New People Partnership. There is no denying that it is hard to change and to adopt new philosophies that are truly meaningful. But we believe that the New People Partnership is essential to the new business model and to a company's success in the future, and there is no choice for most corporations but to implement some form of it.

# CHAPTER FOUR

# MINING THE RICHES IN KNOWLEDGE

**KNOWLEDGE** has been an unshakable and important part of business for a long time. At one point, it was actually synonymous with craft. It was Peter Drucker, the distinguished management thinker, who coined the term "knowledge worker" to show that the knowledge is separate from the production. Rather, it is a more broadly and richly defined set of skills that includes very specific know-how and capabilities.

Nowadays, as companies are beginning to appreciate that knowledge is a source of untouchable strength, many of them are struggling to determine what their knowledge structure should be and how they can build on this knowledge base by becoming learning organizations—in other words, companies that benefit from their parade of experiences and apply what they discover to good purpose. Alas, it's not at all uncommon for a business to reinvent the wheel three or four different times simply because it is too feebly structured to learn from its doings. We had a client who actually did set up three different offices in China, all within the space of about a year. None of them was successful, because the company made a similar series of mistakes in all three instances.

This new focus on knowledge has contributed to a concomitant revolution in thinking on what exactly constitutes a corporation. It suggests a more complicated response to this basic question than has been the custom. Rather than a collection of businesses, a company is being seen as a collection of capabilities based on highly precise knowledge. In essence, a company is what it knows and what it is able to do.

Part of the knowledge structure, of course, is information. The availability and speed of capturing and transmitting information have very much defined the times. Access to state-of-the-art information capabilities has become a competitive necessity for many firms, an inherent component of building a value creation engine.

To appreciate the enabling role of information in business, we like to use an analogy rooted in an entirely unrelated field. A baffling dilemma facing physicists today is how to converge the Newtonian world of our physical surroundings that we see every day and the quantum world too minute for anyone to actually see. Our reality, of course, is a world of objects like the book you are holding. It certainly seems solid. Yet the book is in fact made up of atoms that are mostly empty space. Our heads are mostly empty space as well. Without carrying that thought too far, the issue is why is mostly empty space so real.

Particle accelerators and theoreticians are helping define a quantum world at its most fundamental level as pure potential with both wave and particle attributes. That potential is often thought of in a probability distribution. In other words, you cannot locate the spot of an electron with certainty.

A new branch of physics called the "physics of information" is fashioning a theory which may collapse the Newtonian and quantum world. It regards information as one of the fundamental pieces of the quantum world. According to this thinking, each basic particle or force boasts an information component. We know or can perceive the potential of the quantum world in our reality when the information component is released. That information then dissipates. Again look at the book. If this book were burned in a closed container filled with oxygen, all the molecules would still be locked in the container, but not in the form of a book. And we could not recreate the book from the ashes. The information of what makes the book a book has vanished.

Something very similar goes on in the world of business. Every company has some basic capabilities that it uses to compete. Those capabilities consist of many little things stitched together in a unique way: information, know-how, processes, market perceptions, and so forth. These all add up to the firm's knowledge structure. What we perceive is the performance or competitive advantage of the firm, not the sheer potential of the individual pieces. Each company assembles these in its own singular way. This, in part, explains why some companies are able to forge a dominant position in an industry for an extended period of time even though their competitors can see exactly what they are doing. The competitors cannot reconstruct the advantage simply by observing actions. For that tells them nothing about the firm's knowledge structure.

One of the reasons we stress knowledge so much is because our contacts with CEOs and top management, as well as many published studies, show that most senior executives simply do not yet understand the real implications of the knowledge revolution. Frankly, we believe that knowledge and its applications will upset the balance of power among companies. It will do everything from causing the disappearance or irrelevance of many suppliers of products and services to producing vast opportunities for growth, facilitating globalization, spawning new forms of communication, and demanding more astute leadership. That's merely a partial list, and yet it entails significant investments in people, capital, and other resources, not to mention major implications for business.

## MOST COMPANIES MISUSE KNOWLEDGE

Every company creates and uses knowledge, but few organizations actually learn or manage knowledge effectively. Knowledge isn't new. What's new is systematically creating, using, and improving it.

Unfortunately, in the orthodox business model managers blunder along content to have valuable troves of knowledge dormant and inaccessible. Most companies create and use plenty of bits of knowledge, but not efficiently or effectively. For the most part, knowledge is something that reposes in one person's drawer as some sort of unintentional secret, not in the hands of the people who really need it. It is often intuitive rather than explicit, and it is rarely detailed enough to be especially valuable. All too often, knowledge exists with multiple points of view instead of the collective best thinking. It is occasional but not integral to the business. And, most important, it is available but not used very much.

The majority of companies have their knowledge embedded in the people in the organization. Thus you can't really look it up, and so it gets lost. Every time someone leaves or dies or retires from a company, a mass of knowledge goes right out the door with that person, unless there is some structure to retain it. Whenever three of four key members of a corporate department leave en masse to join another firm, it is astonishing how often that newly barren department finds itself paralyzed by the loss of knowledge, barely able to function. All over the world, you see institutional knowledge getting lost by the minute (indeed by the millisecond). It is not easily replaced.

In a startling number of corporations, knowledge is delegated to the R&D department or to the training people or to the chief information officer. The CEO couldn't be bothered with it. If something important comes up, he assumes he'll be told. Someone else will know. And the advent of technology, particularly the Internet and intranet, has tremendously elevated the significance of knowledge, allowing it to be used in more creative ways. At the same time, it has created a fundamentally different set of opportunities and challenges for today's CEO.

And that is why, important as the New People Partnership is, it is inadequate without active management of the second business enabler—knowledge. The Centerless Corporation puts knowledge on a higher pedestal than it has ever been on.

Knowledge is transformed into a front-and-center CEO issue. Make no mistake, that is a monumental change from its role in the conventional business model.

What is more, our model addresses knowledge in the broadest possible sense, which is far more than what a corporation knows and can know. The definition that Nonaka and Takeuchi express in their book, the *Knowledge Creating Company,* is a useful one to consider. They sum up knowledge as having beliefs and commitment, action, and real meaning. That's saying a lot.

At Booz•Allen, we define knowledge as a set of understandings used by people to make decisions or take actions that are important to the company. It is defined by its use and its relevance to work. Information, of course, is an important subset, and it is key that it is something used by people. True knowledge should be linked to the building blocks of how the organization creates value, especially with unique know-how and capabilities. Thus how-to's, processes, information, insights, and the like are all integral pieces of a company's knowledge.

## MANAGING KNOWLEDGE

Today, most senior managers implicitly understand that knowledge matters and they are almost universally committed to the vague concept of "knowledge management" or of becoming a "learning organization." For the most part, they would agree with everything we have said so far.

The problem is that while most managers believe that knowledge is important, few of them can articulate what the value is or how to become a learning organization. Interestingly, over half of our clients across the world have raised this issue with us. Many have tried to launch a program; all are struggling to figure out how to succeed.

Perhaps the most important thing to remember is that the discipline is still immature, as evidenced by the explosion of meetings on this subject along the conference circuit and by the lack of clear answers. As early practitioners (we launched our own knowledge program in 1993), we have watched our own thinking evolve significantly over the years. But there is still a lot more evolution and revolution to come in the knowledge field.

So what does an effective knowledge program look like? Most companies that have done well in creating one have not conceived it as a separate and distinct "knowledge program," but rather have embedded basic tenets of learning or knowledge management into the core of a broader business transformation. But if you stop to think about it, this is not really a surprising finding, since a broader transformation program is more likely to successfully incorporate the linkage and coherence that will really extract the highest value from a knowledge program.

To bring the idea of knowledge management to life, let's look briefly at two early adapters before we turn to some important theoretical constructs: GE and Motorola. These are our favorite stories, and, in our view, the most viable role models—even though they didn't call their programs "knowledge management."

Motorola is famous for its Total Quality Management (TQM) effort, which, if you think about it, was an early knowledge program. The idea behind TQM was to systematically improve the cost-effectiveness of manufacturing by creating, using, and continuously improving understandings about how to make things. Motorola fundamentally changed its manufacturing paradigm. Through heavy investments in training, people were equipped with the skills they needed to collaborate and develop unique solutions to manufacturing process issues (statistical analysis, fishbone diagramming, facilitation). They were organized into collaborative "quality circles" that were supported by TQM experts and asked to go improve quality.

And they did it, over and over again. Not by focusing on knowledge or learning, per se, but by emphasizing quality and changing the overall manufacturing paradigm to something that embedded learning in all the key business processes.

Quality became part of everybody's job, and some people were assigned to help manage the process full-time. The results have been evident for years. But the point here is that through systematically managing the creation, use, and improvement of understandings about manufacturing processes, Motorola has achieved dramatic results at both the operating and financial levels.

GE provides an equally interesting, though entirely different story. While GE is famous for the concept of "work out," the important knowledge story, in our view, is the company's ability to systematically identify new paradigms from outside the company and then apply them across a set of diverse businesses. Take "Quick Response." Quick Response is a program to dramatically reduce order-to-delivery cycle times that GE adapted from a company in Norway named Sealand Appliance and applied across all of its manufacturing businesses. GE has done this with a whole series of new paradigms. The learning here occurs at the level of senior management looking for important new ideas and then people throughout the organization adapting them to drive performance in their particular business. That's leveraging knowledge.

The principal challenge in leveraging knowledge is to simultaneously drive business value, learning, and organizational change. Let's revisit Motorola to see what that means. Senior management recognized that quality would drive value and worked the dynamics of learning and change to enhance quality at the level of where the work was done, which resulted in dramatic performance improvements. Note that the focus is on a dynamic process, and that value comes from knowledge that is created (in the quality circles) and then used (in specific manufacturing processes).

## THE VALUE IS IN USING IT

As we've said before, knowledge is only relevant when it is used—it has no intrinsic value of its own. This is why initiatives to assign a value to a company's inventories of knowledge are so misguided. While we can argue that knowledge is power and that having it is valuable, there is really no point in trying to calculate the value of knowledge assets as if they were physical inventories like computer chips or loaves of bread. Management energy is better spent creating and using the forces that will drive overall performance and deliver value to the company's key constituencies.

From a theoretical standpoint, consider the Knowledge Dynamic depicted (Exhibit 1):

### EXHIBIT 1: THE KNOWLEDGE DYNAMIC

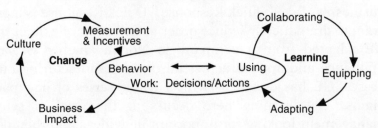

Change and learning are continuous cycles that propel the company to higher levels of performance over time. They are connected at the level of the people doing work or making decisions in all the important parts of the business. The "learning loop" involves people working together to learn and working individually as they conduct their jobs, also to learn.

All learning occurs in some form of collaboration, most powerfully in team collaboration with others (e.g., GE's management team looking for the next idea like Quick Response or demand flow manufacturing), but also in one person collaborating with others in understanding prior knowledge, either through study or casual discussion. When something is learned (like the TQM process), then people need to be equipped to utilize the knowledge. Adapting follows, as the learning is applied and adjusted to the particular situation at hand. It is then used, as learning accrues again and ultimately is formalized through collaboration. Systematic learning, or knowledge management, is the effort to do this in a focused way, aiming at the areas of understanding that are most important to the business.

The "organizational change loop" involves changing behaviors to get past what we call the four unnatural acts of knowledge: sharing, using, improving, and collaborating (we will discuss these more fully later in this chapter). A company's measurement and incentive structure must reinforce the desired behaviors and discourage the undesirable behaviors. Over time, a change in the culture will result if the new behaviors have a positive impact on the business, and this cultural change will reinforce the change loop itself, propelling the company to higher and higher levels of performance.

## FOUR PATHS TO LEVERAGING KNOWLEDGE

Of course, much of this is the traditional view of organizational change, and it is possible to "pick it up" anywhere in the cycle by driving changes in measurement/incentives or the culture or the desired business impact. However, because knowledge is fundamentally about people creating and using knowledge in their work, that is the place to begin—with the behavioral change required to surmount the particular challenges of creating and using knowledge.

To illustrate the variety in types of knowledge initiatives, we have broken them down according to the type of learning and change desired by the company (see Exhibit 2). There are two fundamentally different kinds of learning in business: applied learning, where a company focuses on applying the best of what is known (either internally or externally), or synthesis, where the company makes a determined effort to learn something new.

The choice of learning model depends upon the state of the underlying knowledge. If there are huge gaps between best and worst—either between your best and your worst, or between your best and what you see outside—the learning should focus on the applied learning model. If everything is mostly state of the art, then the "synthesis" model is appropriate. Clearly, a company may decide to undertake both types of learning in different areas of the business. On the change side, the decision is between continuous change or leaps, depending upon the overall strategic business imperative. Both are high impact. The four approaches to leveraging knowledge differentiate along these two dimensions, and all four cells represent powerful ways to leverage knowledge for the Centerless Corporation.

## PURSUING OPERATIONAL EXCELLENCE

The most common and best understood way to leverage knowledge is to organize learning to accelerate improvements in day-to-day decision-making (i.e., capabilities). We call this *Operational Excellence*. A program to enhance operational excellence makes sense when there are significant opportunities to improve by bringing the worst-performing up to the level of the best-performing within a given business paradigm. This is the focus of most best-practices programs: stop reinventing the wheel and make sure that everyone, everywhere is operating with the best available knowledge.

Buckman Labs, which provides specialty chemicals and services for water and waste treatment, papermaking, leather tanning and other industrial processes, is a good example of an Operational Excellence program. One of the objectives of its knowledge program is to ensure that the company's over one thousand associates have access to the best available information and knowledge to solve specific customer problems in the ninety countries and ten languages that Buckman serves. To enable this knowledge transfer, Buckman has built a global network tying together a variety of knowledge bases, including content and the names of experts. While the culture continues to evolve, collaboration is already extensive. In addition, a formal program of capturing examples of best practices for selected customer situations is working well to ensure that the current best thinking is used whenever possible.

While Operational Excellence programs are the most

**EXHIBIT 2: FOUR APPROACHES TO LEVERAGING KNOWLEDGE**

| | **CHANGE** | |
|---|---|---|
| | Continuous Change | Leaps |
| **"Push the Frontier"**<br><br>Continuous synthesis and improvement of state-of-the-art understandings to push the frontier of a given paradigm | | **"Big Ideas"**<br><br>Focused effort to create a fundamentally new idea that changes the rules of the game |
| **"Operational Excellence"**<br><br>Continuous identification and application of best practices (internal and external) within a given paradigm to close a large gap between best and worst internal practices | | **"Capability Paradigm Shift"**<br><br>One-time shift to a broad set of state-of-the-art understandings (when external is better than internal) followed by continuous improvement |

**LEARNING**
Synthesizing
Applying

common type of knowledge effort, they are also the hardest to pull off, because people have to change how they behave while doing the work in largely the same way, or at least within the same context. This kind of change program absolutely requires top management's sponsorship. It can have a profound impact on the company's performance. Focus is critical. The program needs to include a systematic effort to understand what is "best" and then to move toward it. Too many early initiatives that would appear to fall into the Operational Excellence category have failed because they were really only efforts to share knowledge having low impact, which could not justify the level of senior sponsorship necessary for success. It is these types of failure—usually bottom-up efforts—that have led many to believe that knowledge management is just another passing management fad.

The principal lessons we have learned about Operational Excellence programs are:

- Focus on achieving significant business benefits in a few activities
- Measure improvements to the bottom line, linked to operating measures
- Change the underlying business process (usually including changes in the skills of people)
- Execute a comprehensive change program
- Ensure the learning cycle is carefully structured to identify and select what is really best
- An intranet is a good vehicle for distributing content
- A corporate university is a powerful vehicle to enable adaptation and use

## PUSHING THE FRONTIER

An increasingly common type of program involves the ongoing synthesis of state-of-the-art understandings to push the frontier and solve specific problems. We call these programs *Push the Frontier.* The trick here is to get experts to collaborate on coming up with the better way.

An instructive example is the Innovation Teams that we established at Booz•Allen as part of our own knowledge program (which we will discuss later). We united global teams of experts on selected topics and gave them a set of very tough objectives. The idea was to push the thinking to come up with a common view on the best ideas about strategic alliances, organization, marketing customer care, and wargaming, to name a few.

Most research programs, while not in the new wave of the knowledge craze, fall into this category as well. Well-run research efforts enable experts to collaborate to drive to the next idea. It's learning to the core.

Olivetti Ricerca is the center of Olivetti Research and Development. It is a network of research laboratories and competence centers. Its mission is to work closely with Olivetti's various research and development organizations to develop new products, solutions, and services. Olivetti Ricerca uses an intranet to create a "virtual laboratory" where its researchers can push the frontier. This intranet links the Olivetti Ricerca sites with other Olivetti labs in Italy and around the world to help foster collaboration. Claudio Adriani, the director of technical strategies, says that Olivetti's goal "is to use the intranet for 'knowledge management,' making critical knowledge available wherever and whenever it is needed. In a research and development environment, the free exchange of ideas and information is a powerful catalyst for innovation."

The intranet is both a collaborative forum and a tool to equip researchers to do their work, and it has significantly reduced the amount of time they need to find both internal and external information. Researchers perform searches for articles, news, bibliographies, and they link to relevant Web sites all through the intranet. Collaboration is possible through "dedicated discussion areas," whereby researchers are encouraged to share ideas and information.

"We are beginning to see increased productivity and creativity with this new research and development model," Adriani says. "The Web is providing tools to form a renewed and more competitive Olivetti Research and Development."

The principal lessons learned about Push the Frontier programs are:

- Make sure the change program adequately addresses new levels of collaboration required among experts
- Build incentives into use processes
- Demonstrate impact through early "wins"
- Use different processes to attain the frontier than used to push the frontier
- Partner with external leaders

## THE PARADIGM SHIFTS

The third type of knowledge initiative focuses on what we call *Paradigm Shifts* in how key business activities are performed. Paradigms are evolving rapidly in many areas. For example, in marketing there is a shift from intuitive, expert-based marketing to deeply analytical capabilities for critical tactical decisions about pricing and product-line management. Customer service and support are changing from a paradigm where customer service either fielded calls (e.g., American Express's call centers) or dispatched a technician to fix something (e.g., your copier) to a fundamentally new world where customers actually take care of the problem themselves through the use of knowledge-based tools (e.g., Federal Express's Website for tracking packages, remote diagnostics for facility equipment).

Manufacturing is moving from Materials Requirements Planning (MRP) and activity cost-focused paradigms to demand flow and TQM. And that's only the beginning of the list. What makes these shifts in capabilities knowledge programs? A successful paradigm shift typically results in an initial order of magnitude increase in performance/cost, followed by continuous improvements. The whole idea is to embed the unnatural acts in the new paradigm. This type of change program is actually much easier to manage than the other two we have described so far because, by definition, it is part of a much broader, top-management change initiative.

The Internet appears to be driving paradigm shifts in sourcing and channel management. Strategic sourcing is one of the most important extended enterprise applications for knowledge. This is one area where companies can realize truly significant near-term profit improvement. Typically, better sourcing has three distinct phases:

*Phase 1: Buy better.* Companies need to profile their buying patterns, understand vendors, segment what they buy, and do better at selecting and targeting vendors. Generally, this will cut costs between 5 and 10 percent.

*Phase 2: Design better.* Companies need to improve vendors' capabilities, solicit vendor input, restructure product lines, and coordinate their buying patterns across business units. The benefits here are an additional 10 percent.

*Phase 3: Partner better.* Companies need to integrate subsystems, share benefits with their suppliers, and increase outsourcing. Another 5 to 10 percent in savings can be realized here.

Do not expect these results to come quickly. These are often multiyear, multistage efforts to improve buying patterns. Progress is dependent on the development of a stable vendor base and on clear-cut changes in people's behavior.

A proper knowledge structure, enhanced with an intranet access to shared agreements, specification databases, tools to track and analyze spending patterns, end-user buyer tools integrated with vendor and order management systems, and inventory visibility can furnish a wide variety of capabilities that will improve your sourcing.

Wal-Mart and Procter & Gamble use a sophisticated electronic data-interchange link (EDL) that allows P&G to manage Wal-Mart's P&G product inventory. Data is continuously fed to P&G via satellites. This data includes sales figures, inventory levels, and price information from each Wal-Mart store. P&G uses this data to anticipate sales, determine the amount of P&G product required, and automatically ship the merchandise directly from the factory to the specific store. P&G then invoices Wal-Mart electronically. Wal-Mart pays P&G the same way.

What benefits does this provide? P&G has experienced lower costs for order processing, billing, sales visits, and inventory. Wal-Mart has achieved reduced inventory holding charges, fewer stock outages, and less paperwork. In the end, the consumer wins by paying lower prices for P&G products when shopping at Wal-Mart.

Many companies today are realizing that they can create useful new channels through knowledge-laden Web sites. Retail channels like stores and mail-order catalogues are likely to disappear as their venue changes from paper to the Internet. Many companies are already providing such services to their clients: Spiegel and L.L. Bean sell clothing, Omaha Steaks and Hickory Farms sell specialty foods, Tower Records sells music (after letting you listen to a 35-second sample of your selection). And Peapod Services allows you to order groceries from a local supermarket's inventory for delivery to your door.

We have spoken of how one of the crucial parts of the Centerless Corporation is the New People Partnership. Consider a paradigm shift around how human resources are managed—across businesses to significantly enhance people programs.

Aetna, Alcoa, Eli Lilly, IBM, Monsanto, and Procter & Gamble started an Internet-based job search site in 1992. The site, known as the Online Career Center (http://www.occ.com), provides job ads, resumes, and career-related information. At last count, it had 262 corporate members, who pay $3,900 each to join the site and then a $2,400-per-year fee for the right to list job openings. Future employees can search the site and at no charge can add their resume for possible employers to read. This on-line site is part of a broader program to help employers find the right skill sets from a worldwide pool, while allowing employees to discover opportunities that they might otherwise have never heard of or even considered possible. AT&T recently initiated a similar consortium called the Talent Alliance.

Another example of a paradigm shift is Cadence Design Systems' new knowledge-based sales and delivery capability. Cadence Design is a $500-million provider of software and technical support for the semiconductor and computing systems industries. Cadence's CFO, H. Raymond Bingham, explained Cadence's motives behind its knowledge program: "We wanted to move beyond being a company that did business the old-fashioned way, with smart technical people creating products that were shipped to a sales and marketing force and explained through unidirectional communications. Sometimes they [the sales force] got the message, and sometimes not, so we set about creating this knowledge resource, initially for the sales force."

Cadence began building its intranet in February of 1995. It required an initial $100,000 investment and six months of development time. As it built the system, the company realized that it had to move toward products allowing for dynamic input from customers, technologists, service providers, and salespeople. Barry Demak, the manager of worldwide sales automation projects, said, "By putting everyone on the Web accessing information in both directions (internally and externally), we suddenly had a cohesive view of our markets, customers, and technologies."

Cadence's 300 salespeople receive key data on customers and competitors from 2,000 worldwide sources of information. Each salesperson can create a personal profile for every customer. According to Corey Leibow, vice president of worldwide marketing, "Our new sales and delivery process on the intranet gives us the ability to offer a wider range of solutions to existing customers and helps us to identify new markets and new customers."

Finally, consider Bank of Montreal. Under the leadership of Matthew Barrett, they have introduced a number of new paradigms as part of a broad transformation of the business. One of these was a shift from a classic accounting-based measurement system to evaluate branch performance to one based on evaluation against performance potential estimated from an in-depth understanding of controllable, exogenous, and structural factors. It is a brilliant knowledge program. Branch managers use a set of statistical models to assess potential, and results are available to all levels of management—all the time. By focusing on potential, instead of competing with each other, people seek help from one another. Branch managers look for colleagues who are outperforming them, but who face similar situations, and then find out what they are doing and implement the best practice.

Most companies focus on one paradigm shift at a time, largely to control the amount of change the organization has to absorb at once. However, it is possible to learn how to change and accelerate the introduction of new paradigms. As we discussed earlier, GE is systematically introducing a series of paradigm shifts in various capabilities, one or two at a time. The strategy appears to be to gain competitive advantage by adopting breakthrough concepts more quickly and effectively than its competitors, not by developing new paradigms.

The principal lessons learned about paradigm shift programs are:

- Focus on stimulating adoption of the new paradigm by setting aggressive performance targets and providing training and tools
- Hire people with the new skills required
- Demonstrate top management leadership
- Build learning into the transformation from the beginning
- Leverage the broader change program to drive the cultural change needed for learning

## GOING FOR THE BIG IDEAS

A different type of knowledge program focuses on the development of *Big Ideas*, or what we call strategic innovations.

Strategic innovations can change the rules of the game through marked improvements in the entire business system that delivers value to customers. As part of an ongoing research effort at Booz•Allen & Hamilton to assess the drivers that create long-term shareholder value, more than 1,300 large publicly traded companies in the United States during the past three decades were evaluated, along with case studies of 65 companies in the top 10 percent of shareholder value creation for at least a decade. One of our findings is that strategic innovations result in 25-to-30-percent annual increases in earnings, sustained over periods of 10 to 15 years, and that these occur most frequently in mature industries.

The knowledge dynamic is crucial to enabling strategic innovations, because our research indicates that most strategic innovations did not start out with the concept that ultimately proved successful. Innovations that in retrospect appear to be a single idea were in fact the result of a series of linked innovations and adaptation.

For example, Federal Express was started to provide guaranteed overnight delivery, which was a breakthrough idea. However, the initial target market was critical products like medical supplies or parts. The discovery that most of the actual volume was paper and the subsequent positioning around reliable delivery of important business material were what really drove growth.

Booz•Allen's research indicates that four broad concepts have been responsible for nearly 80 percent of the strategic innovations in the United States in the past thirty years (see Exhibit 3).

Learning to adapt a proven strategic innovation concept like power retailing, which has transformed a series of retail categories (including appliances, home improvement, tires, and toys), to a new category is difficult and time-consuming. One telling indication of just how hard is the fifteen years required for any of Home Depot's competitors to create an equally successful format—even though they could build upon Home Depot's experience. A strategic innovator's competitive advantage is not the breakthrough idea, but rather the

**EXHIBIT 3: Strategic Innovation**

| Concepts | Examples |
|---|---|
| Power Retailing | Circuit City<br>Home Depot |
| Bypass Step in Industry Value Chain | Tyson's<br>Frito-Lay<br>Dell Computers |
| Focus and Remove Complexity | Southwest Airlines<br>Nucor |
| Fully Leveraged Brands | Walt Disney<br>Coca-Cola |

myriad details of the successful business system and the ability to adapt rapidly and improve.

With the advent of the Internet, we are seeing a potentially new avenue for strategic innovation that could have dramatic effects on many industries, as the Internet allows companies to develop new relationships with customers and suppliers and to extend the boundaries of the company in areas such as sourcing and customer care. Dell Computer, already a successful strategic innovator, is selling over $1 million of orders per day over the Internet. Amazon books pioneered the Internet-based bookstore, and this notion is now being mimicked by Amazon's traditional bookstore competitors like Barnes and Noble, even though this could cannibalize B&N's existing businesses. As Internet-based strategies such as these are adapted and evolve, real strategic innovation may result.

So as we can see, the real power lies in a company's ability to adapt an idea over several years before rolling it out. Competitive defensibility resides in the know-how to apply the concept to create dramatically superior value for customers. Thus, Big Ideas are fundamentally about knowledge and learning. Knowledge initiatives directed toward Big Ideas focus on concept creation and validation, and on the feedback loops required to rapidly improve the concept.

The most important lessons learned about Big Idea programs are:

- Focus on building the learning (especially experimentation) and rapid feedback loops rather than detailed planning processes. Done right, Big Idea initiatives quickly generate the learning dynamic.
- Find some good concepts and wrap ideation processes around them (like the four main concepts of the past twenty years and the Internet).
- Involve three different kinds of people in the process: the gifted person with "foresight," those with a knack for research, and the select few who can manage both of the others.
- Evaluate the change challenge: it's either impossible—or relatively easy—depending upon senior management.

The most important thing to note about the framework and examples we have cited is that these powerful "knowledge programs" aren't knowledge programs at all. They are fundamental changes to the business which are driven by high-level business imperatives, and they embed the knowledge dynamic of learning, change, and business impact. Recognizing that knowledge isn't separate, but is one of the critical enabling factors to a more powerful management model, is the first step to getting it right. Failure to recognize this is probably why the discipline remains so immature.

## KNOWLEDGE NEEDS STRONG SCAFFOLDING

Knowledge needs the proper scaffolding to do its work. In the Centerless Corporation, a carefully designed knowledge architecture becomes crucial to the company's success. It gets away from the idea of compartmentalizing knowledge. It functions seamlessly inside the company, as well as with key suppliers and customers. Most important, it connects people and ideas continually. Intelligence is embedded into operations rather than extracted from it. That is when the company can be truly described as connected, learning, flat, customer-centered, and extended.

With this scaffolding erected, learning can occur—across the enterprise. This means that best practices can be transferred rapidly and replicating worst practices is thankfully avoided; new paradigm shifts can be implemented; collaboration that pushes the frontier can be enabled; and new big ideas can be created and evolved. And all of this can be done more quickly than was ever possible before, providing the Centerless Corporation with a powerful source of competitive advantage.

So what does this really mean in practical terms for the corporation? For one thing, it means that a company like Exxon no longer has to install different financial systems in different parts of the world. It means Exxon doesn't have to learn how to optimize a refinery all over again when it can find out about the latest developments instantaneously. Twenty-four-hour a day productivity in innovation also means getting products to market much faster. In essence, we're talking about a company that works across time zones, without walls, and with a common language and understanding. That translates into advances in product development, problem solving and troubleshooting, customer information, and all the other critical drivers of business success. Services are offered in a seamless manner from supplier to customer.

If you want to see knowledge used exquisitely, listen to Bob Shapiro, the CEO of Monsanto, as he discusses his R&D process: "We have facilities in the United States, in Asia, and in Europe. A problem will be worked on in our U.S. lab during its business hours, and all the data from that day's work will be on line and transmitted to our people in Asia, who continue work on their problem while the U.S. is sleeping. When they go to sleep it is transmitted to people in Europe who work on the same problem. What you are doing is shortening the cycle time in product development." Of course, the challenge in making this work is ensuring that collaboration is actually occurring across members of the extended team.

The Centerless Corporation recognizes that while individual learning always has been and will continue to remain important, real competitive advantage is derived from understanding how to systematically create, use, and improve knowledge to make the leap from individual learning to institutional learning, which has a much greater business impact for the firm. What makes this so difficult, and more art than science, is the fact that it requires working so many interrelated dynamics at once. There aren't any single solutions that can be applied everywhere, and so understanding how to quickly adapt and implement new ideas is key. A carefully designed knowledge architecture (see Exhibit 4) must address infrastructure (both the technology and full-time people), an understanding of the targeted knowledge itself, metrics, a focused program to ensure behavioral change, process (both business and knowledge), and the set of interrelated communities that collaborate and use the knowledge. These elements provide the scaffolding essential to enable knowledge to do its work.

By knowledge *infrastructure,* we mean people (dedicated staff) and technology. People are always a requirement—as either trainers, knowledge managers, or collaboration support/facilitation. Why? Because knowledge cannot be a nights-and-weekends activity. The people out there doing work and making decisions need support—either to be trained, to enable capture and access to learning in a knowledge base without enormous extra work (the role of a set of highly skilled knowledge managers), or to facilitate the work of experts engaged in collaboration.

Technology, while not a part of early knowledge programs, is a powerful enabler and a must for future knowledge programs. Newer and more powerful tools like the Internet and intranet can provide easy, high-visibility success by making previously hard-to-get-at knowledge readily accessible. And new advances in technology will make today's state-of-the-art quickly obsolete, enabling even more amazing advances.

Nevertheless, it is important to bear in mind that learn-

EXHIBIT 4: KNOWLEDGE PROGRAM ARCHITECTURE

Business Context and Imperatives

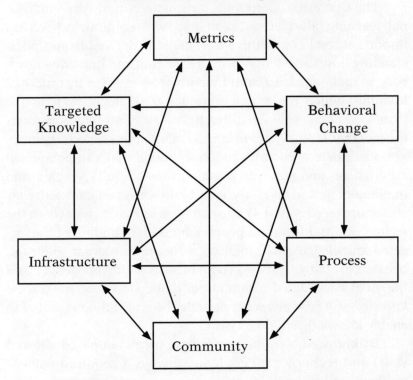

ing, not technology, is what knowledge initiatives are all about. The challenge is not to get over enthusiastic about all that technology can do now that it is no longer a constraint. Top management of the Centerless Corporation must quickly embrace and implement new technology enablers, but they must also keep a tight rein on the vision and avoid getting carried away by the technologists and "functionality freaks" in their organization who may have lost sight of the learning cycle that technology is supposed to enable.

## TARGETING YOUR KNOWLEDGE

Understanding who-you-want-to-learn-what is another important element of the design. We call this *targeted knowledge.*

The idea isn't to overengineer the knowledge dynamic, but to know what it is that you're trying to learn about and who in the organization is the best to do the learning, not to mention who should be equipped to use it. For example, if it's customer insight you want, think about what kind of insight and where it will be used. If it's a set of decision rules for a customer service agent, think about how to develop them, improve them, and equip agents to use them. The idea is to consciously plan for learning while leaving it open enough to be flexible. An art, to be sure. But it needs to be carefully planned and tightly focused to ensure that real value will emerge.

Most knowledge creation and learning occurs when people are reacting to someone else's thinking. This is why the concept of *communities* is so important and should be included in a knowledge program architecture. The most effective communities generally include a core of five to fifteen people, with a broader community of interested people. A learning organization consists of a network of overlapping communities like organizational units (business, function, geography), natural affinity groups, and special-purpose learning communities. Communities should be designed around both learning and change, and they should be overlapping to enhance the diffusion of learning through the organization.

As we've said before, knowledge has no intrinisic value on its own—it only has value in use. Therefore the value of knowledge is measured in its application. We suggest three levels of *metrics,* linked by logical argument, since at this point we haven't seen anybody who has been able to do it empirically. At the highest level, measure financial impact tied to the overall objectives of the program as defined by the company's strategic imperatives. One level down, measure operating impact, for that's the place where knowledge really drives change in terms of improved cycle time, lowered cost, and higher quality. At the bottom level, measure the knowledge and learning activity itself to make sure that the program is on track in usage and number of people involved.

The truth is, managing knowledge is a gnarly and often tortuous undertaking. As we saw in the knowledge dynamic, successful management hinges on changing people's behavior. An effective knowledge initiative includes an all-out *behavioral change* program with all the usual components (communication, communication, communication; top-management sponsorship; sponsor-agent-target effort; incentives), but the emphasis needs to be on changing specific behaviors. This may surprise you, but the primary obstacle happens to be people themselves, since knowledge requires four acts that are so difficult that many individuals find them downright unnatural.

### THE FOUR UNNATURAL ACTS

1. *Sharing* your best thinking (which is often an important part of your personal competitive advantage) with others. And we mean sharing data and understanding, as well as opinions.
2. *Using* what other people have developed. A simple concept but one that requires breaking down the dreaded not-invented-here syndrome.
3. *Collaborating* by building on the expertise of other experts.
4. *Improving* by synthesizing new ideas continuously while purging yesterday's conventional wisdom.

In the Centerless Corporation, these four previously unnatural acts become automatic. Everyone must abide by them, from the bottom to the very top of the company. That gets drilled in and made permanent by a new structure for the use of knowledge.

The challenge and the shape of a company's behavioral change program depends upon the company's culture and how unnatural each of the unnatural acts actually is for the people in the company. The change program needs to be explicitly built around these challenges. Very often, these programs involve the creation of incentives which elegantly reinforce the desired behavior (and therein reinforce the change loop in the learning dynamic).

We can't stress enough the importance of overcoming these unnatural acts and sharing best thinking in today's world. When we talk with CEOs, no matter what the industry, they tell us that the transfer of best practices is one of the biggest issues driving cost, efficiency, and satisfaction in most companies. We had to smile when the CEO of one major oil company confided that he spends a fair amount of his time transferring the worst practices and practitioners, those individuals who make the same mistakes over and over again— that's like injecting a human version of a computer virus into your business.

One of the problems is that knowledge transfer has often been a case of who you know versus what you know. It is hit or miss, and it is usually within the corporation rather than across the company's boundaries. With speed being a key determinant of competitive success, companies must do a lot better.

As Sir John Harvey-Jones, the former director of IT of Northern Telecom, said recently, "Information technology has failed to move from data processing to becoming a key strategic weapon to change businesses and ways to beat the competition. The real value of it is only real if you change the way business is done."

The *process* component is the most commonly overlooked in the programs we have seen. All too often, knowledge initiatives are started at the grass-roots level with the expectation that people will automatically create and use knowledge. The unnatural acts aside, it still takes a process. The most difficult process in many ways is the use process itself. This has to be engineered directly into everyday work processes. On top of the work processes, you must actually engineer the creation processes. For example, in our knowledge program at Booz•Allen, we have incorporated specific work steps into client engagements for our teams to document nonproprietary new or improved insights, approaches and methodologies that may have been developed in the course of doing work.

## ACHIEVING COHERENCE IN A KNOWLEDGE PROGRAM

Knowledge initiatives are much more difficult than they appear to be. Out of all the knowledge programs that Booz•Allen has investigated, only a small percentage have had a significant near-term impact, meaning within two years. Some of the programs have had some modest success, but over a very slow implementation horizon (it has taken three to five years to get value) and with a very limited scope (an application within a business or geography). A sizable number of the programs are out and out failures, in which technology was deployed without an effective change program and/or where applications were of low business value.

The greatest challenge in managing knowledge effectively is combining top management leadership and understanding with an approach that ensures linkage among critical business priorities, knowledge initiatives, and an overall change program. As we discussed earlier, most senior managers are committed to a vague concept of "knowledge management" or "becoming a learning organization," but very few have a concrete understanding about what they should be doing for their business today. Coherence (which will be discussed more broadly in the next chapter) is the essential element in bringing it all together. The Centerless Corporation's knowledge initiatives must emanate from the overall business strategy. They must be linked coherently through the intermediate steps required to implement knowledge initiatives, driving all the way through to the broader architecture of the firm, including performance measures, incentives, communication, and culture. The "Five Hows" framework demonstrates these linkages (see Exhibit 5):

## A KNOWLEDGE PROGRAM IN ACTION

Before wrapping up, we would perhaps do well to take a look at a professional services company, in which knowledge is ab-

EXHIBIT 5: THE FIVE HOWS FRAMEWORK

| | Question | Focus |
|---|---|---|
| **Starting Point** | | • Business strategy<br>• Financial targets |
| **How #1** | How will the company achieve its strategic objectives? | • Key capabilities |
| **How #2** | How will we do it? | • Specific business initiatives |
| **How #3** | How do we leverage knowledge to achieve the business objectives? | • Targeted knowledge |
| **How #4** | How can we systematically create, use, and improve these understandings? | • Process<br>• Infrastructure<br>• Community |
| **How #5** | How do we make this happen? | • Behavioral change<br>• Metrics |

solutely essential to success. We're talking about our own firm, Booz•Allen & Hamilton.

Knowledge is a central element of our strategy, which requires more collaboration, more leverage of our best thinking across practices and geographies, and less reinventing of the wheel. We needed both an infrastructure that was better, faster, and easier to use, and a real change in the culture of how we work. We needed to create, capture, collaborate, consume, contribute, communicate, and change the culture. We needed a vehicle to stimulate the capture and exchange of ideas, without compromising proprietary client information. We needed to provide Booz•Allen staff all over the world with easy and immediate access to our best thinking, with a link to external sources of knowledge and with a guide to the experts behind the ideas. We wanted platform independence (not hostage to any vendor), value for cost, and zero disruption. We invested several million dollars in two years to build and use a knowledge system, and we make ample use of it every day.

The knowledge program we developed has all five components of the architecture we advocate:

- Targeted knowledge
- Infrastructure (both people and technology)
- Processes to create and use knowledge
- Communities
- All-out behavioral change
- Metrics

We got started by looking broadly at what we wanted to learn about. The challenge here was to narrow our focus, since by nature we wanted to learn about everything. After some hard discussions at the level of senior management, we decided to focus our learning primarily around our service offering (the CEO agenda and the understanding to put ideas into action), our functional capabilities (how we work with clients), and basic skills. Some of the areas that fell out included competitor understanding and industry-specific insights. This isn't to say that we don't worry about those things too, but our learning in those areas was already very good. We wanted to do better in other areas. So we focused.

With this viewpoint in mind, we set out to bring the knowledge dynamic to life—really to speed it up, since by definition a consulting firm does a lot of learning. The sequence of what we did says more about our change program than a logical sequence for building a knowledge architecture. It simply isn't a linear process.

We took two initial steps simultaneously. Think of it as a big jump. One was an effort to bring together communities of experts (we called them innovation teams) around the top CEO agenda items, to begin to sift through our various perspectives and drive a "Push the Frontier" program to advance beyond state-of-the-art. At the same time, we undertook a significant backfill, or knowledge capture, effort to gather up all of our best thinking for our innovation teams to digest and as an immediate way to address issues of reinventing the wheel and delivering our very best thinking to our clients. It was a sort of "Operational Excellence" program. Note the relationship between the efforts. On the one hand, we set out to gather up all the really good nuggets that we had and make them broadly available; on the other hand we were synthesizing these nuggets into new, broader insights. Fortunately, the backfill part was a one-time effort. On an ongoing basis, it boils down to a process of collecting bits of intellectual capital and techniques through knowledge managers and innovation teams.

The most visible part of our knowledge program has been what we call our Knowledge On-Line (KOL) system. We rolled out KOL within the first six months as a part of the change program. Within two years, we went through three different models of the system. The first one, KOL, was a rapid application of a mature bulletin board technology. The second, KOL 1.1, involved additional collaboration and functionality, and experts' databases. Our current system, KOL 2, is a state-of-the-art intranet which connects our internal intellectual capital with our business information systems. Our KOL architecture includes knowledge repository, expert skills inventory, financial reporting, training, recruiting, marketing, human resources systems, external databases, and other applications. This approach will ultimately lead to a full executive information system. A small team from our Corporate Systems & Technology Department manages the technology.

The other part of our knowledge infrastructure is a dedicated team of knowledge managers who are the keepers of KOL. This cross-functional team spends all its time maintaining and feeding KOL, which has a large appetite. As we said before, we have learned that knowledge management cannot be an additional duty. It requires senior staff who understand what value-creating knowledge is and information professionals who participate in client engagements. Our information professionals or knowledge managers have insights into how to organize information, understanding of specific industries, and an ability to build the bridge between user demands and technology applications. Our knowledge managers are matrixed between an industry group and an information professional department.

In carrying this out, we have learned a lot about the processes necessary to get people to create, use, and improve knowledge. Processes for creating knowledge involve culling nuggets from both our client engagements and informalized teams. Both mechanisms work well.

The real challenges for us are around use and improvement. All it took to get junior staff to use knowledge was simply to make it available. Alas, that approach works a lot better with junior levels than with senior people. Junior staff quickly adapted to technology and routinely use KOL for references to previous best practices or to learn more about their colleagues. Improving is another story altogether, since no one likes to see their ideas purged from a system. We're still working on that one.

For senior level staff, the value in the system is more in finding experts among their colleagues or in determining the latest thinking on an issue. But the real value in our knowledge program for senior staff is the work that gets done on the innovation teams. It is here that we have created a formal mechanism to share the firm's best thinking on a particular topic (often borne from real client work) and synthesize these experiences to forge new insights. The challenge is to get experts to reach for one another.

Our success in the knowledge architecture was probably due to our focus on change issues, which was most evident in our willingness to commit a senior partner to lead the effort. We were fortunate that we were able to build on a culture where everyone is interested in content and team building and eliminating artificial boundaries. Our principal obstacles have been familiar ones: the unwillingness of some partners to accept others as experts and changing the way we use knowledge in developing relationships with clients. We found that there was a strong need to have incentives to reward those who actively participate in knowledge activities. We use two incentives: our appraisal process and our recognition program in various practice teams.

From our standpoint, the impact has been staggering. We believe that our knowledge program has been a major enabler of the growth of our services. It has fulfilled some long-recognized needs by making people aware of what we know and who knows it. There's no more wasteful reinvention of the wheel, and fewer nights and weekends devoted to manic attempts to locate information. It has really pushed our thinking.

One of the most gratifying results is how widely accepted KOL has become. It's turned into the company's best friend. Over 95 percent of our people use KOL each year, and about half use it each month. Because knowledge is shared and recognized within the company, articles and books published by our professionals have increased by 90 percent and media citations by 50 percent. We find ourselves able to continually discuss leading-edge ideas with our clients. And so we have rolled out fundamentally different approaches to brand building and training that explicitly use our knowledge.

We learned some key lessons from this exercise that companies should keep in mind as they undertake their own knowledge programs. The essential ones are:

- Senior sponsorship is critical.
- Early investment and ownership by the business is mandatory from the start, and should be sustained throughout with cross-functional teams.
- The development process must be disciplined and staffed adequately to avoid pitfalls and deadline slippage, budget overrun, nondelivery, underdelivery, poor quality, incorrect business fit, and so forth.
- Integration of best of breed technology is a complex venture, but it can pay off over the long term in flexibility, reduced costs, and vendor independence.
- The Web spreads fast, and we must create law and order to wrest control.
- Organizations are content providers in this intranet world.

## KNOWLEDGE CREATES BUSINESS SPACE

As knowledge becomes more critical to a company's strategy, it will require a different set of skills to be developed and a new kind of leader. Many companies like our own are now establishing the role of the Chief Knowledge Officer (CKO). The CKO can be a major player in the company's strategic success. It will be incumbent upon this person to guide the knowledge program and see that knowledge is constantly being created, utilized, and available. Nicholas Rudd, the CKO at Wunderman Cato Johnson, a subsidiary of the advertising agency Young & Rubicam, says, "It's a question of understanding there's a business benefit to be gained from managing experience, as opposed to watching it flitter out the door."

Companies that integrate knowledge into their business strategy will be rewarded with vast new Business Space. This will be achieved by understanding what they are offering the customer, how they are offering it to the customer, and how they can leverage this knowledge into a new offering or the same offering using a new transaction mode. Until companies fully tap the riches of knowledge, there is no appreciating just how valuable those riches can be.

# CHAPTER FIVE

# THE FINE ART OF COHERENCE

**COHERENCE.** That's a concept that you hear about in physics (calling to mind electromagnetic waves that have a definite relationship to each other) and in music (Beethoven without coherence is not Beethoven), but it may seem like a rather funny and squishy word to apply to a corporation. And yet anyone who wants to achieve solutions to the problems of tomorrow must acquire this vital trait.

There seems little doubt that the successful companies in the future will be the ones wise enough to harness the full potential of the entire organization. It will not be enough to draw on a majority of the potential, to operate at 70 or 80 or even 90 percent of what the company is capable of. The world is going to be too tough and competitors too ingenious as companies are shaken loose from traditional ways of conducting business. The winners will be the unbridled firms that are responsive to challenges and adroit in both creating and capturing opportunities. To match a business environment that is more networked within and among companies, the ability to manufacture value will have to be distributed across the company to a much greater extent than in the past.

One should recognize that the qualities of speed and responsiveness and the ability to tap in to the full potential of an organization are not endowed. They are not genetic. They are built. Companies that simply expect them to be there to automatically unleash the organization's power are sadly mistaken. There is only one way to achieve these necessary qualities and abilities. Companies must develop what we like to call "coherence" among the many disparate and far-flung pieces of the company.

By this, we mean establishing a potent binding force and sense of direction and purpose for the organization. We must never forget that a business is a complex system. Complex systems have characteristics that amount to more than the sum of the parts (a living cell, for instance, is more than its constituent chemicals). What makes a system complex is that the relationships among the parts are typically nonlinear. There are few or no one-to-one relationships. Coherence is what makes a corporation greater than the sum of its parts.

While we can see the pieces used to create coherence, there is no one-to-one relationship between any one piece and coherence. For instance, implementing the world's best performance measurement system will not in and of itself create coherence. Coherence is achieved when all of the pieces are mutually reinforcing. It is particularly important to have no weak links in the pieces that create that coherence.

How coherence is achieved is unique to each corporation. The good ones find a way to get it done.

By achieving coherence, each part of the company and each and every individual will be better able to drive purposefully toward a common goal that is clear, communicated, and understood by everyone. That is why the job of creating coherence is one of the major missions of the CEO. No one else can do it. It is a heroic leadership challenge, and the final piece in the success enabler puzzle.

What qualifies coherence as a key business enabler? Well, it belongs to that special class of higher-order levers so important because of their distinctive ability to energize the company and generate fresh vitality. Once in place, coherence facilitates the initiative and drive that are required of leading companies. It enables the organization to become quick, nimble, and responsive. How? By providing a compass for decision-making. It's common sense that decisions can be more decentralized and of better quality when everyone understands where the company is headed. Decisions are better when everyone has access to the right knowledge at the right time. Decisions improve when the right people are working the problem.

We can state flat-out that you can't realize the benefits of the Centerless Corporation without coherence. It is the glue that holds together all the elements of the model. As we have said, one of the major objectives is to make the business model more dynamic and less mechanical than the traditional corporation. This becomes important as the environment evolves to one with profoundly more complex industry dynamics and more obtuse industry boundaries. The basis of competition is capabilities and knowledge. The value-added potential of many businesses is shifting toward knowledge and service-based activities. Partnerships and joint ventures, part of the extended enterprise, are becoming standard pieces of the competitive puzzle.

Coherence is what allows the company to deemphasize a rigid organizational structure. With coherence, corporations can be built on more flexible configurations of people, processes, and systems. The goal is to encourage access to and sharing of capabilities across the company. The organizational units themselves may always be in flux, but with effective linkages all the relevant pieces are tied together in a grand unit of common purpose and direction.

This integration will foster better teamwork and communication. It will facilitate knowledge-sharing, which in turn will enhance the corporation's overall capabilities. The integration is accomplished when there are a means and a willingness to cross organizational boundaries, to work as a team while being physically distant. Coherence is especially challenging and of greatest importance to large companies that must shepherd multiple businesses, operate across many geographies, and interact with a substantial network of alliances and similar relationships.

We can't tell you how often we hear, as consultants, companies describe themselves as insular, introspective, or independent. In this day and age those are sorry attributes. These characteristics inhibit success, and the tribulations of so many once-great companies bear mute witness to the consequences of these traits.

One of the staggering failures of the old and dysfunctional command-and-control business model is that by stressing the control part, it chokes the potential of the company. In an earlier era, where companies were learning how to be big, pioneers like Alfred Sloan of General Motors were able to attain a tremendous edge by creating a bureaucracy to collect and synthesize information and then to dole out commands. This was an invaluable advantage when no one knew how to manage such a large enterprise, but today it is something best cast overboard.

Today, information collection, synthesis, and transfer are almost instantaneous and can be done by machine. It has become axiomatic that speed is now the advantage. With the rate of information transfer so much faster than decision processes, it is the latter that must improve. That improvement begins with coherence.

## COHERENCE COMES FROM LINKAGES

So how do you accomplish coherence? It is a deliberate and rational process of change, a strenuous process that can be successful only if it is driven from the top. The way to achieve it is through linkages (see Exhibit 1). These linkages come in two basic varieties: hard-wired ones that are organizational in nature and soft-wired ones that are cultural mechanisms. In the manner that we think of them, linkages are broadly defined. Vision must be linked to strategy which must be linked to execution. One part of the organization must be linked to another. The company must be linked to its people and to the outside world. In this fashion, the successful corporation of the future will be extensively linked both internally and externally, every part of it one more bead on a gigantic necklace.

**EXHIBIT 1: THE NEW BUSINESS MODEL IS
"GLUED" TOGETHER WITH ITS LINKAGE MECHANISMS**

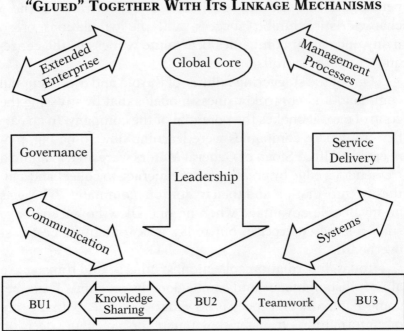

To a great degree, it is the formation of these linkages that is the innovation of the next generation of leading companies. Indeed, integration of increasingly complex systems will be analogous to the ability of companies fifty years ago to control large organizations.

If coherence is so important, what will be the consequences for companies that successfully acquire it? We suggest that the handsome benefits of improved linkages will be evident on both the revenue and the cost side. The top-line growth will come from three primary avenues: (1) new businesses created from combining capabilities across existing business boundaries; (2) improved coordination and transfer of products, services, and know-how across the corporation to optimize its geographic coverage; and (3) more rapid dissemination of capabilities and know-how to magnify performance within the current business definitions.

On the cost side, the transfer of best practices and lessons learned will make good performance more uniform across the organization and optimize the knowledge base of the company. This will give the firm a continuous transformation process, a goal to which every company should aspire. Change should be continuous and as seamless as possible. Moreover, with an improved Global Core and effective use of shared services, more streamlined business processes will further simplify the complexity of the business. In essence, linkages build coherence in values, beliefs, and decision-making.

Creating coherence is a deliberate act that requires careful thought and planning. Not only should each piece of a company's business model be linked, but those linkages should be tailored to a specific set of outcomes. To establish linkages, you need to implement an actual set of linkage mechanisms. These consist of the management processes, organization structure, and systems of the firm. They also incorporate the leadership style, teaming approach, incentives and rewards, and communication strategy. Exhibit 2 details the key categories of linkages.

The benefits of creating the right linkages can be large. Often, one or two key mechanisms are all it takes to gain a discernible advantage. Imagine the potential of putting a coherent system together. Let's look at several companies that have been able to construct coherence through different types of linkages. Then we will outline a general process that any company can go through to figure out what is the right way for it to realize its own coherence.

## The Integration of Banc One

Banc One, a bank holding company based in Columbus, Ohio, is operating in several states. They perform commercial banking operations, mortgage banking services, insurance services, and other related financial activities. Banc One concentrates on serving retail and middle-market customers through community banks that operate with considerable local autonomy, coupled with strong, central financial and credit controls.

**EXHIBIT 2: THE CATEGORIES OF LINKAGES THAT CREATE COHERENCE**

| Linkage Category | Issues/Requirements | Mechanisms |
|---|---|---|
| Management Processes | • Systematically and actively manage and leverage the knowledge and information that exist in the corporation <br> • Identify, plan, develop, deploy, utilize, and transfer the corporate core capabilities across the business units to drive growth | • Human resource programs which rotate top players into different areas <br> • Temporary task forces/committees <br> • Cross-unit strategy development involving line and functional staff |
| Systems | • Effectively link the numerous organizational units to realize system openness and two-way communication <br> • Realize object-oriented programming and provide effective data warehousing, search engines, and enterprise reference systems | • Market intelligence transfer systems <br> • Entity management systems <br> • Open-access financial systems |
| People | • Enable the development, deployment, and transfer of corporate capabilities across the entire corporation | • Executive development <br> • Corporate structure <br> • Compensation Systems |

Each of the company's affiliates has its own board of directors, its own business plan, its own strategy for marketing and product pricing in its local operations, and is responsible for its P&L (profit and loss). The company originally maintained what it calls an "Uncommon Partnership" philosophy that was rooted in three principles: decentralizing the people side of the business; standardizing and centralizing the business's paper and electronic transaction aspect; and operating under a financial management system that continuously measures and reports successes. However, Banc One has recently abandoned the "Uncommon Partnership" model. Although this model had served well during the firm's initial growth spurt, it was presenting obstacles for future growth. Individual bank chief executive officers enjoyed too much autonomy. Banc One found that deploying new technology or reaching a common consensus on strategic plans was made extremely difficult by this philosophy. The prospect that there may not be a single product or service offered by all Banc One affiliates was worrisome. Moreover, it became virtually impossible to communicate to customers all benefits of banking with Banc One affiliates.

As a result, Banc One has changed its structure to reflect a National Partnership, where each major line of business has its own unique vision. No longer does Banc One labor under a separate vision—for each bank—as it did under the Uncommon Partnership. Instead, it is able to exploit economies of scale more fully and to leverage its size and standing as a global enterprise. On the other hand, by establishing a vision for each line of business, Banc One is able to maintain the flexibility necessary to create more values for customers in different market segments. Interestingly, Banc One has retained certain elements of the "Uncommon Partnership." The firm continues to emphasize the "importance of strong, local leadership, the need for local credit decisions and for local management of [its] people." It believes that these principles will enable it to differentiate itself from its competitors.

For some time now, Banc One has merited the reputation

of being the best bank in the United States, with the fastest-growing stock price, earnings record, and asset base. Over the ten years ended 1995, it had recorded the highest average return on assets and fourth highest return on equity among the current 25 largest U.S. banking organizations.

But because of its strong balance sheet, particularly relative to its peers, Banc One made innumerable acquisitions in the early 1990s. Between 1990 and 1996, it broadened its asset base from $30 billion to over $90 billion, its network from 587 to 1,558 branches, its work force from 19,300 to 46,900 people, and its geographic presence from 6 to 12 states. With such breakneck expansion, Banc One was faced with the considerable challenge of properly integrating these acquisitions seamlessly into its current operations.

What did it do? It pursued coherence. It resorted to a mutually reinforcing set of processes, systems, and structures to provide integration and to encourage the exchange of best practices among its independent affiliates.

In the systems arena, Banc One made it mandatory that every affiliate's back-office system meet the Banc One standard. All data-processing operations were transferred to a central office in Ohio. Then Banc One set up a detailed monthly reporting system called Management Information Computer System (MICS) to allow affiliates to gauge their performance against a range of forty product and market variables, identify areas of improvement, and discover which affiliates could teach them something. In addition, the company developed a distributed system, the Strategic Banking System, to place up-to-date customer data on the desktops of customer service staff to improve service.

So far as processes, Banc One requires all of its affiliates to serve their local communities and to focus on three measures of service quality: customer retention rates, response time for customer requests, and proportion of "highly satisfied" customers. The exchange of best-practice information is encouraged through an internal posting of affiliates' monthly performance on MICS. In this way, people know unmistakably which institutions are doing things well. Banc One consulting teams travel from bank to bank transferring knowledge to the banks and learning from them. Corporate management reviews MICS performance data with each affiliate on a monthly basis, concentrating on variances and relative performance based on return on assets.

Banc One also produces manuals centrally to capture company-wide learning on topics like home equity loans. Quality Councils address specific projects which affect all of the affiliates. What's more, Banc One informs affiliates about broad issues and specific products through conferences. It has created a "college" that schools senior executives in the philosophies and policies of the company and allows people to exchange their thoughts on topical banking issues.

So far as structural linkages, Banc One has all of its affiliates operate under the Banc One brand name. Each affiliate must adopt a standard range of products and services. Specialist services like corporate banking and trust activities are centralized at those banks boasting expertise in that specific area.

As a result of this coherence, Banc One has realized some significant benefits. It has enjoyed rapid and successful growth. Over the past ten years, it has enjoyed a compound average growth in assets of 22 percent per year. Banc One has become convinced that integration of a newly acquired affiliate into its network can increase the institution's earnings by nearly 40 percent. Early tests from the implementation of the Strategic Banking System indicate that it can reduce system operating costs by 20 percent. All of this is testimony to the power of coherence.

## COHERENCE COMES TO JOHNSON & JOHNSON

Johnson & Johnson, one of the best-known pharmaceutical giants, has been able to develop coherence in a decidedly more diverse set of businesses than banking. J&J, as the company is known, develops, manufactures, and sells consumer pharmaceutical and professional medical products through 160 separately chartered companies in about 50 countries. Its products include everything from toiletries and hygienic items to a vast array of prescription and over-the-counter drugs, diagnostic products, and surgical instruments.

J&J's credo, a statement of its values, has been a key element of its success. During the Tylenol crisis, J&J's credo enabled everyone to know what to do. That's coherence.

Since the 1930s, J&J has had an extremely decentralized organization. Presidents of its disparate companies have complete autonomy and authority over research and development, product selection, hiring, manufacturing, marketing, and sales. The presidents are strictly accountable for profit and loss results to nineteen product group chairmen, who report in turn to three product sector chairmen (one each for the consumer, pharmaceutical, and professional businesses). This extreme decentralization into small, self-governing units provides a sense of ownership, speeds reaction to markets, and maintains clear accountability.

Over the years, however, the company's decentralized mode of creating and operating new businesses had led to high overheads because of redundancies across businesses. For instance, in 1991 overhead at J&J was 41 percent of sales. In contrast, Merck was at 30 percent and Bristol-Myers Squibb was at 28 percent.

J&J was also not producing the type of integrated and coordinated service across products demanded by its larger customers. These customers wanted to simplify their dealings with manufacturers by reducing the number of contacts they had to maintain. Finally, many managers felt their long-term career opportunities were limited owing to the small size of the business units and the reluctance to hire and promote people from outside the individual companies.

From 1989 to 1991, Ralph Larsen, J&J's CEO, instituted several changes intended to achieve more integration across the independent units without losing the benefits of decentralization. These included:

- Establishment of customer support centers where employees from separate units work as a team at the customer's location to facilitate the ordering and distribution of all J&J products. Separate sales representatives from the different units still call on the customers, but the customers receive their products in common, large shipments.
- Development of Pathfinder, a joint customer service and credit department which combines four separate departments that had often performed similar work for the same customers. It also provides a contact point for customers who are experiencing difficulties.
- Pooling of back-office functions across multiple units like payroll processing, computer services, purchasing, distribution, accounts payable, and benefits.
- Integration of companies, particularly internationally, to achieve economies of scale and scope where local market control is not critical.
- Creation of an executive development program where company presidents share their yearly managerial reviews with the group chairman. The group chairman can then suggest personnel transfers across companies.
- Requirement that the group chairman help the independent companies identify potential areas of temporary or permanent resource sharing. For instance, one company borrowed some underutilized salespeople from another company to help on a new project launch rather than hiring new people. The exchange was conducted under a formal contract, spelling out terms and payments.

The considerable coherence gained from these linkage mechanisms has produced notable benefits. In its quest for integration of uncompetitive, small-scale facilities, J&J has consolidated 47 operating units and closed more than 25 plants worldwide over the past five years. The programs to share administrative, financial, and information services among companies and locations, mergers of operating companies, and consolidation of manufacturing locations have reduced J&J's work force from 84,900 in 1992 to just over 80,000 in 1995. Overhead-to-sales ratios, though, still remained high at 40 percent in 1994.

## LINKING THINGS AT SKANDIA

Skandia AFS (Assurance and Financial Services) is a Stockholm-based international corporation offering insurance and financial services from offices in fifteen different countries. Its parent company is Skandia Insurance Company Ltd., which was established back in 1855. The AFS group is the company's biggest and fastest-growing division, providing 50 percent of Skandia's gross premium income.

Finding itself in 1991 still heavily dependent on a mature Swedish market, Skandia needed to move rapidly into other global high-growth markets and take advantage of the worldwide trend toward deregulation of insurance and other financial services. Thus it implemented the following linkages:

- Captured and packaged the firm's intellectual capital and best practices on branch management by creating a "branch prototype"—a collection of customizable software applications, manuals, and other structured know-how to support branch operations.
- Created the world's first position of Director of Intellectual Capital, whose primary responsibility is to transform human capital, the source of innovation and growth but not an asset the firm can own, into structural capital, which belongs to the organization.

What benefits did Skandia gain? For one, it realized its goal of establishing a presence in high-growth markets. By 1995, U.K. operations accounted for nearly half of AFS's assets under management and showed strong profitability. The corresponding figure for U.S. operations was over 35 percent, and American Skandia was the tenth largest company in the

United States in its market segment. As of 1994, business outside Sweden accounted for about 85 percent of Skandia's total premium income, and the company is successfully expanding its operations beyond Europe and the United States into other potential high-growth markets in Latin America and Asia. Use of the branch prototype allowed Skandia to cut the investment involved in opening an overseas office by 50 percent, and the time required was reduced from 24 to 6 months.

The Skandia knowledge system gives more than 7,000 brokers detailed, up-to-date knowledge on investment options and asset allocation, while also assisting in sales and client proposals. Similar knowledge transfer initiatives within the firm have encouraged cross-border sales so that products developed in one country are made available to customers in another. Cross-border sales now account for about 15 percent of Skandia's premium income.

## LINKAGES DEFY ANY RECIPE

One thing these examples clearly show is that there is no all-encompassing recipe for creating coherence. Each firm must construct its company-specific set of linkages. The important thing is not so much what the linkages are as that linkages are created. But we have identified what we hope will be some useful guidelines that can help you determine the necessary degree of customization for your company as you pursue coherence.

Each of the broad groups of linkage mechanisms—management processes, corporate systems, and structure—have their own particular determinants to keep in mind when attempting to customize linkages.

Coherence is created for a purpose. The company's business strategy and operating philosophy should be the pillars of coherence. Coherence is a highly customized system. It is built for a unique purpose from components that are often very company-specific. They are specific because the how-to in a firm is almost always related to its unique culture and history.

In the examples we cited, coherence was the result of a clear concept or strategy for creating value and the means to put it into operation. Banc One believed that through a knowledge system and best practices it could capture value by acquiring new banks. It aligned its purpose, people, and processes to create the coherence that enabled it to capture that value.

J&J looked elsewhere to create value. It believed that greater pooling of resources, more teaming at the executive level, and the elimination of redundancies could capture significant value. Skandia looked to globalize by applying best practices with its branch prototype.

The key to coherence is first to establish, or articulate, the purpose. Then the people and processes can be designed to fit. Although this seems straightforward, think about how many companies actually achieve it. Not many.

While the degree of customization from company to company may be large, there are some key organizing principles which help define some of the interrelationships among the parts. These include:

1. Leaner organization, with reduced levels of hierarchies, minimized number of bureaucratic regulations, and focused to realize synergies
2. Clearly defined objective orientation of each individual organizational unit
3. Flexible, adaptable organization structures with simple decision processes and responsibilities
4. Economic, efficient structures, systems, and processes avoiding redundancies

What is more, each company must figure out what has to be linked corporately and what should be linked within a given business. The types of processes that more and more must be linked across corporate boundaries include planning, innovation and product development, technology and capability transfer, human resource management, and knowledge management. Processes that are more suited to the regional or business unit level include areas like marketing and sales, manufacturing, distribution, and order processing. However, these categorizations are not inviolate. The general rule is that firm-wide processes address issues of identification, deployment, development, and capabilities transfer across business lines. Business unit or regional processes are more specific to those parts of the business.

For the most part, linkages should facilitate sharing, especially the building and distribution of corporate knowledge.

Good linkages make it possible to create a more robust organization, one that otherwise would be too complex to manage. But with coherence, good management is made easier, and that's a big advantage.

## MATCH MECHANISMS WITH PURPOSE

Linkages should also establish better corporate-wide identification and foster greater motivation. One way this can be accomplished is through various leadership linkages. Leaders, can, for instance, formulate and ensure that all staff understand the common mission and values of the firm. This will coordinate effective decision-making across the business units. Another mechanism could be performance measures and incentives that are consistent with the company's overarching objectives.

Still another way to accomplish this is through the linkage mechanism of teamwork. This consists of things like task forces, workshops, committees, and councils. Needless to say, communication serves as one of the most essential linkage mechanisms. By establishing a comprehensive corporate communication program and direct interaction with employees, timely, top-down information can be dispersed to support decision-making throughout the firm.

In establishing coherence, it is important that the specific integration device is matched to a particular purpose. Although in one sense just about every device imaginable has been tried, it is the linking to purpose that makes a mechanism successful.

## COMMUNICATION IS A PROCESS FROM THE TOP

Communication strategy is itself a linkage never to be over-looked. Communication needs to be top-down and spontaneous, as well as bottom-up and comprehensively planned. Communications are not events or individual memos from the CEO's office. They are a process. Indeed, they accomplish all of the following:

- Provide a forum for input into decisions
- Describe direction and status along the way
- Answer questions
- Surface resistance
- Link individuals horizontally and informally

Communication processes must be tailored for each constituency and purpose. These include the target audience, the message, the means of communication, the frequency, the rationale, and the selection of key communicators. All of these imply an understanding of the overall communication environment—the opinion leaders in the different target audiences, the resistance and support to be expected, the group think, the expectations, and the objectives.

It is worth spelling out some communication principles that should be kept in mind.

- Link messages to the strategic purpose and direction. In that way, employees will understand need and you will build credibility. Be open and honest, for that is critical to maintaining credibility. "Open" doesn't have to mean all information is available every step of the way.
- Set realistic expectations. Begin early to outline potential implications, and don't gloss over potentially negative messages. Share parameters and limits to prevent the anticipation of worst-case outcomes.

- Provide for two-way communications. Allow opportunities for employees to submit the questions they really have. Give employees the chance to provide their ideas.
- Put greater emphasis on being proactive versus reactive. This means to send out messages in advance, before the "hue and cry" becomes too great. Avoid the defensive posture.
- Send the same message repeatedly through alternative channels. Frequently individuals need to hear a message multiple times before it is internalized. Multiple channels increase the chance of the message being internalized.

## COHERENCE BREEDS RESPONSIVENESS

To recapitulate, the greater the coherence, the greater the responsiveness of a business to external stimuli. The greater the coherence, the more the company can become flexible and fast, and the better it can function within its growing extended enterprise.

Coherence is created only through a wide range of linkages across and extending out of the corporation. These linkages must be driven by the company vision and values and be institutionalized through high involvement by the top executive managment. The linkages will form a highly integrated set of connections which will involve lots of sharing and exchange across organizational lines. They should be performance-focused, meaning that they are put in place with the expectation that there will be an improvement in value creation, and they should be highly customized to each company. One shoe does not fit all.

Once the linkages are set in place and put into operation, the advantages will show up in many welcome ways. Coherence should help align all of the business elements in the desired direction. It should foster an improved corporate identity. It should leverage the best ideas independent of where they are in the corporation, build on diversity within the firm, and create a significantly higher level of motivation across the company.

By tapping in to the best corporate knowledge and experts, coherence should hasten development, deployment and transfer of capabilities. This will lead to greater value creation. Since it entails better shared understanding and specific mechanisms for working together, coherence should foster entrepreneurship, trust, and empowerment. This all should result in far more astute decision-making.

In the end, coherence, along with the other two key enablers, People and Knowledge, strengthens the hand of corporate leaders to manage the company beyond its day-to-day performance. Together they transcend the prosaic command-and-control model by putting in place an organizational capability geared to making the corporation run better and grow faster. These higher-order enablers afford great leverage to the CEO in running a business. Like all good things, it takes a fair amount of effort on the part of the executive team to bring these enablers into effective being, but coherence will surely be a major differentiator of which companies will prevail.

In the following chapters we will explore the four basic elements of the Centerless Corporation, beginning with the all-important Global Core, and look at how the roles are revamped from what they are in the conventional business model.

# Chapter Six

# A CORE NOT A CENTER

**WHAT** is the role of corporate in a corporation? We realize that is about as basic a question as one can ask. But we raise it not as some sort of trick theoretical exercise. We feel it is well worth pondering, because the question cuts to the heart of existence for many of today's large businesses.

For the most part, the modern corporation is essentially a collection of business lines, often diversified, and almost always covering distinct geographic markets and customer segments. In fact, many large corporations are collections of large businesses in themselves, usually called business divisions or business groups. These in turn are also often an assemblage of businesses.

In the middle of all this activity and churning commerce you have the corporate center. It sits at the very apex of a hierarchy of management and administrative activities with tentacles that touch almost every part of the company. Lately, these corporate centers have been reeling under ferocious, and entirely justifiable, attack. They have been downsized, resized, outsourced, reengineered, and at times nearly eliminated. All of this remorseless battering has been done under the rubric of cost savings.

The ongoing frontal assault on the corporate center has been necessitated by an almost universal truth of these organizations: many of their activities entail high cost and add low value. The truth of the matter is, in a world of rapid global communications and information flows, the typical corporate center is in the way. It slows up the workings of the corporation and delivers far too little in light of the heavy demands it places on the businesses. Thus the standard approach to remedy this unfavorable value-for-cost equation has been to shrink the center, in terms of both its size and its effect on the business. The result is that shareholders pick up the incremental value of reduced costs.

In many respects, the condensation of the corporate center has been a free lunch. Although rather painful for those in it, its reduction can easily be seen as a plus to shareholders and to the people running the businesses. Not only do the direct costs of corporate disappear, but also the indirect costs imposed on the businesses of a large center making too many requests. A double whammy!

Yet something is missing. True, the corporate center has been an easy mark. But its complete dismantling might not be the right answer.

## WELCOME TO THE GLOBAL CORE

This brings us back to the fundamental question we asked above, "What is the role of corporate in a corporation?" We believe that the implications of the answer are so great that we must stop calling corporate a center. Rather, we have adopted the concept of the "Global Core" as more fitting to its new purpose in the Centerless Corporation.

The terminology here is important. A center suggests something that is in the middle. Information flows into it and directive flows out of it. In short, a holdover of the familiar command-and-control model.

A Core is something else altogether. It suggests a sense of essence and purpose, of heart. It is essential in that it creates the context for growth. It ensures that the pieces are in place for growth and that they are working effectively and not clogging up the works. It sets the tone, while not always beating the drum. Most important, it adds value, not sheer overhead.

The role of the Global Core is not merely to perform a predetermined set of activities. It is not the management of the businesses, the reporting of results, the keeping of the faith. These are things that the businesses in all likelihood can do very well by themselves. Indeed, in many respects, they can do them far better than can a corporate center or an executive team that is several levels removed from the heat of the action.

The real test of value for the role of the Global Core is that it is the key piece within the corporation that makes the whole worth more than the sum of its parts. Simply and purely, the role of corporate is value creation. The metric for that value creation is the value of the business as a corporation versus the value of the pieces. This is a rather hard test, but it is the only one that makes sense. Any other role will destroy value. These days, no cost reengineering can save a corporate center if it is only overhead costs and does not create value.

Thus the role of corporate revolves around corporate strategy—how to create that incremental value above and beyond what the businesses can do on their own. It should be based on the strategy of why the particular pieces are put together in the first place. This is a very dynamic and positive role and one that, if done right, should be recognized as positive throughout the corporation. It is also a role that should be mandated by effective boards. The board on behalf of the shareholders should ask the question, "What is the role of our Core and how is it creating value?" No corporation should tolerate any piece that does not add value. The burden of proof is on the Core.

The context for this value creation is a highly distributed yet networked business community. The networking is facilitated by high-speed communications and information flows. Businesses are networked across geographies, between and among corporations, and within corporations. Greater networking is due to the natural interdependence of activities. Doing this well means faster, more responsive entities.

More and more, the inefficiencies caused by a lack of information are dwindling. Information is readily available and moves quickly. No company is really able to maintain a monopoly for long by hoarding information within its borders. Instead, companies are moving to the next level of creating value with the information they have, and to do this well they need a lot of it and very fast.

In this context, the role of corporate acting as a middleman or broker of information is no longer valid. Information is widely available and seems to find its home in a seamless fashion. Thus we see an exploding number of alliances between and among companies. These alliances link complementary skills and know-how. The largest number is between competitors, but there are numerous ones between supplier and customer, manufacturer and distributor. In fact, Booz•Allen & Hamilton's research into strategic alliances has clearly demonstrated that alliances, on average, earn higher returns on investment than the returns generated by the participating companies on investments not related to an alliance.

We hasten to add that corporations have to completely change their mind-sets if they are going to create the intracompany workings to yield the higher results of the intercompany alliances that lead to value above the sum of the parts. And they must be able to capture these benefits without incurring the high cost.

What this boils down to is, the Global Core must create its value in this networked world. It must facilitate the creation of a more effective internal network, where appropriate. And it must be willing to delete from the portfolio any piece that does not contribute to the "greater-than-the-parts" process of value creation.

Needless to say, the Core's role is a large one. It represents the cornerstone of the Centerless Corporation. If it fails, the essential purpose of the Centerless Corportion cannot be achieved. It must create the *raison d'être* for the corporation. Yet it is not large or bulky. Quite the contrary. It consists of no more than the CEO, his direct reports (including the heads of the businesses), and requisite supporting activities. It is about as flat as a dime.

## TINKERING BUT NOT A GLOBAL CORE

Some companies may think that they have already achieved something like a Global Core, but few have. Before going into the missions of a true Global Core, it is worth briefly reviewing some of the hectic events that are assailing the corporate center.

As the traditional corporate center has become a bloated, high-cost bureaucracy weighing down heavily on the Business Units, we've seen a lot of tinkering with corporate centers. By casting off unnecessary layers of bureaucracy, today's corporations are appreciably flatter. These layers, which once may have been a needed channel for information flows and checks and balances, are obsolete with modern computing technology. Information should be readily available. The challenge is what to do with it.

So flattening is not enough. Business process redesign is not enough. Corporate's role must change, and it must change to one of value added. Most restructuring really captures the value added only through a one-time hit on high costs. The true restructuring must be of the role of the center.

Too often when clients ask us to look at the role of their center, they are focused on cutting costs. This is a shortsighted and inadequate road to improvement.

Efforts to attack the inefficiency and ineffectiveness of the traditional corporate center have helped spark two trends which continue to have a healthy run at the modern corporation—business simplification and corporate center cost reduction.

Big corporate centers often place a high cost on the businesses without adding value. Moreover, diversified businesses are more complex to manage, and the traditional corporate center has difficulty adding value across a wide range of businesses. Thus spinning off businesses unleashes significant value. The number and the value of acquisitions and leveraged buyouts have been large by any historical standard. KKR and other buyout artists have had a field day scooping up businesses that could not thrive, much less survive, under an ineffective corporate center. Often, what is sold is an underperforming unit that the corporate center can't fix. Or the corporation may have a problem in its main business which needs lots of attention. Hence, goodbye to the distraction.

And so Xerox unloaded its property/casualty insurance business. Sears sold its interests in Prodigy, Dean Witter, and Allstate. Kmart disposed of its auto centers. Daimler Benz got rid of its automation technology and power distribution businesses. Baxter sold its hospital supply business. 3M sold or spun off its data storage, audiotape, and videotape lines. The list goes on and on. Companies can manage only so much complexity. Or in other words, they can add value to only so many businesses.

In addition to streamlining the corporate portfolio through fire sales and spin-offs, some companies have actually chopped the business into smaller, more defined pieces. In what is perhaps the most prominent recent example, AT&T created Lucent Technologies so that it would have a broader market and not be tied to its largest "customer." Unisys fashioned three businesses out of one—computer systems (hardware and software), computer consulting, and computer support. James Unruh, the chairman and chief executive, described these businesses as "large enough and mature enough to be self-sufficient." Westinghouse and Monsanto are shifting their portfolios to reduce diversity—Westinghouse is spinning off its industrial businesses to continue its renewed focus upon entertainment, and Monsanto has sold its chemicals business to concentrate on agriculture, food, and pharmaceuticals.

It makes sense that the simpler the business portfolio, the easier it is to create value. But is that really true? Some very large, diversified companies have created tremendous value. General Electric has a highly diversified set of businesses ranging from old-line industrials to entertainment. Yet it has generated great value for its shareholders. Even the giant oil companies, like Exxon or Mobil, which appear to operate in a single industry, are actually in several very different businesses: resource extraction; manufacturing and logistics; and retailing. Many of these companies have been tremendous creators of shareholder wealth. Why, then, can some firms find a way to add more value to a diversified set of businesses while others cannot? Before we answer that, let's quickly look at the other trend, the downsizing of the corporate center.

As part of the simplification movement, corporate centers have become "lean and mean." Many of the high-profile downsizings are of bloated overhead functions at corporate. Percy Barnevik, the current chairman and former CEO of ABB, helped redefine the era of corporate downsizing with his 30-30-30 rule for his corporate center. Under this dictum, 30 percent of the center work force was parceled out to the Business Units, 30 percent went to a services company, 30 percent was dropped, and 10 percent was left to run the activities of the corporate center. By adopting this rule, he shrank a corporate center of about 1,500 people down to a mere 140. That is major-league shrinking.

Business simplification and corporate center downsizing often seem to go hand in hand. Take the case of Olin Corporation. Prior to its 1991 restructuring, Olin had a diverse mix of businesses: chemicals, metals, ammunition, ordinance, and defense. It streamlined its portfolio to focus on only a few areas—chemicals, ammunition, and brass. As part of this portfolio restructuring, it reduced its corporate headquarters staff from 1,100 to 450.

No question about it, wringing out the costs and simplifying the business have been vital steps in the evolution of the corporation. By and large, these efforts have been implemented so that corporate does not hamper the ability of the businesses to create value. What's missing is a clearly articulated approach for corporate itself to create value—to create enough value to make the whole greater than the sum of the parts. And so the question becomes, What proactive steps can corporate take to add to the overall value? How should the center be structured? What should its role be? How should it interact with the businesses?

## THE FIVE MISSIONS OF THE GLOBAL CORE

The answer to all of these questions, we feel, is the Global Core.

In our view, the role of the Global Core is far more ambitious than that of the corporate center. It is nothing less than to help the corporation capture or create Business Space. Beyond its natural role as an integrator, it is also a feisty initiator, helping each of the pieces of the corporation realize its full value potential, while not being burdensome for the businesses.

The Core drives the corporation to be more competitive and to seize larger expanses of Business Space through a more proactive and strategic management of the three key enablers of the new business model we have spoken about: knowledge, people, and coherence. To our mind, these are the factors that will dictate current and future competitiveness. These are the factors that assure that the Business Units have the right foundation for growth and initiative.

Too often, corporations leave these enablers to be managed by the businesses with insufficient impetus from the center. As firms have diversified or spread geographically, the businesses themselves have become of adequate scale to stand alone. It's reasonable to wonder, What does corporate add beyond costs? What is the rationale for having these businesses under one corporate banner?

In our model, the Global Core becomes an integral component of the value-adding engine of the firm. We call the value contributed by the Core "system value." It is value that cannot be created by the businesses alone. To be sure, this sets a very high standard for the Core, but it is the only one that makes any sense. If the Core cannot create value beyond that generated by the businesses themselves, then it serves no real purpose, and the firm will have greater value broken into pieces.

Unfortunately, most corporate center organizations have been shaped over time in an incremental manner and without a clearly defined value-added mission. Typically removed from the primary customer and production processes by multiple hierarchical layers, they have tended to lag rather than lead in the corporation's organizational evolution. In the typical multidivisional firm, encumbered by as many as hundreds of Business Units, corporate is too distant from the real action to add value in most areas. What, then, should it do?

When most companies start to tackle the role of their corporate center it is from the cost side. For firms with a large center, this is not a bad place to start. For nearly any corporation, a head count of over a thousand at corporate is absurd. Such a mini-army of staffers is more burden than blessing. On the other hand, the minimalist center—the extreme variation is the CEO and a very busy assistant—is just as unlikely to produce meaningful value.

The right way to think about the Core, then, is to build from the bottom up, by putting in place the proper resources to do the right work to meet the burden-of-proof test and see what you get. At a minimum, corporate has to have some understanding of the business from an investor's point of view. It must also perform a certain amount of monitoring and reporting. But it must go beyond this to add the value needed to justify the existence of corporate.

Our analysis tells us that the Global Core has five key missions (see Exhibit 1) that allow it to create value for the corporation. They are strategic leadership, identity, capital, control, and capabilities.

The "burden of proof" is on corporate to show that it can create value where the businesses cannot. Thus the missions of the Core must be corporate missions, not Business Unit missions. Centralized services, for example, do not meet the burden-of-proof test. These could be done jointly by the businesses (often with an impetus from corporate) in a shared-services Business Unit or outsourced. Activities that do not meet the burden-of-proof test should be removed from the Core and placed elsewhere or eliminated as warranted by a business case test.

### EXHIBIT 1: MISSIONS OF THE GLOBAL CORE

| Mission | Objective |
|---|---|
| Identity | • Formulate a shared vision and set of values, and create the most favorable and strongest corporate IDENTITY possible in each relevant constituency. |
| Capabilities | • Act as a sourcing/disseminating "market maker" to ensure corporatewide access to world-class, low-cost CAPABILITIES. Provide "matrix capabilities" in nonmatrix organizations. |
| Capital | • Minimize cost of CAPITAL and fund growth. |
| Strategic Leadership | • Provide the vision, leadership, and purpose for GROWTH. Initiate "outside-the-box" thinking to generate future growth. |
| Control | • Exercise CONTROL on behalf of the board and the shareholders. Understand and manage the risks of the business. |

The five key missions meet the burden-of-proof test. These missions are corporate in that they transcend individual business boundaries. They are the vehicles by which the individual businesses benefit directly or by which the corporation spawns new business activity and captures additional Business Space.

While the Core is responsible for ensuring that these missions are carried out, almost always it will be the businesses themselves that do the execution. Thus some of the Core is distributed across the organization and across the globe. It is distributed to the businesses of the corporation. There may be no center. But there is a Core. And there is great value.

Let's run through these five key missions.

## STRATEGIC LEADERSHIP

Strategic leadership means to provide the vision, direction, and context for the success of the corporation. In short, it means to sketch out a road map for the organization that will allow it to unleash its full potential. The map should reveal how to create value as well as how to establish a stronger beachhead on new Business Space. Oftentimes, creating new territory to conquer does not involve invading a new industry, but rather redefining what is currently being done, though at a different level of intensity.

There are lots of examples of companies that have redefined themselves while never venturing far from home. British Airways, long known for lackluster service, was able to reinvent itself guided by Sir Colin Marshall and Lord King. It opted to compete through service to become "the world's favourite airline." Facing stiff competition by Japanese manufacturers, Motorola reversed its fortunes with the "Six Sigma" quality approach instituted by Bob Galvin. These programs were led by corporate and then were institutionalized.

Strategic leadership should also include a sense of how this value will be accomplished within the construct of the organization. Lew Platt, together with the company founders Bill Hewlett and David Packard, reaffirmed the "HP Way," digging into the company's roots of dealing with people and customers, to frame an approach for the future. In order to enable global growth, Percy Barnevik has shaped ABB into a "multidomestic company" that feels at home in any country. Jack Welch is creating a "boundaryless" GE to break down all barriers to communication and action by empowering all employees to go wherever they need to get information or input on decisions. In each case, these leaders are describing a way in which the company should think about growth opportunities.

Strategic leadership is also crafting the corporation's portfolio, determining what businesses should be there, what the performance requirements of the businesses are, and what types of alliances make sense. Not all business activity has to be part of the corporation. The Core should continually reevaluate what should be in and what should be out of the corporation. The basic rule is that activities which add greater value through the five key missions should be in the corporation.

One challenge of strategic leadership is developing an understanding of how fast the company should be growing, how fast it is growing, and what is the nature of the gap. The Core should develop, or cause to be developed by the businesses, a corporate-wide perspective on how to plug that gap, if it exists. The right growth metric at the Global Core level should be connected to shareholder value.

Our research has looked at how some firms have consistently been able to outperform the market, and it has shown that even large corporations can maintain a high degree of shareholder value creation (see Exhibit 2). The role of the Core for all companies regardless of size, should be built around growing value.

Strategic leadership is all about creating the context for growth. It provides the vision and purpose of the corporation, and defines the means (the culture, values, and way of working together) needed to achieve these goals. It is not about micromanaging business strategies. Rather, it should provide the umbrella under which businesses devise appropriate strategies and create value.

## IDENTITY

The identity mission of the Global Core boils down to formulating a shared vision and setting values across the corporation, so that the most favorable and strongest corporate

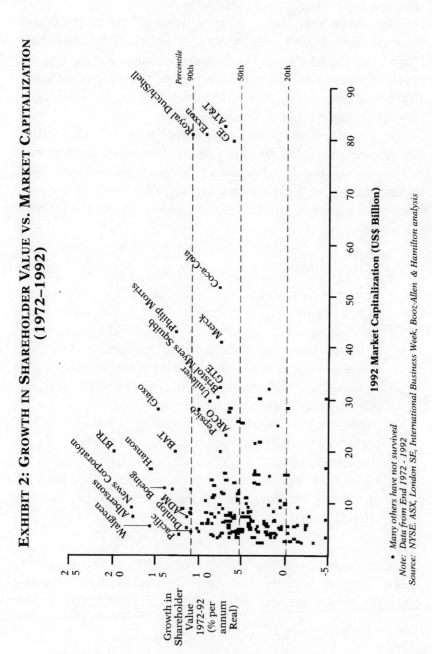

EXHIBIT 2: GROWTH IN SHAREHOLDER VALUE VS. MARKET CAPITALIZATION (1972–1992)

• Many others have not survived
Note: Data from End 1972 - 1992
Source: NYSE, ASX, London SE, International Business Week, Booz-Allen & Hamilton analysis

identity unfurls in each constituency. Let us be clear here. This does not always mean the same identity across the corporation, but rather the most appropriate one.

And remember, the constituent base is both internal and external. Faced with ever-increasing forces, firms are challenged by critical external and internal issues that have to be resolved through the effective management of corporate identity. These involve employees, shareholders, customers, regulators, and governments, among others.

In a nutshell, corporate identity is the "glue" holding the organization together by providing a consistent platform to communicate the firm's values and purpose. In many respects, it must be linked to the strategic leadership mission. Corporate identity impacts on the corporation in the following ways:

- *coherence* — relating different parts of the corporation to each other and to the whole to act as a seemingly unique entity. This is one of the three key enablers.
- *symbolism* — transmitting culture, attitudes, values, beliefs, and norms so they can be shared and understood by people both inside and outside the organization.
- *positioning* — differentiating the corporation and its products/services in the marketplace.
- *trust* — enhancing the firm's credibility by communicating its identity in a way that reflects the realities of the corporation.
- *reputation* — managing the expectations of the different audiences by transmitting what the company is and what it stands for.

The corporation communicates its identity through four major areas of activity that must be managed in concert. These are broken out in the following chart (Exhibit 3):

**EXHIBIT 3: KEY ELEMENTS OF IDENTITY**

| Element | Brief Description | Key Identity Implications |
|---|---|---|
| Vision | • What the firm is all about: mission, core values and beliefs, distinctive capabilities, and fundamental purpose. | • The basic precepts of an organization's identity are derived from the corporate vision.<br>• The identity and all of its elements must be aligned with the corporate vision in order to be effective. |
| Culture | • How people within the organization behave to each other and to outsiders.<br>• Corporate culture has five major elements: leadership, teamwork, behaviors, traditions, and values. | • Culture is the most pervasive element of the identity, but it certainly can be adapted to respond to competitive changes.<br>• Firms may have multiple cultures associated with functional groupings or locations — identity helps resolve potential conflicts and provides a basis to a seamless whole. |
| Communications | • How the firm describes and publicizes what it does, both inside and outside the organization.<br>• The organization's core messages and visual style. | • Corporate communications is a key element to establish the firm's identity, both internally and externally.<br>• Effective identity must be communicated with appropriate emphasis on all of the firm's audiences. |
| Products and Services | • The products and services that the firm delivers; their design, performance, and standards of quality. | • Management of the firm's identity must be consistent with the products and services it delivers — cosmetic identity can lead to disastrous consequences for the firm's reputation and credibility. |

In our model, companies should emphasize distinct identity elements to respond to specific strategic imperatives. A product like a soft drink would simply be an anonymous commodity without its packaging and advertising. Coca-Cola, for example, derives much of its global success from the ingenious marketing and communication of its world-famous imagery. Other organizations, particularly service-oriented firms like consultants, depend for success upon the way in which their people interact with the outside and within the organization. Their identity is greatly influenced by their culture and behavior. In a product-dominated company, it is the product itself that is most responsible for shaping and maintaining the firm's identity, both at the internal and external levels. Sony's identity, for example, is largely conditioned on its endless range of innovative products.

We can't stress enough that effective corporate identity must be communicated, with appropriate emphasis, to both the firm's internal and external audiences. Traditionally, most firms have concentrated their identity efforts on external audiences, primarily customers. The reality, however, is that successful corporations must be able to market themselves to *all* the different groups of people with whom they interact, particularly their own staff.

Because of the potential size and diversity of its audiences, firms must learn to correctly segment, understand, and address the different internal and external audiences, and communicate accordingly. To avoid discrepancies, the firm must "synchronize" the message being delivered to these different audiences. Consistency, in both content and delivery, is crucial in building and maintaining a cohesive identity.

Communicating the firm's identity in a way that reflects the realities of the corporation is also critical. Claiming to be innovative when the principal innovations are in advertising, for example, is bound to severely damage the firm's credibility at both the internal and external levels. Different internal and external audiences can, and in fact most certainly will, overlap, one more reason why it is important to foster consistent corporate communications.

Specifically, there are three circumstances when defining and reviewing the corporate identity are particularly useful:

1. A need for major corporate change. Redefining the corporate identity can help announce, symbolize, and facilitate change if the company needs to be turned around or expanded into new markets.
2. Mergers and acquisitions. One strong umbrella identity can help weave the previously independent organizations into a single seamless whole.
3. A crisis that threatens identity. Refocusing and reinforcing the corporate identity during a crisis allows the firm to reestablish its position and to increase credibility among its different audiences.

Identity should never force the strategic direction of the company. Companies like J&J are able to leverage their external identity in times of crises, as they did with the Tylenol emergency (their "credo" also guided behavior of executives during the crisis). Others like Hewlett-Packard used their internal identity with employees to overcome a business crisis in the 1980s—born out of a gradual buildup of bureaucracy that eventually began to slow-down critical decision-making processes and separate the company from its customers. Identity is a corporate property, and although many businesses may appropriately foster separate identities for different parts of the corporation, that should always be done with intent, not by chance.

## CAPITAL

There is little question that the Global Core must be responsible for the capital mission of the corporation. After all, it alone is able to exert significant leverage in sourcing low-cost capital, especially for smaller regional Business Units.

Moreover, it acts as an arbiter for capital allocation across the extended organization because of its unique ability to gather information most efficiently, in particular information about global capital markets and the peculiar needs of the Business Units. Often it is able to furnish specialized financial expertise to the units on matters like building capabilities to assess risk and return trade-offs, and it can support business decisions by supplying analytical tools and frameworks to operating managers.

For global companies, the capital mission has gotten more complex. We are talking about the challenge of gaining access to capital in global environments, managing capital investment across borders, maintaining relationships with an increasingly global financial community, protecting the organization against more varied risk exposures (transactional, translational, competitive), and supporting transactions of the operating units in multiple countries and currencies.

Capital structure is an important part of the capital mission. This mission goes beyond the standard leverage question, but rather addresses issues of ownership. Should part of the corporation be spun off to shareholders as Monsanto did with its chemicals business? How should ownership of an alliance be structured? How different should the capital structure of the pieces be? Enron, for example, used very different capital structures for its pipeline and independent power businesses. The issues are getting more complex.

Companies are redefining a set of key activities for which the financial core is responsible—gaining access to and optimizing the cost of capital, channeling capital toward productive investment opportunities, maintaining relationships with the investment community and financial markets, developing capabilities to effectively manage corporate risk, lending technical expertise to support transactions across global markets, and ensuring appropriate vertical and horizontal integration with the rest of the organization to communicate financial results and share financial expertise.

Because capital has become so mobile across borders and currencies, gaining access to it is an information-intensive activity. As financial markets become more integrated, global companies will be forced to joust for the same capital. In some instances, a more corporate-wide perspective makes the most sense. That way you can be certain that capital-sourcing is consistent with the goals of the overall organization. It also allows the company to leverage scale economies in borrowing across potential sources, as well as to create shared-service support for transactional needs.

However, appropriate capabilities must also be developed at the Core and used in support of distributed Business Units. We suggest creating teams to assist the Business Units in analyzing high-leverage investment opportunities and to provide expertise to identify optimal capital sources at local levels.

Without a doubt, optimizing the company's cost of capital is a critical imperative for funding global investment opportunities (see Exhibit 4).

The Global Core must then effectively use this capital by matching the appropriate financial strategy to valuable invest-

**EXHIBIT 4: GLOBAL INVESTMENT DRIVERS**

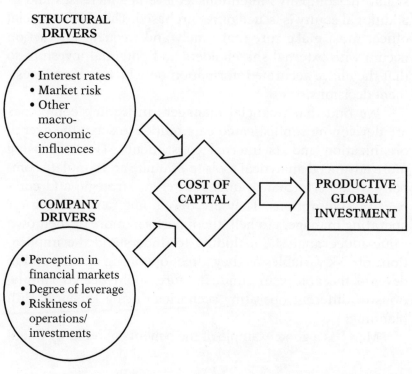

ments. It should determine the organization's needs for capital in both the short and long term. This means it must develop consistent methodology to estimate future cash flows from operating units that will help to fund investment opportunities, understand where leverage is appropriate and its relative cost, and manage the tax implications of the financing structure across the global organization. It should carefully allocate capital across the Business Units. To do that, it has to understand the unique needs of individual operating units and to figure out where capital can be used most effectively, keeping in mind the importance of risk to cash flows. It should make trade-offs where necessary to maximize returns.

Beyond this, the company's financial position, dictated by the choice of financial strategy, must be communicated to the global investment community. It is incumbent upon the Core to ensure that its financial decisions are interpreted consistently and accurately by financial markets. As financial strategy changes over time, senior management must clearly signal the company's intentions as leverage increases and as additional equity is issued or repurchased. The chief financial officer must make sure that timely and frequent interaction occurs with external shareholders and potential investors so that they have accurate information on which to base investment decisions.

We find that financial managers in leading companies are developing sophisticated capabilities to serve the overall organization and its internal constituents. They are using more advanced analytical tools to evaluate and simulate company-wide performance under different strategic and competitive assumptions. They are developing new training for operating managers to help them perform more of their own value-added analysis, including to understand the implications of risk variables as they affect operating results, and to develop the ability to conduct more sophisticated simulations of different operating scenarios during Business Unit planning.

Merck is a good example of the benefits of building financial capabilities to cope with global uncertainty. A major issue at the pharmaceutical giant was that R&D and new product development were the primary driver of growth and profitability. Yet high risk and cost were associated with bringing new products to market. There were also significant financial risks as a multinational operating in approximately forty different currencies. The company was under strong price pressure due to increased global competition and high health-care costs in industrialized countries. Hence it needed vehicles that would allow managers to quantify the impact of risk and uncertainty on key operating strategies.

Using sophisticated Monte Carlo simulation techniques, Merck created the Research Planning Model (RPM), a capability to help managers assess projected risk and return of projects prior to making R&D commitments. It then expanded RPM to analyze projected profitability of project groups and to better formulate larger strategies. It also instituted "divisional partnering," an initiative to deeply integrate financial analysis into business decisions made by operating units. Finally, it focused on shaping strategic options with sophisticated financial techniques *ex ante*, rather than *ex post*.

The benefits were considerable. Merck has been able to more precisely allocate R&D funds by quantifying the likely effects of multiple risk variables. It has leveraged financial expertise and analytical capabilities throughout the organization to better respond to competitive threats and shape strategic alternatives. And it has encouraged continual innovation in sophisticated financial techniques and analysis which could support specific functions, in addition to overall strategy.

As the finance organization evolves to better meet the needs of operating units, the role of the CFO and senior finance management changes markedly. It moves away from internal steward of corporate resources to integral contributor in formulating external corporate strategy. The role becomes that of the key leader in identifying and evaluating strategic acquisitions, mergers, and divestments, as well as active involvement in budgeting and strategic planning with the Business Units, allowing them to challenge financial assessments and assumptions.

Organizations must rely on CFO and senior management's understanding of global macroeconomic trends and their likely impact on the company's strategic goals. The CFO must also lead the effort to develop local finance expertise and guarantee that appropriate linkages are in place with the Core. The CFO needs to both consider the appropriate organizational structure and provide the proper incentives to meet the capital mission of the global core.

## CONTROL

One of the first things we, as management consultants, typically do on an engagement is an assessment of where the client's businesses are making money and where they are not. Part of that exercise involves understanding the cost and value added structure in an economic rather than an accounting way.

For the most part, companies are too wrapped up in doing better the things they typically do. Who looks after what they should be doing? We had one client who, for years, had been trying to find out how much his firm produced on a daily basis across operations. It is hard to imagine managing without that type of information.

The control mission of the Global Core must perform two basic functions, and not much else: satisfy legal and fiduciary requirements, and ensure that there is sufficient and appropriate management information to enable the smooth, efficient operation of the business and an assessment of its inherent risks.

Fiduciary and legal requirements are primarily dictated by laws and regulations—securities market disclosures, tax reporting and payment regulations, directors' fiduciary responsibilities, environmental laws, employment rules, and so forth.

On the other hand, the control needs varies quite a bit as the firm's environment and structure changes. This can encompass orchestrating diverse activities across the firm, designing work and allocating responsibilities efficiently, motivating people to pursue the firm's overall objective, and identifying and managing firm-wide risks. Given that the legal control mission is fairly straightforward, we focus here on the enabling role.

Setting aside its fiduciary role, the control mission adds value to the Core by coordinating diverse activities throughout the organization and making sure that they all promote the same strategic vision. We break this down into several ingredients.

1. Coordination: multiple activities across the firm must not contradict one another, but must fit sensibly together to form a coherent, unified strategy.
2. Work design: accountability and authority must be allocated to produce the most effective, efficient production given the firm's environment.
3. Motivation: people's efforts must be clearly and unambiguously directed toward achieving the overall objective.
4. Risk management: the impact of risk, from any single activity or group of activities, on the entire organization and on share price must be understood and managed.

In essence, the control function translates the firm's strategic vision into actionable goals, designs authority and incentive systems to support their pursuit, measures progress toward those goals, and manages risk throughout the organization. While the firm's strategic vision is primarily set by the strategic leadership mission of the Global Core, the control mission helps to translate that vision into goals. The "rules of the game" define individuals' roles and responsibilities, and the details of the performance and reward system to which each will be held accountable. Individual and group performance are measured against objectives, and performance is rewarded according to the predetermined rules.

The organization's progress toward the strategic vision is continually monitored, and the actionable goals and rules of the game are adjusted when necessary. Risks from market expectations, the composition of the business portfolio, and business operations are watched and managed on a firm-wide basis.

The "rules of the game" are vital in all of this because they essentially dictate how individuals should behave within the organization.

Through the identity mission, the firm's culture provides an important element of the code of conduct that controls and coordinates individuals' behavior. All cultural elements, including leadership, teamwork, behaviors, traditions, and values, should be consistent and compatible with other control mechanisms. Explicit standards help coordinate activities that are relatively straightforward to quantify. These standards economize on learning and training costs, reduce redundancies in system support, establish procedures for routine activities, and standardize and speed workflow. Explicit codes of conduct promote compliance with legal requirements. Implicit codes become especially important when the "right" behavior is hard to quantify explicitly, or hard to identify in advance, in rapidly evolving environments, or when new opportunities are very different from past opportunities or are otherwise difficult to predict. "Team-playing" or other peer objectives are widely recognized and clearly valued, and are often looked on as limits or boundaries for acceptable behavior.

British Airways used a mixture of both implicit and explicit controls when it transformed itself to a customer-and service-oriented organization and discarded its old transportation-oriented past. The implicit control imparted by a strong and cohesive culture was created by extensive training and human resource initiatives. For example, they developed an innovative "Managing People First" training program led by external psychologists and utilizing intensive learning experiences both inside and outside the classroom—the program focused upon fundamental beliefs and values and on how these beliefs could direct one's behavior. In addition, British Airways developed a network of "families" who would work together on a continuing basis to support and nurture fellow staff who were in the most stressful front-line customer-contact jobs. The more explicit controls included greater scrutiny over the types of people that were hired and a determination to remove employees who did not meet new standards. This was underpinned by a revamped performance evaluation process that included both measurements against predetermined goals and peer review.

The control function of the Global Core also makes regular assessments of the organization's performance against its established targets. It calculates the contribution of each Business Unit to corporate goals, focuses management on performance drivers, provides a framework to drive decision-making at all levels of the organization, furnishes "results" feedback for modifying budgets, action plans, strategies, and corporate goals, establishes detailed accountabilities for achieving results, focuses and motivates the organization's efforts and fosters communication within the company, and provides input to the employee evaluation and reward system, making adjustments when necessary.

A final avenue through which the control mission of the Global Core adds value is by managing and monitoring risks from all sources across the entire firm. It is evident to us that companies that manage risk poorly will consistently fail to meet profit forecasts. This failure will be recognized by the market through a discount on the value of future earnings. Identification and evaluation of risk ensures that projects selected for implementation are the most effective use of shareholder funds. Identification of risks during project evaluation allows them to be proactively managed over the course of the project to maximize project returns. Like project risks, the risks associated with whole businesses must also be tracked and managed. The specific tools for managing financial risks were discussed with the capital mission of the Global Core.

Risks can be grouped into three areas, all of which can be managed:

1. Expectations risk. Nothing seems to change faster than

the market's perception on the prospects of a corporation. In July 1996, Motorola announced that its earnings would be below what it had forecast and an entire industry suffered a drastic correction in its share prices. That's expectation risk. It involves several factors, all of which can be influenced through shareholder communications programs. The key things are the message to the market or growth target, the current potential to meet growth targets, what projects are in the pipeline and what capabilities the company possesses to generate and convert its opportunities, the market's confidence in the company's ability to meet longer-term growth targets, and the company's ability to consistently find new opportunities. Managing portfolio risk requires understanding the risk/return profile of the business portfolio and the risk diversification and accumulation effects, and adjusting the portfolio mix accordingly.

2. Macroeconomic risks. These include inflation, exchange rates, and economic growth. Then there are political/policy risks like tax changes, environmental regulation, and health and safety compliance. And there are industry risks, including industry cycles, new competitors, and market concentration.

3. Business risk. This is specific to existing businesses or proposed projects, and can often be more actively managed than other types of risk. Here we are talking about input market risks like supply availability and quality and labor relations, operating risks like production failure and operations efficiency, and output market risks like product price and new product development.

The Global Core is the only place in the corporation that can take a completely firm-wide look at risks and see that they are appropriate and not excessive.

## CAPABILITIES

The final of the five missions of the Core is that it facilitates a flexible business framework that spurs interaction among the units and enables the organization to compete at full strength. The purpose here is simple: to increase value by creating and capturing growth opportunities, as well as by adding new business to produce value beyond the current corporate boundaries.

This corporate-wide growth agenda requires that the Business Units have access to all of the world-class capabilities. These may be accessed outside the corporation through strategic alliances or shared with the corporation. With a renewed focus on growth, Business Units must often work together flexibly to combine capabilities across the units to engender new opportunities outside the current boundaries, to coordinate current activities across the corporation to optimize geographic coverage and customer orientation, and to facilitate the use of corporate-wide capabilities and know-how to develop opportunities within the current boundaries.

How do they do this? Management skills transfer, knowledge sharing, best-practices exchange, and enhanced communication between the units are the keys to building and enhancing sustainable competitive advantage. The Global Core is the broker of capabilities within the organization. Ultimately, the corporate design should be a flexible configuration of components within which knowledge and capabilities can be exploited, and which changes as the organization's strategy and environment evolve.

Remember, our leadership model focuses on managing total corporate resources (e.g., people and capabilities knowledge which span organizational boundaries) rather than just assets (see Exhibit 5):

## EXHIBIT 5: NEW MODEL CHARACTERISTICS

| Traditional Model | Emerging Model |
|---|---|
| **Managing Assets** | **Managing Resources** |
| • Built around assets | • Built around capabilities |
| • Focus on managing numbers | • Focus on creating value |
| • Hierarchical | • Networked |
| • Independent parts | • Interdependent |
| • Reactive | • Responsive |
| • Command and control | • Empowered |

To understand this clearer, let use give you our definition of capability: the ability to perform better than competitors using a distinctive and difficult to replicate set of business activities.

Capability, then, has the following characteristics:

- Is built around a tight business focus closely linked to the company's mission and values.
- Is based on a value proposition which can be measured in terms of time, value, or cost.
- Is a corporate property, and therefore it is a corporate responsibility to ensure its development and deployment.
- Is broadly based across the value chain.
- Consists of an integrated set of enablers across business functions.
    Organization's knowledge and skills.
    Business process and organization structure.
    Supporting systems and technology.
    Positional assets and/or resources.

It is the Global Core's job to coordinate, facilitate, and broker the Business Units' efforts to select, acquire, develop, and leverage capabilities firm-wide. First of all, it establishes and facilitates mechanisms among the units and the Core to identify and select strategic capabilities. It ensures that these chosen capabilities match the overall corporate vision. It supports the units in building, maintaining, and expanding their capabilities by providing the information and motivation necessary (to broaden and leverage capabilities). It should afford easy access to capabilities to be shared across units as well as those that must be sourced or acquired from outside, and ought to encourage the combination of capabilities across the units.

To assure the easy access and exchange of capabilities, it is the role of the Core to enhance capability-focused cross-BU processes including:

*Capabilities transfer*, under which leading-edge capabilities/processes are disseminated throughout the organization. This enhances competitive advantage, minimizes duplication and development costs, and leverages the Business Units' relatedness and regional focus.

*Knowledge sharing*, in which there is global accessibility to the organization's best knowledge and the experts behind the ideas. This avoids reinventing a lot of wheels, and it continuously enhances the organization's know-how. What happens is the company expert database replaces the central staff.

*Best-practices exchange*, under which better ideas, processes, and systems are exchanged between related functions and businesses. This upgrades the performance of the individual business entities to the highest possible level, minimizes duplication and development costs, promotes better understanding of unique needs for each business entity, and fosters cross-group relationships while encouraging Business Unit innovation.

Let's look at a few examples. Canon made a bold move when it redefined itself as a repository of expertise in core capabilities, rather than just a camera manufacturer. Then it made significant investments in developing eight core technologies, including precision mechanics, fine optics, and microelectronics. Out of these eight core technologies, it developed a wide array of more than thirty world-class products, including cameras, video equipment, laser printers, copiers, fax machines, calculators, computer screens, and typewriters.

Dow Chemical has achieved great success in sharing knowledge. It created a structured portfolio of the firm's 29,000 in-force patents, and it mapped existing patents against the corporate capabilities and businesses. Then more effective patent processes were put in place to allow better management of the potential multibillion-dollar business opportunities that could come from licensing and sharing the patents across the firm.

Komatsu uses formal human resource programs to leverage capabilities into new areas. Its "Return Ticket" policy provides a means for staff to move back, which encourages transfers to areas that had been viewed as banishment. Then its "Strategic Employee Exchange" lets staff work on projects in other units on a short-term basis. Sharp institutes project teams to pursue cross-unit initiatives, known as "the chairman's projects," to attract the best resources from across the company.

In many cases, the capabilities mission is carried out through the implementation of information technology, for this allows easier sharing across organizational lines. Ford Motor Company, for instance, is moving toward the global design of cars. Its objectives are to globally design cars and parts more efficiently and to eliminate duplication of product development and engineering activities between regions. To accomplish this, Ford has developed new digital information and manufacturing exchange technology to express product information in a standard format. By now, some 10,000 people use a single system for product releasing (transferring a product from design to manufacturing). The company is working on a telecommunications infrastructure to provide worldwide digital data access to design simulation supercomputers. They link suppliers into Ford's network via e-mail. The benefits include the maximum utilization of global resources, an expected return on the technology investment of at least 50 percent, the elimination of costly and time-consuming translation of data, the development of a worldwide car (Mondeo), and streamlined interactions with suppliers that have lowered their costs and eased their operations.

To cite another example, Citicorp is working to leverage its market coverage. It wants to secure and maintain a large market presence by more effective work processes and to increase the focus on customer rather than internal administration. And so it has established a work-group computing environment whereby employees are able to access a wide range of information throughout the company from their desktop. Also, it has redesigned work processes to change job definitions and improve internal communications. What benefits has Citicorp reaped? Profit center earnings doubled, the amount of time spent to process loans was cut in half, executive time spent on administrative activities dropped from 70 percent to 20 percent, and the number of customers managed by account executives increased by 170 percent, resulting in higher revenues.

It is important to point out that much of the responsibility for managing and deploying corporate capabilities lies with the Business Units. Being closer to the market, they often become cognizant of opportunities faster. Thus it is imperative that all Business Units commit to the development of the selected strategic capabilities and participate in cross-group development programs. They know best of all their capabilities' strengths and weaknesses.

But since one of the Core's key functions is to guarantee the best use of corporate-wide capabilities, a flexible business framework is required that encourages interaction among the firm's units so that the firm competes with its full complement of capabilities. As capabilities span the entire corporate value chain, the Core plays a fundamental role in coordinating, facilitating, and brokering the efforts of the Business Unit to select, acquire, develop, and leverage capabilities firm-wide.

In this regard, we stress the importance of the three key enablers—people, knowledge, and coherence. Knowledge is a major component of the firm's capabilities; people leverage these capabilities; and coherence provides the context for action. The Global Core's job is to make sure that these capabilities are readily available and used. The examples cited above show the potential of fully exploiting capabilities that already exist within the corporation.

One of the major drivers in the recent increase in the number of strategic alliances is the power of combining complementary capabilities to create growth. Leading companies must learn to overcome obstacles and create the same advantage internally.

## DISTRIBUTING THE CORE

There is one final and rather important issue having to do with the Global Core. The five key missions of the Core are the vehicles through which the corporation creates system value. These are missions that meet the "burden-of-proof" test and are the responsibility of corporate. Paradoxically, while they are corporate missions, their execution is often best done on a distributed basis.

With rapid advances in information and communications technology, the once-thorny obstacles of distance and time zones can be surmounted. With a more appropriate business model in place, the obstacle of organizational boundaries is overcome. Thus corporations can locate Global Core activities very close to where they are needed or where they are more effectively executed (see Exhibit 6).

There is no reason why activities can't be geographically dispersed. For example, the identity mission could include maintaining external relations with constituents in twenty countries. A corporate presence could be established in a country by locating part of that function locally. There are several ways to accomplish this. A single Business Unit of the firm with a presence in that region could perform the function on behalf of the corporation. Or the activity could be delegated to a strategic partner or outsourced. Either way, the activity would be networked as part of the extended Core. It

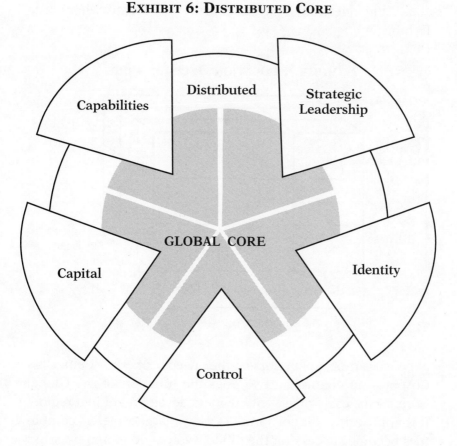

Capabilities

Distributed

Strategic
Leadership

Capital

GLOBAL CORE

Identity

Control

would report to the Core executive responsible for that function and remain an extension of corporate.

The advantages of distributing the Core are considerable. The corporation's presence is significantly expanded so that remote geographies are no longer remote. A number of companies have been quite effective in distributing parts of their Core. Philips does it through its network of geographic offices that are used by all of the businesses. GE has set up a hub in Hong Kong headed by corporate to provide support by businesses pursuing opportunities in Asia. BHP created a senior executive of its international division who put in place a network of country managers to build the company's identity across businesses in target markets.

A big question is what activities to locate where (see Exhibit 7):

## EXHIBIT 7: LOCATION DECISION CUBE

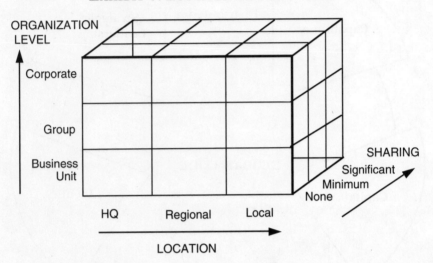

Over time, of course, the needs of the Centerless Corporation change and so does the function of the Global Core. In the early phases of business development in a region, it is appropriate for corporate to play a larger role. As companies become successful, the model evolves. Regional pressure must become local. Businesses should carry a greater portion of the load. And thus the Global Core becomes distilled even more, moving inexorably toward its ideal.

At times it may be appropriate for a regionally dominant Business Unit to carry the responsibility of executing one of the five key missions. In this way, more and more companies are learning not to replicate resources and to build on what is already there. In the end, the Global Core becomes the leader in guaranteeing that the corporation has the right resources and that these are deployed in the best and most efficient manner. Only in this manner will the organization fulfill its true promise and come to reign over the Business Space it rightly deserves.

# CHAPTER SEVEN

# THE ELASTIC BUILDING BLOCK

**IT** is a conceit to imagine that the hardy Business Unit could hold up, unaltered, under the siege of change and freewheeling conditions that we have seen in recent times. Several lifetimes ago, no one could have conceived of a world grown so complex and so small, where one makes an overnight trip to Argentina on an hour's notice, when international money transfers take milliseconds.

The Business Unit has long been considered the fundamental building block of the corporation, and for good reason. Imagine what a company would look like if we had never had the evolutionary step that created these basic structures. Corporations would be confronted with managing a tangled mess of activities, a stew of enterprises bubbling away in one giant pot. You would have to do some serious ladling to gather up all the potatoes or to search for just the meat.

We are acutely aware that no corporation could operate without Business Units, and we would hardly suggest that you do away with them. It would be difficult today to conceive of a large organization that was not sliced up into these more manageable elements of focus and accountability. The arrival of the Business Unit structure was the welcomed step that has enabled corporations to attain remarkable new levels of size. Indeed, they have been a necessary vehicle to reduce the dense complexity of diversity.

Be that as it may, we are just as acutely aware that fealty to the Business Unit as we have known it must cease. It is too inflexible. In the Centerless Corporation, with a Global Core in place of a corporate center, we also introduce a new type of Business Unit. It is a spunky entity that is more reliant both on its brethren units as well as on the external world. We think of it as the highly elastic building block. You can stretch it and twist it so that it brushes against the other units and can be connected to whatever outside elements can bring it value.

There is far more rigorous appraisal of these blocks in the Centerless Corporation. No Business Unit gets a free ride. Harder questions get asked about whether a particular unit "fits" into the overall portfolio. They get asked about when do we add and when do we subtract. They get asked about how do we manage them.

As we have said, the strategic challenge of the corporation is to make the whole worth more than the sum of the parts. An alternative translation of that challenge is that the business model of the corporation had better add appreciable value to what the individual businesses could generate on their own. Ultimately, that added value is the test of the business model. It is the reason that firms can no longer accept the cost of corporate overhead without the benefits of added value.

Rarely, though, can you achieve enough value by just picking the right portfolio of businessess. Financial theorists lecture us that the share market is efficient and that investors are better off picking their own portfolios. Corporations do not have to do it for them. In fact, highly diversified companies often find their stock price penalized. In part, this may be due to how market analysts are organized, which is by industry. Companies that cut across industries have businesses that are not well understood and appreciated by the analysts and hence performance in that sector gets discounted to some extent. The exceptions to this practice are companies like General Electric, almost an industry in itself, that are large enough to have analysts dedicated to dissecting their every breath.

Simplifying business lines—embracing the notion that small is beautiful—is leading some firms to sell off non-core businesses or assets. Taken to the extreme, this leads us down the path to single-business firms.

Many of these principles have been applied to how firms create and manage Business Units. For the most part, the business units are highly autonomous with clear bottom-line accountability.

## Add Value Through the Five Missions

Obviously, Business Units exist at many levels. Small units get aggregated into divisions and groups within the corporation. By the time the aggregation is complete, many large companies like to brag about their Business Units in terms of where they would rank in the Fortune 100 or 500 if they were stand-alone entities. The way many of them are managed, they actually should be set free. The corporation just doesn't add sufficient value.

The only way a corporation adds value to the individual businesses is through its "five key missions"—strategic leadership, identity, capabilities, capital, and control. This is where the value in excess of the sum of the parts comes from. Accordingly, the right businesses for the corporation are those that benefit from the five key missions. They are the ones that fit.

The design of the Business Unit, the role of the unit, and the role of the Business Unit head all must evolve to take full advantage of the five key missions. If a particular part of the business sits outside this envelope of added value, it should not be part of the corporation.

Thus we see a revolution in how companies construct their organizations. Competitive pressures are driving companies to be faster and nimbler. Yet they must compete with a highly developed set of capabilities to be successful. In this environment, it is imperative that the Business Unit framework be flexible enough to encourage interactions among units within the firm. In this way, the firm can compete with its full complement of capabilities while still retaining accountability.

## THREE DRIVERS OF CHANGE

We see three distinct drivers of change influencing the role of the Business Unit. One, a firm should be able to compete with all of its capabilities regardless of organizational boundaries. This requires more explicit linkages among the Business Units in certain, though not all, areas.

Two, the basic building block of the firm is really its capabilities, not its Business Units. Thus, new opportunities are as likely to fall between existing Business Units as they are inside the units. This means not only that greater cooperation is needed, but greater flexibility in defining what in fact a Business Unit is.

Three, key capabilities may also reside outside the corporate boundaries in strategic alliances and joint ventures. This makes businesses more interdependent externally as well as internally.

### No Entity Unto Itself

To accomplish the potent flexibility of the Centerless Corporation, the role of the Business Unit has to be augmented. It must still be the fundamental building block of accountability, but greater interdependence means that it cannot be monolithic, an entity unto itself. Too often the price of increased accountability has been barriers within the organization. Corporations must step outside the dimensions of such a trade-off.

Naturally, implementing the new imperative across the businesses is a challenging undertaking. Some of the pioneers in this area have encountered some thorny issues. After all, moving to a more open model is contrary to the deep-seated nature of business managers. But while the track record in the early stages is typically spotty, once the new paradigm is successfully achieved it proves to be a powerful lever of business performance.

The Disney Company is a good illustration of a bold attempt to exploit synergies between Business Units. The seeds were planted with a plan first articulated in 1985 by Michael Eisner and the late Frank Wells to get divisions to promote other divisions within the corporation, as well as to get corporate-level teamwork. Indeed, Disney's chief rationale for acquiring Capital Cities/ABC, as it outlined in its 1995 annual report, was that the "linking of the two companies will produce heightened opportunities for synergy in production, programming, and distribution that neither could achieve alone."

To prod the BUs into acting on potential synergies, Eisner has them engage in regularly scheduled "synergy meetings" that bring together the heads of each division, along with their top area management. These sessions encourage the cross-pollination of Disney movies in all parts of the company.

Everyone recognizes that these meetings are high priority. Division heads and other key management are expected to prepare well for them. In fact, to underscore their strategic importance, they are never canceled. Indeed, Eisner maintains that the meetings "are one of the prime reasons that our company has grown as rapidly as it has."

More informally, Disney has held staff lunches every Monday for the last twelve years, which serve as open forums in which creative ideas for "cross-pollination" are exchanged and explored.

What's more, the company is pursuing plans to select one or two of its properties each year and then transform them into what it calls blockbuster live-action "event" films under the Walt Disney banner. The idea is that all of Disney will promote, publicize, and support the chosen pictures in the energized way that Disney converts an animated film into a company-wide effort. The first property tried under this approach was *101 Dalmatians*.

Another interesting case is Cisco Systems, the world's largest networking equipment company. Cisco operates as decentralized Business Units, each with its own marketing and engineering organization. The setup enables the company to combine the manufacturing and distribution efficiencies of a large company with the entrepreneurship and responsiveness to business opportunities of a small one.

But the linkages between the BUs go beyond those that underpin the most obvious economies of scale. One of Cisco's key objectives is to become a one-stop shop for the networking needs of all clients. While the BUs are mainly product-focused, they are expected to jointly manage client relationships. This means offering a single point of contact for global support and maintenance.

To deliver on its one-stop shopping strategy, all the BUs operate under the umbrella of the Cisco Internetwork Operating System, software that regulates the networking hardware. Implementing the Cisco IOS on all the hardware sold by the company allows its products to work seamlessly together. This makes one-stop shopping at Cisco particularly compelling to potential customers. Clearly, customers desire comprehensive solutions rather than a grab bag of parts that they have to assemble and tweak.

Indeed, this IOS and the process for implementing it in all of Cisco's businesses and hardware products make up a powerful linkage between the BUs. To target specific market segments, Cisco has formed special marketing units whose scope cuts across individual BUs. After the acquisition of StrataCom in 1996, Cisco formed a Service Provider Marketing Unit to drive product requirements across the BUs for the important client segment that includes telcos, cable operators, and Internet service providers

Cisco, however, has encountered some significant difficulties implementing its linkage mechanisms. It has had trouble maintaining a single version of its Cisco IOS on all its hardware, which has proved bothersome to some customers. The company will undoubtedly need to push harder with initiatives like the Service Provider Unit. Analysts have already voiced concern that the Business Units still don't truly send a consistent message to their targeted audiences about the company's technologies and strategies.

For some more insight, consider the case of BHP, Australia's biggest company. It has four large business lines: copper, minerals, steel, and petroleum. They are arranged in several sizable and relatively autonomous business groups which compete on a global basis. Growth for these resource-based businesses was driving them more and more outside Australia. In particular, many of the businesses had targeted Asia for key growth areas. For the most part, these independent units implemented their own growth strategies entirely separate from each other.

By 1994, chief executive John Prescott reached the inescapable conclusion that BHP needed a common face to many of its constituents in the target countries. He decided that penetration into high-growth areas around the world required:

- greater local presence and knowledge
- the ability to leverage capabilities across businesses and geographies
- a common, recognized identity and one-company approach
- integrated strategic management of key external entities
- development of more global, culturally aware, and adept managers
- core risk management capabilities

In mid-1995, BHP began implementation of a host of new programs aimed at changing some of the processes, systems, and structures of the company. It did things like establish global management training programs and courses that were held in different locations around the world. These focus on high-impact, topical issues like risk management, and can spawn a cross-unit task force to research a particular high-profile issue. The human resource function was distributed into regional growth areas to improve recruitment and training, and there was stepped-up emphasis on cross-unit transfer of personnel within functions and in operations.

Geographic strategies were developed for target areas by a team of cross-unit line and staff personnel that focused on the needs of the country as well as BHP's needs. Group projects led to new businesses.

Then a company-wide information intelligence network was established to access and share critical competitive market information. "Owners of information" were responsible for making information accessible, creating useful knowledge from raw information, and getting the knowledge to the key players.

Strategic relationship management was developed across the company to coordinate strategies and approaches, to leverage contacts and knowledge, and to improve long-term positioning within and across industries. Senior managers identify and coordinate the strategic approach and development of long-term goals for companies that have significant interactions with multiple businesses in several geographic areas.

A senior executive was appointed to promote international growth and facilitate movement and interaction across businesses. It was his job to appoint and develop in-country executives to identify new opportunities and create a unifying approach across businesses. He also was to develop and implement the BHP identity with internal and external constituents, and create cross-business strategic plans within a country to leverage in-country and worldwide capabilities to the fullest extent.

In essence, BHP's change in its approach to its Business Units is to give each the leverage of the company as a whole. The change, which may seem subtle, has many different initiatives at various levels. Businesses had to become part of the larger company identity. They had to learn to be more open in sharing certain information and working more effectively across traditional organizational lines. While the businesses still have strong profit and loss accountability, they must do more. In short, the businesses have to build from the strength of the company as a whole by both using and contributing to the whole. The organizational model continues to evolve, as they reduce the number of layers and increase the number of cross-functional capabilities.

And so companies are quite emphatically moving in the direction of establishing explicit links between their Business Units, but it is also evident that many of them are stumbling somewhat in making those links work effectively as yet. An important thing to remember in the examples we have just cited, as well as others, is that without changes in the broader business model companies are going to have mixed success in these attempts.

## Centering on Capabilities

Conceiving of the organization in terms of its capabilities rather than specific businesses is an essential step in building the company of the future. As business shifts to stronger knowledge-based competition, the organization itself becomes centered around the firm's know-how and know-what. Although the business may be managed along more traditional lines of businesses, often these businesses are more temporary than the more fundamental blocks of capabilities.

Subordinating the Business Unit structure to the knowledge structure can yield significant advantages, especially in businesses that have a rapid pace of change. It drives the company to focus on what's important for creating value. This more direct focus of senior management on value creation has the potential to make the definition of the Business Units themselves more fluid. It also focuses Business Unit heads on the larger picture, in addition to Business Unit performance, since the capability may last longer than the specific organization around it.

Often the focus on capabilities achieves two important results. First, it generates new businesses, new products, and new services. This occurs because the firm looks more broadly at what it can do with what it has, its capabilities, rather than only trying to expand what exists today. Second, it can cause a restructuring of the company's portfolio as activities that fall outside the umbrella of what's needed to generate competitive advantage become candidates for divestment.

Canon Corporation is a global organization dedicated to the design, manufacture, and service of products like photographic cameras, copiers, computers, computer peripherals, business systems, and optical gear. It is a world leader in research and technology development, and considers leading-edge technology one of its main assets.

In the late 1970s, Canon started searching for alternative growth opportunities outside its core market. As a power in the photographic equipment industry, Canon had developed extensive expertise in about a dozen core technologies, including precision mechanics, fine optics, and microelectronics. To successfully expand into other markets, the company needed to wring maximum value out of its expertise by building on its core technologies to develop a broad array of products and services.

And so it redefined itself as a repository of expertise in core technologies—rather than just a maker of cameras. The firm launched an ambitious program to identify, develop, and lay out routes for getting its core capabilities to other parts of the company. At the same time, Canon made significant investments in developing knowledge in eight core competencies. Out of these streams of expertise came a wide array of more than thirty world-class products: cameras, video cameras, copiers, laser printers, fax machines, computers, computer peripherals, electronic typewriters, and calculators.

This effort paid off in some notable benefits. Over the years, Canon has managed to maintain its leadership role in the photographic camera market, while successfully expanding into the office equipment, computer, and consumer electronics markets. It is also a world leader in research and development in fine optics technologies, microelectronics, and precision mechanics.

By focusing and developing its core technical competencies, Canon has been able to forge a highly competitive position in many global markets, a status its competitors are finding exceedingly hard to duplicate.

By implementing a core capabilities strategy which emphasizes the development of key expertise, Canon is able to make much more efficient use of its internal resources, focusing only on the businesses it is good at and not putting needless effort into areas that will not carry the company over the long term.

Lew Platt used a shrewd capabilities focus to revitalize Hewlett-Packard. The company sees its basic business purpose as being to create products that accelerate the advancement of knowledge and improve the effectiveness of people and organizations. The computer, communications, and consumer electronics industries in which Hewlett-Packard competes are rapidly converging. As the entertainment, publishing, health, and consumer electronics businesses go digital, multibillion-dollar markets are opening up in areas like personal communications, video on demand, interactive games, and home shopping.

In 1993, Hewlett-Packard found that it confronted a serious handicap. Unlike competitors like IBM and Apple Computer, it was absent from the digital deal-making scene with media giants like Sony and Time Warner. Despite its current success, HP's future would be limited indeed without a significant role in the new digital era.

And so HP adopted the following strategy:

- It mapped the firm's unique mix of core technologies: a broad and highly competitive family of computers, industry leadership in test and measurement instruments, and HP's extensive expertise in computer networking. These were core technologies that no single rival could match.

- It created the HP=MC² Council (for measurement, computing, and communications), composed of top technical and marketing people from the company's measurement, computing, and communications divisions, to identify new multibillion-dollar opportunities drawing on all capabilities of the company.
- It combined its three core business divisions and technologies to create an all-new-product category, with about a third of HP Labs' $137 million budget going into fundamentally new products.

The results were gratifying. The unique blend of core technologies gave the company a crucial edge in many potential markets. The HP=MC² Council has already identified a significant number of market-creating products, including remote medical diagnostics equipment, home video printers, interactive TV devices, digital cable TV decoders, and video servers. As one example, HP entered into contracts to supply Ford with a diagnostic system that uses an innovative flight recorder to analyze automobile problems. HP beat IBM to the $63 million Ford contract because IBM lacked in-house measurement expertise.

The HP=MC² strategic architecture is guiding behaviors and projects across the company's many decentralized business units to leverage individual efforts and projects for the entire organization. The approach has led to cutting across and bringing together HP's computing, communications, and measurements businesses.

Both the Canon and Hewlett-Packard examples highlight the benefits of thinking of the business as a collection of capabilities rather than of today's businesses. In both instances, it led to an expanded concept of the business. Following their example allows a company to ask the question "What more can I do with what I have?" rather than the more typical and mundane, "Should I keep this or not?"

## Going External

The third expanded role for Business Units is an external role. Companies are increasingly becoming more networked as they reach outside their existing structure to acquire capabilities. We see more joint ventures and strategic alliances as vehicles for filling in gaps in the capability portfolio, changing the geographic reach of the business, or as a means to acquire capabilities instantly.

This means that the very concept of the Business Unit must change. Access to world-class capabilities, one of corporate's five key missions, can be accomplished through either ownership or alliance. The existing definition of a particular Business Unit is more a function of how the company decides to acquire and exploit a set of capabilities than it is of just working with the same set of businesses as a given.

Merck provides an interesting example of how a company reached out through both alliances and acquisitions to bundle the set of capabilities it believed it needed to be successful.

The 1990s have forced Merck, along with the entire pharmaceutical industry, to adapt to rapidly changing health-care systems worldwide. There has been a profound change, especially in the United States, in the profile of pharmaceutical purchase decision-makers. Large customers, including managed-care organizations, now account for 67 percent of all pharmaceutical purchases in the United States, up from 40 percent in 1985. Then there has been a shift away from local pharmacy-based distribution to mail-order pharmacy and pharmacy benefits manager-mediated distribution.

At the same time, profit margins have eroded, because of growing competition from generic drugs, heavy pressure from governments to "contain" health-care expenditure, and the increased ability of large drug purchasers to force price concessions. Meanwhile, the cost and minimum efficient scale for undertaking R&D to innovate have escalated. Also, as living standards rise, developing countries have become more attractive for generating revenue and profits.

Merck's corporate strategy seeks to build and strengthen the capabilities that are identified in its vision as the bases for its success: innovation, effective product delivery, and value demonstration. An unwavering commitment to pharmacological research is the cornerstone of the strategy.

To adjust to changing conditions, the company embarked on an effort to extend its own research and development capabilities through strategic alliances. Du Pont Merck, a joint venture with du Pont, was established to support du Pont's basic biochemical research with Merck's development and marketing skills in the pharmaceuticals business. Astra Merck, a joint venture with Astra AB of Sweden, has given Merck access to Astra's innovative pharmacological research and has given Astra a presence in the U.S. market through Merck's marketing and distribution infrastructure.

Merck's priority in product delivery is to gain access to the consumer products markets and to international markets, particularly in the developing world. Merck has used the joint venture, Johnson & Johnson • Merck to market and distribute consumer pharmaceutical products. The venture has allowed Merck to extend the life of some of its prescription drugs by distributing over-the-counter formulation, and it has enabled Merck's research to more effectively utilize the consumer products market. By giving Merck access to Johnson & Johnson's expertise in consumer product marketing and distribution, it has obviated the need to develop this expertise in-house. At the same time, it has given J&J access to Merck's research and products. One major product that resulted from this marriage was Pepcid AC, an over-the-counter version of Merck's Pepcid.

Merck has grown its foreign presence by building domestic operating units and manufacturing facilities, as well as by entering joint ventures with domestic partners. It has recently put up manufacturing facilities in China and South Korea, as well as operating units in Chile, Croatia, the Philippines, and Romania.

To trumpet the value of its products, Merck has established an extensive network of relationships with all the key parties to the pharmaceuticals purchase decision. Merck continues to support the traditional channels for pharmaceutical sales, including a sales force that targets physicians individually and clinical trials and outcomes research to generate information about its products. Through its 1993 acquisition of Medco, Merck gained more direct and effective access to managed-care organizations and health plan sponsors. Managed-care organizations account for 40 percent of all pharmaceutical sales, and their share is expected to climb to 60 percent by the year 2000.

Merck has aggressively pursued strategic alliances as a means of extending its capabilities and, indeed, has developed a competitive advantage in being able to structure alliances efficiently. It has used alliances to gain new products, technology and research capabilities, marketing expertise, and global presence. And it has developed the expertise to make alliances a cost-effective alternative to acquisitions as a means to gain necessary capabilities.

Merck's purchase of Medco, for instance, has allowed it not only to more effectively target its traditional products to cost-conscious customers but also to develop novel products and services specifically for these markets. Medco is the largest pharmacy benefit manager in the country, managing both retail pharmacy and mail service prescriptions, and serving 47 million people in 1995. It provides its services through contractual relationships with managed-care organizations (MCOs) and employers' health plan sponsors. It maintains supply relationships with drugmakers.

Merck has used Medco's sales force to increase its market share of MCOs, and this has allowed Merck to more aggressively price its products for these customers and to efficiently deliver product information in these nontraditional markets. In the long run, Merck expects the acquisition to allow it to develop products and services specifically for Medco's markets. For example, it hopes to develop new bundled services like disease management. Medco's extensive relationships with drugmakers, MCOs, and physicians will allow Merck to build marketing strategies around integrated therapeutic plans, rather than around individual drugs.

Merck's strategic initiatives have significantly benefited the company. R&D efforts resulted in the launching of six new products in five therapeutic categories in 1995, the largest number of new product releases in Merck's history. Meanwhile, Merck's joint ventures have strengthened its long-term growth potential. Johnson & Johnson • Merck's Pepcid AC Acid Controller is the Number 1 product in the acid relief category, and Astra Merck's Prilosec is also a strong performer.

Medco has enjoyed substantial growth since its acquisition by Merck. The market share of Merck drugs on Medco formularies has increased from 10 percent to 12 percent since the acquisition. By 1995, there were 46 million people eligible for pharmacy benefits managed by Medco, up from 41.5 million in 1994. Managed prescription volume rose from 130 million to 170 million prescriptions from 1994 to 1995.

## NEW DIRECTION MEANS NEW RESPONSIBILITIES

The new direction for Business Units means that they have to shoulder greater responsibilities. They must work effectively within the corporation and effectively within the more extended enterprise. Their leaders have to manage greater interdependence. As a result, they have to take a more enterprise-wide perspective, yet still deliver results. They must be able to benefit from the five key missions, have a capabilities base, and link into the extended enterprise.

As practitioners, we see the challenges of changing the mind-set of management, both at corporate and at the business level, to adopt this novel framework. In many respects, heading a business is akin to being granted a fiefdom, and it is commonly used as a telling testing ground for future CEOs. This made a lot of sense in the days of command and control, but not today.

As leadership of the corporation sweeps to new heights and involves managing a more complex organization, one that is most likely part of a greater extended alliance, so too will leading a Business Unit demand new skills. These skills are best developed in a more networked environment, even at the line of business level.

So, as companies evolve to the Centerless Corporation, the Business Unit structure must also evolve if it is going to function effectively in a network. And the leaders of those businesses must develop a new ethos and a broader set of disciplined skills if they expect to be adept managers. We should go on cherishing the Business Unit. But we must ask more of it.

CHAPTER EIGHT

# GOVERNING IN TURBULENCE

**AS** long as there has been recorded history, corporate governance seems to have been a necessary and contentious part of the landscape. For a good portion of that history, governance has been regarded as a suspect and limp arm of the organization, which has had unfortunate consequences. In many ways, our understanding of governance's beleaguered history has often been based on symbol-clotted myths.

In the United States, the United Kingdom, and Australia, corporate governance has evolved through several stages. From the Age of Dynasties through the Depression, interests of owners and managers were almost perfectly aligned. Then, from the Depression through the early 1970s, we had the Age of Hired Kings, when shareholders became more dispersed, professional CEOs gathered immense power without significant ownership, and the link between owners and managers was ruptured.

Between the early 1970s and the early 1990s, the Age of Reformation roared in, characterized by the rise of institutions as major owners and the struggle to reconnect ownership and management. The Age of Reformation included some turbulent times; it was encapsulated by the late 1980s, the notorious takeover era. It was marked by hostile

takeovers, corporate raiders, LBOs, and myriad other techniques to gain quick control. These transfers of power rarely
produced the desired effects and their costs, in terms of
wasted human and financial resources, led to a backlash from
the public and in the business community itself. The fallout
from these episodes not only spurred institutional shareholders to assert themselves with renewed vigor, but also put the
issue of governance on the front pages.

Now, not only in the United States, the United Kingdom,
and Australia, but everywhere around the world, we seem to
be entering the Age of Reconstruction, in which companies
are grappling with the new realities of competition, alliances,
and global businesses. In this churning environment, shareholders are exerting far more pressure on their boards and demanding entirely new forms of governance—no more of the
old smoke-filled rooms occupied by a group of rubber-
stamping directors who would put their imprimatur on just
about anything. This new era in corporate governance was already apparent in the United States when, in 1993, Dale
Hanson, then the CEO of CalPERS (the California Public
Employees Retirement System) told a group of corporate
managers, "We are no longer into CEO-bashing. We are now
into director-bashing."

Scandals and high-profile corporate crises are another in-
gredient of the tumultuous environment for corporate governance. In the United Kingdom, for example, the scandal of
Robert Maxwell raiding his employees' pension plan was
played out in front of a national audience, and directly affected thousands of people. In Japan, financial scandals have
also undermined the public's confidence in the political and
economic structures that have supported a tightly interwoven,
and even secretive, system of governance for so long.

Indeed, what makes governance such a hot topic today is
that the environment is changing swifter than the turnover of
directors, and this is causing enormous friction and adjustment problems. Boards are more willing to oust a CEO than
ever before, as they find themselves targets of institutional investor activism and escalating concern about the steep level of

CEO pay that often seems to have no relation to company performance or any other reality.

Consider the following:

- Ten CEOs of technology firms left their posts between January and August of 1996. All heads of high-technology companies are said to "keep one eye on the door."
- In March 1995, according to *The Economist,* the College Retirement Equities Fund bullied WR Grace into cutting the size of its board from twenty-two to twelve and imposing a mandatory retirement age of 70. For good measure, it forced it to get rid of its chairman and replace half of its directors.
- Institutional investors now hold over half of all publicly traded equity in the United States, versus less than 10 percent forty years ago.
- More than 650 shareholder proposals were filed by investors in the first part of 1996—up 10 percent over the year before.
- In one 1995 study, 21 percent of the corporate directors surveyed had been formally contacted by institutional investors.

To be sure, governance is a broader concept than is commonly appreciated. As we see it, it has three facets—the governance of the entire corporation by the board of directors, the governance of intercorporate entities, and the governance of intracorporate entities.

Virtually all the signal changes at work in the world are coming to bear on all aspects of corporate governance. We speak of international alliances that require new cross-country solutions for governance. We speak of new forms of joint ventures, cross-holdings, and participation that demand innovative corporate governance systems. We speak of regulatory action, as privatization fosters new governance models and deregulation insists on comprehensive reviews of the existing structure.

In almost every respect, CEOs are having to redefine their basic relationship with the board. Those in the vanguard of such changes believe that their success depends on treating directors as equal partners. M. Anthony Burns, the chairman and CEO of Ryder Systems, Inc., says, "I really want to work with the board and make decisions with board members all the time." Indeed, he championed a corporate bylaw change that barred him from serving on any board committee of his company.

The board of directors, therefore, is one of the crucial linkages in the Centerless Corporation. A successful board will bring coherence to the system. It will allow diverse stakeholders in the extended enterprise—the shareholders, employees, governments, competitors, and partners—not just to cope with their independent perspectives but to benefit from them.

## NEW SHAPES IN THE GOVERNANCE LANDSCAPE

What new forms of corporate governance will emerge as a result of all these changes remains to be seen. Yet some of the shapes in the new governance landscape are coming into focus. Consider a few examples.

As part of an extensive review of its corporate governance policies, Chrysler's board spent several months holding one-on-one meetings with approximately forty of its major institutional shareholders. As Chrysler reported in its 1996 Proxy Statement, "An outside, independent member of the board attended each of these meetings and engaged in a candid exchange of views with the representatives of the relevant investment organization." Furthermore, the company executives who were present at the beginning of the meetings excused themselves after a period of time so that investors could have a more frank exchange with the independent directors.

The company published the results of its review in its Proxy Statement—not only did the board thoroughly examine its structure and operation, it also redefined its relationship with its shareholder base. That is, Chrysler's board developed a broad mission statement guiding its approach toward corporate governance—a framework, essentially, both to evaluate its existing structures and processes and to guide any future changes.

Among the highlights of Chrysler's boardroom review were the changes made to the compensation structure. Directors are no longer paid an annual retainer; rather, they receive their retainer in the form of common stock. In addition, there is a minimum ownership requirement of 5,000 shares and the cash retirement program has been terminated. All of these changes are clearly designed to make sure that corporate performance and improvements in long-term shareholder value are foremost in the minds of the directors.

The new partnership between management and the board is typified by the following statement: "Board members' activities at Chrysler are not restricted to board meetings. Directors are involved in a continuing, informal dialogue with management and have frequent contact with the company."

In short, the board is becoming a more active participant with the Core in defining and attaining the overall corporate mission—a proactive and interdependent partner in key strategic decision-making processes.

Think about it. Even five years ago, could you imagine a board of directors actually lobbying their shareholders, institutional investors, asking for their input and striving to satisfy their needs, rather than waiting until a crisis brought them together.

United Airlines has gone one step farther. To prepare for the future in one of the most brutally competitive and rapidly evolving global industries, it has sold a majority of its stock (55 percent) to its employees, effectively reconnecting the owners of the invested capital with those who decide how to spend it and those who earn it. Its shareholders are its managers and its front-line employees.

United's employee stock ownership program (ESOP) is widely regarded as one of the most successful attempts of its kind, and its accompanying approach toward corporate governance is also groundbreaking, especially for an American company. Its reconstituted twelve-member board now has three employee directors (selected by the pilots' union, the machinists' union, and the salaried management employees respectively), four independent directors (elected by the previous independent directors on the board), and five public directors (elected by the public shareholders). Much of the work on this new board is done by committees. The board has ten committees, twice as many as the typical U.S. board, and the members of each committee are carefully selected from the various stakeholders represented on the board. For example, there is a Labor Committee that represents the company's interests in collective bargaining agreements. It is composed of three directors, including at least one independent director and one outside public director. There is also a committee to nominate and appoint outside public directors after their initial term. It, too, is composed of three directors, all drawn from the pool of outside public directors.

United's structure is far from perfect. As of this writing, the flight attendants have chosen not to participate in the ESOP and, according to some observers, this has created a sense of two "classes" of employees—owners and nonowners—that is becoming a source of tension at the company.

In addition, the governance structure at United has caused some concerns among analysts. Their main worry is that the airline will sacrifice profitability in favor of job preservation. The evidence from other airlines, like TWA, in which there is employee participation at the board level, is inconclusive. Nevertheless, the efforts under way at United are truly ground-breaking, and there are few precedents against which they can be judged. Success in the future will require all stakeholders to balance their interests and take into account the many other demands and constraints upon their situation.

The changes at Chrysler and United provide a window into the future. Actually, the wide representation of stakeholder interests is closer to the traditional German system of governance than the U.S. system. The use of well-defined and transparent processes has been made popular by the shareholder movement in the United States and the United

Kingdom. In the Centerless Corporation, best practices from around the world are used. The intention of the model is to break traditional paradigms, and to bring change to one of the last sacred cows in the world of business—the board.

## THE CENTERLESS CORPORATION GOES PROACTIVE

The board of directors in the Centerless Corporation faces unprecedented pressure to change. Not only must it come to grips with the ferment and trends in the global business environment, it must also address fundamental changes in its shareholder base. The call for something new in the boardroom of the Centerless Corporation has been amplified to a point where it can no longer resist.

Stakeholders now realize that they have more leeway with governance forms than they ever thought possible. They want boards to perform, and are willing to take action if they don't. The Centerless Corporation heeds this call. In the Centerless Corporation, with the corporate center replaced by a Global Core, old governance models are discarded as inappropriate.

Instead of the board playing its traditional passive guardianship role, it is transformed into an active supporter of the business imperative. That is not to say that the board's most fundamental responsibilities have changed. Quite the contrary. The board's fundamental role, to safeguard shareholder interests, remains the same. But what that task now involves *has* changed. Under our new model, the board does things like bring insights on customers from a cross section of industries and services. It benchmarks inside knowledge with outside intelligence. It challenges the efficiency of the CEO and top management, and challenges the role of the Global Core. It makes sure the company is developing key business capabilities. It transmits trends. In every sense, it is an advisory as well as a control body.

This last point, that the board has both an advisory and control function, is particularly important. Just because the

board of the Centerless Corporation must become more outwardly oriented does not mean that it will abandon its traditional internal conformance role. In many respects, the risks
attendant upon a corporation in the new era of global competition make the conformance role more important than ever.

Our focus in the current chapter, however, is on the
changes in the role of the board that must take place, for successfully navigating these changes will be the crucial difference between companies that will thrive in the future and
those that will flounder. In addition, the conformance role of
the board of directors has been extensively studied by many
authors. What is important for us to realize, however, is that
the board of directors, one of the most crucial linkages in the
Centerless Corporation, is under more pressure to reconstruct
itself than at any time in the past.

## GLOBAL FORCES IMPACTING CORPORATE GOVERNANCE

The changing face of global competition and the evolution of
the shareholder base in the Centerless Corporation are creating the powerful forces that are driving change in the boardroom. To be effective in its new proactive and strategic role,
the board of the Centerless Corporation must understand
these forces, for the overall result is that there must be a renewed focus on performance, creating shareholder value, exploring new or novel forms of governance, communicating
with governments and regulators, understanding cultural differences, and cooperating with business partners. Three
forces in particular have come into play:

EXPANSION AND PROLIFERATION OF CAPITAL MARKETS. The expansion and proliferation of capital markets across the world are
redefining the role of corporate governance, and have two
major implications for the Centerless Corporation. The first
implication is that corporate performance is becoming more
critical. In the old less turbulent, less competitive world, many
U.S. companies could finance expansion largely through

retained earnings. In Europe, additional capital needs were often met by government subsidies. Many companies, therefore, were able to formulate strategy and fund new projects with less "interference" from their board or their shareholders. The worldwide growth of capital markets, however, is creating competition for capital on a global basis and increasing the pressure for better performance. Even in Japan, with its traditionally strong dependence upon bank financing, the use of equity capital is on the rise. In 1980, equity represented 12 percent of Japanese corporate financing; today, that figure is closer to 30 or 40 percent.

Associated with the proliferation of capital markets is another trend: the increasing mobility of capital. This, too, has served to strengthen the demand for performance. Large foreign holdings in local markets are not unusual. In France, the director general of the Commission des Operations de Bourse estimated that in 1995 as much as one third of French stock was held by nonresidents. In this new equation, where investors have more choices, it is the corporations that are put under pressure—pressure to deliver greater returns. Put another way, shareholders increasingly have the option to vote with their feet.

At the same time as boards are demanding better performance, the expansion and proliferation of capital markets is increasing the demand for new, perhaps even novel, forms of governance. As family businesses reach out for capital, new shareholders are insisting upon an audible voice and true participation. China has bounded into the capital markets, and other countries are not far behind. With many privatizations occurring in the developing world, often involving alliances between foreign investors and local players, family businesses are reaching out for a copilot. The West is investing in the rising and maturing stock exchanges around the world at an accelerating rate, as it seeks market positions and greater return on capital. Conflicting forces of a strong family tradition in Asia and Latin America, in tandem with different governance models, will cause major friction, especially when the investors are far from the Western world. These forces will require redefinition of the role of corporate governance. Existing cultures and governance models will have to be reconciled, and companies will have to select the best practices around the world to reshape their governance models.

REGULATORY ACTION. As governance has become front-page news, regulators have become more heavily involved. From southeast Asia to the United States, governments are in the boardroom as never before.

According to Robert Pozen, the general counsel at Fidelity Investments, the recent proxy reform rules in the United States have revolutionized the whole way in which directors view their role. The new rules made it easier for shareholders to communicate with each other, allowing them to issue press releases and declare how they will vote, all without having the SEC approve their comments in advance. Although many observers believe the regulations could have gone further—indeed, in many respects, they were simply following rather than leading an increasingly active shareholder body—it is also clear that the ripple effect of the regulations is having a profound impact on many U.S. corporations. Shortly after the new ruling, Ed Durkin of the Carpenters' Union recalled that, in the past, "the only thing we'd hear from them typically was, 'I've received your letter.' " Shortly afterward, he was gaining audiences with the responsible people in the corporations, including the CEO.

In the United Kingdom, the London Stock Exchange (LSE) has chosen to follow a path of self-regulation. It has adopted the reforms of the so-called Cadbury Report as recommendations, rather than law. Nevertheless, the threat of regulation if companies cannot reform themselves is clearly present, and as is already apparent in the United States, the threat of regulation can be even more potent than regulation itself.

In Japan, the legal system has also recently added new momentum to fledgling changes already under way. Revisions that were enacted in the Japanese Commercial Code in 1993 seem likely to have some far-reaching effects. Changes in the procedures for shareholder lawsuits, shareholder access to company accounts, and the audit system are now on the books. Of particular interest is the reduction in the cost of a derivative lawsuit from prohibitive levels to less than $100, a move that will considerably strengthen the hand of the shareholders. The changes to enhance the audit system, requiring companies to appoint a three-member audit committee containing at least one "independent" member, are also likely to have substantial long-term effects.

In addition to the new regulations, there is also increasing pressure from the general public, various interest groups, and politicians on issues of social and environmental responsibility. The public is reacting more strongly than ever when CEOs get raises while laying off thousands of workers. Likewise, boards are now being called to answer for the environmental records of the companies under their stewardship. This trend seems sure to continue. Shareholders are aware of the potential risks and financial costs of environmental crises, and these concerns are reflected in a growing number of proxy proposals.

ALLIANCES. Alliances are becoming increasingly international, longer term, larger, and more entwined with the core business. This raises questions of how to guarantee equitable distribution of returns, how to govern without a conventional control orientation, and how to address cross-cultural differences. International growth through alliances is a widely accepted approach. Many of these unions involve complex combinations of foreign players, local firms, and governments, each with a different mix of abilities and expectations. Over 20,000 alliances were formed by U.S. companies in the past five years, compared with 5,000 the previous five years, and just 750 in the 1970s.

In general, alliances present governance challenges on two levels. The first is at the level of the corporate board (i.e., what issues should the corporate board take into consideration?) and the second is at the level of the alliance board (i.e., how should the entity itself be governed?). A corporate board

might consider, for example, how to evaluate potential partners, how to understand the impact on existing operations, or
when to become involved in negotiations. An alliance board,
on the other hand, might consider how to manage cross-
cultural misunderstandings, what decision-making processes
to establish, or what personnel should sit on the board.

Booz•Allen's extensive research and practical experience
in making strategic alliances work has identified what, we believe, are the two most fundamental drivers of the increased
number of alliances: globalization and the need to build capabilities.

That is, alliances are being driven by the need for companies to globalize their operations, build capabilities, or both.
This framework not only rationalizes existing observations on
the formation of alliances, but also provides us with a way to
address the issues and challenges pertinent to their governance.

Alliances that are driven by the need for globalization present a distinct set of challenges. The participants are typically
looking to achieve channel access and market penetration—
common in industries such as automotive, energy, and chemicals. The main board must undertake careful risk assessment
and valuation of the foreign partner. Alliances force partners
to develop new governance procedures that not only are different from the parent's own corporate governance procedures but create the basis of an effective working relationship
spanning cultures, management philosophies, and political
systems.

Ford's joint venture with Fiat's IVECO unit is an interesting case in point. The venture is operated on a day-to-day basis
by the IVECO unit of the Italian Fiat and is based in the United
Kingdom. The board meets only three times a year, but its responsibilities are clearly defined. First, all of the items on the
board agenda are discussed ahead of time to avoid major sur-
prises or embarrassments for either party. Second, all matters
for discussion fall into one of three categories: (1) major items
that require unanimous agreement, e.g., withdrawal from markets, changes in products, or changes in employment practices

that could affect Ford's other operations in the United Kingdom; (2) lesser issues or day-to-day operational questions that require only a majority vote, e.g., the annual profit or capital investment budget, or the borrowing program; and (3) a final class of topics that require board review but not approval before management can act.

As a result of these arrangements, Ford may occasionally disagree with the decisions of the board, because IVECO holds a majority of the seats. However, in this case, Ford is at least guaranteed an opportunity to air its opinion before any action is taken. Despite the potential for a disagreement regarding a vote at the board level, the parties are nevertheless motivated to work together in good faith, not only to maintain their relationship for the future, but also because they have agreed to equally divide all the profits and losses.

Alliances that are driven by the need to build capabilities present another, distinct set of challenges. The parents are typically looking to establish critical mass—common in industries such as health care, aerospace, or defense. The main board must undertake careful capability assessment and partner screening. If a domestic partner can be found, then this will, most likely, be the first choice. Members of the alliance board must work at capturing, developing, and sharing the capabilities that drove the alliance in the first place.

Finally, alliances that are driven by both globalization and capabilities present the most complex set of issues. The main board must undertake careful capabilities and risk assessment. Alliances in electronics, computers, or telecommunications are often driven by this logic. The alliance board will have to address many issues—working across cultures, languages, and time zones—while simultaneously trying to access new, and potentially unfamiliar, capabilities. Consider the issues raised by the launch, in February 1996, of the alliance between five major photo-manufacturers—Kodak, Nikon, Minolta, Fuji, and Canon—to develop the new Advanced Photo System (APS). Not only are these companies operating across cultures, but they have been longtime bitter rivals. What type of governance procedures, we might ask, are capable of developing an effective relationship through which the maximum benefit of the alliance can be realized?

The biggest danger in governing alliances, however, remains the problem of polarization—when board members become split along company lines. Corning, one of the recognized leaders in making alliances and joint ventures work, favors a very practical approach to avoid this problem: create a 50-50 partnership. In their alliance with the Swiss firm Ciba-Geigy to create Ciba Corning Diagnostics (CCD), Corning insisted upon a 50-50 split, believing that this was the best way to create an atmosphere of cooperation. Ciba, however, believed that such an arrangement would result in a stalemate. It took a meeting of the chairmen from each parent to finally agree upon the 50-50 arrangement.

A 50-50 split, however, is not always possible or desirable (especially if there are multiple partners). In any case, it may be no substitute for partners coming to a better understanding with each other. It must be remembered that board members in joint ventures have additional responsibilities, not only protecting their own interests but also meeting their alliance partner's needs and creating and sustaining a good working relationship. The boards of joint ventures or alliances are also unusual because their members are often drawn exclusively from the management of either partner. These directors, therefore, may be placed in a particularly difficult situation, that of serving simultaneously as a manager and a director, and of understanding and implementing the different roles of each. Sir Adrian Cadbury, one of the U.K.'s leading governance experts, calls the role of an executive director one of the most difficult and misunderstood roles on the board. In alliances and joint ventures, this problem is especially acute.

The CCD venture also illustrates another recurring feature of alliances—the difficulties of working across cultures. Corning, a U.S.-based company, had a more informal decision-making process than its Swiss partners. Whereas the Ciba representatives believed that no proposal or agreement was serious until formal papers had been circulated, the Corning representatives often believed that a spoken "okay" was sufficient to seal an agreement. Thus, by the time Corning thought it had reached closure on an issue, Ciba still did not yet believe that anything had been proposed! To resolve the problem, and accommodate both parties, a more formal process was chosen. However, the example underscores how misunderstandings between genuinely sincere and committed partners are entirely possible, if not inevitable, especially when working across different cultures. The point is not to prevent them, but to deal with them in an effective and constructive manner. For companies still struggling with problems inside their own corporation and with little experience in governing alliances, this is a tall order. Yet developing these critical skills is vital to the Centerless Corporation.

## COUNTRY-SPECIFIC FORCES IMPACTING CORPORATE GOVERNANCE

These three forces—the expansion and proliferation of capital markets, the impact of regulatory action, and the growing importance of alliances—are augmented by country-specific trends that intersect with the global trends already in motion. Let's look at three representative countries—the United States, Germany, and Japan—to get a feel for the type of changes that are impacting various regions of the world as they enter the Age of Reconstruction.

In the United States, in particular, institutional investors and small shareholders are flexing their muscles, and are leading the call to improve corporate performance. CEO turnover has reached unprecedented levels, and incumbent CEOs are facing demands to have their pay linked to performance. As a result of continued debate—not only in business circles but also in the popular press and the legal and academic communities—there is an emerging set of boardroom "best practices." These best practices, calling for strict and transparent standards for board composition, structure, and processes, have become rapidly accepted by the shareholder community.

In 1996, *Business Week* published its first compilation of "Best and Worst Boards," and academics are beginning to amass a large body of empirical evidence to establish, in particular, the link between governance practices and superior company performance.

In Germany, there are rising labor costs at a time when the labor force is working fewer hours per week. There are more non-German operations and touchy issues about code-termination (in particular, whether it applies just to German employees or to all employees). In addition, billions of dollars of equity are now available to the public for the first time. Privatizations such as Deutsche Telecom or initial offerings such as family-run drugmaker E. Merck are stimulating the growth of a potentially potent new shareholder group: the general public. Yet Germany's biggest challenge is in the international arena. The groundbreaking listing of Daimler Benz on the New York Stock Exchange illustrated that Germany's traditionally successful and stable form of governance is now facing new challenges as German companies seek to become truly global. Not only did Daimler's listing highlight differences in disclosure requirements between the two countries, but it revealed deep and fundamental differences between the two cultures—America's shorter-term profit imperative versus Germany's longer-term aims of maintaining the entity and catering to multiple stakeholders.

In Japan, the liberalization of financial markets and the internationalization of its corporations has had profound effects upon its once unshakable model of cross-holdings, which linked company ownership. The increased use of capital markets has begun to reduce corporations' dependency upon bank financing. Furthermore, concomitant changes in regulations seem likely to guarantee an increasingly important voice for the new shareholders. Other internal changes in Japanese society, including an end to the guarantee of lifetime employment and several scandals that have rocked the business and political establishment, have bred an increasing distrust of the interconnected political and bureaucratic system that governs the major corporations. What's more, political and economic demands outside Japan are increasing pressures on the Japanese government to change its trade policies.

## THE NEW REQUIREMENTS FOR BOARDS

In the Centerless Corporation, the board's responsibility for the long-term health and success of the enterprise translates into a decidedly more active role than many boards currently play, especially in the United States. The board now gets involved with setting the agenda, developing strategy, assessing performance, and strong and candid two-way shareholder communications.

In our model, the board interacts much more frequently with the Core. Instead of the board being viewed as a potential problem to be managed or as a set of cronies of the CEO, this newly empowered board is very much part of the team of decision-makers. The Core increasingly gets involved in making certain that the board really understands the corporation's strategy, situation, and prospects. In this way, it moves from being a provider of information to a provider of knowledge.

The need for the board to assume a more proactive and strategic role, and redefine its relationship with the Core, has many implications. The changing role has ripple effects upon board composition, structure, and organization, and many other processes. We must remember that in designing our ideal board—just as in designing any management structure—we are designing a system. A change in one part of the system may have profound effects in another part of the system that, at first glance, appears totally unrelated. The board of the Centerless Corporation, therefore, must not only improve upon traditional board processes, it must also develop new processes. Let's look at what we consider the most important of these.

A vital, yet problematic issue even before the advent of the Centerless Corporation was that of information flow. The Centerless Corporation has both raised the profile of this issue and brought it into sharper focus. It has long been noted by many observers of corporate governance that information received by board members is often "filtered" through management. Not only is the information often too diluted to allow for any meaningful conclusions, it can also be downright misleading. It is hardly surprising that when crises occur, we hear that "the board was the last to know."

The heart of the problem has traditionally been that the board is simultaneously trying to advise and evaluate management. The conflict that arises from this dual role is not easy to solve. It requires the board to develop a new partnership with the Core, a partnership in which the Core becomes a provider of knowledge, rather than a filter of information. This partnership is not dissimilar to the one we described earlier in the chapter that is developing between boards and shareholders. Both parties must recognize (and accept) the vital role played by each other. In short, both parties must recognize their *interdependence.*

In addition to improving upon traditional forms of information flow, improving things like the quality of board papers, the Core must embrace more radical approaches—site visits, advisory panels, access to customers or suppliers, to mention but a few. Boards must also be more proactive in developing the knowledge they need. General Motors empowers directors to seek information from anyone in the company. It also ensures that other managers besides those already on the board are present, or at least available to the board, for some part of the regularly scheduled board meetings. Home Depot encourages directors to visit its stores on a regular basis to get customer and employee feedback.

Furthermore, it is now more important than ever that directors receive board materials well in advance of meetings, not only to give them time to prepare for meetings, but also so that board time can be used more productively. If boards are to act as a forum for meaningful discussions concerning strategy and performance, they should not get bogged down in the details of formal presentations. Precious board time should be used for debate and questions. General Motors has established that, at a minimum, any material that is going to be presented at a board meeting should be distributed in advance (the only exception is if the material is too sensitive to appear in print). Monsanto asks its board for an assessment of the information it receives from management, and has increased the percentage of time spent on strategic direction.

Issues of board education and orientation in the Centerless Corporation are also related to this critical issue of information flow and developing knowledge. If boards are to add value in their new role, they must be brought up to speed more rapidly and have a deeper understanding of the business. They must also be able to work together productively as a team, and board orientation programs should provide at least some understanding of this.

Another central issue that is brought into focus by the Centerless Corporation is the recruitment and selection of directors. Given the change in the board's role, the qualifications for directors must include superior business and technical skills never before required. However, they must also include the type of personal and professional skills that will ensure that directors can take leadership roles on the board. Directors must have the strength of character, self-confidence, and independence of mind to speak up, raise issues, and solve problems. They must be the type of people willing to take a proactive role in leading the board and, most likely, with a proven track record of having done so in other spheres of their life.

The issue of board evaluation, both of individual directors and of the board as a whole, has recently taken on a particularly high profile in the United States. The Centerless Corporation, with its increased pressure for corporate performance, not only accelerates the need to develop efficient evaluation processes, but also changes the nature and content of such evaluations. For individual directors, as we have already indicated, the qualifications are getting tougher. These tough new qualifications mean a long list of new dimensions against which to measure performance, from technical competencies, to leadership skills, to integrity and strength of character. In short, the director in a Centerless Corporation must be an exceptional individual.

For the board as a whole, the standards are also rising. Boards must not only evaluate whether they are fulfilling their most fundamental responsibilities, but also make subjective judgments on the quality and integrity of the processes they use. The conflict of interests inherent to this process, i.e., the process of self-evaluation, are apparent to all observers, so the board must make every effort possible to establish simple, transparent, and workable procedures. Medtronic, for example, solicits opinions on board procedures by asking all directors and a group of managers to complete a questionnaire, the results of which are reviewed by the board.

We have suggested that to be effective in their new role, directors need a deep understanding of the company's strategy, situation, and prospects. This requires time. A recent Conference Board survey of U.S. companies revealed that directors could spend nearly two hundred hours a year preparing for meetings—at least five full forty-hour weeks. Directors of General Motors spend as many as twenty-five days a year. To address this issue, the National Association of Corporate Directors has recently recommended that active senior executives serve on no more than three boards and that retired executives serve on no more than six.

In addition to the mix of personal and professional attributes we have already described, a vital requirement for the board in the Centerless Corporation is that it possess a global perspective. The Global Core, quite simply, demands global governance. The boards of world-class global enterprises already realize that they need new perspectives in order to assess the risks and opportunities of global expansion. They can't get it from reading reports, and they shouldn't rely solely upon corporate management to explain it. A board must possess, or develop, a profound and intimate understanding of the culture and regulatory structures of the countries in which its company is operating.

There are a great many instances of companies that have blundered badly when they have entered new countries, simply because they didn't know enough about the playing field they were entering. As a result, outside directors with expertise beyond the home country will be an important addition to a company's board. In its publication *The Global Outside*

*Director,* the executive recruiter Heidrick & Struggles provides a useful summary of the kind of attributes that companies should now be looking for:

- *International experience,* with candidates having typically worked in several countries and having held executive positions of increasing responsibility. They understand and relate to the issues of operating a global enterprise.
- *Global outlook,* where directors can be characterized as citizens of the world. They view many businesses in borderless terms while being sensitive to nuances that may inhibit the attainment of both corporate objectives and underlying profit performance.
- *Cultural diversity,* with directors at ease in several cultures, having assimilated social skills and corporate customs of various regions.
- *Stature in their home universe,* where the directors have wide networks of contacts and high respect in their home countries, where they are recognized as business figures of stature.
- *Different life experiences,* which include different educational systems, values, beliefs, and cultures.

Notice that these guidelines go far beyond just international experience. They describe a type of global mind-set, a person with deep knowledge and unique leadership skills, and this is consistent with the proactive decision-making role required of directors in the new age. No longer are directors ornaments to be collected atop the corporate Christmas tree, but they are active partners in the decision-making process.

While several companies are already using global directors, there is a real difficulty in attracting them to corporate boards. Often the most qualified potential directors are the ones who are unwilling to commit to the days required to travel long distances for board meetings. The issue, therefore, boils down to the matter of time.

When restrictions on directors' time and the increasing

qualifications and standards are considered, it is clear that all parties need to be more creative in tapping the talent of exceptionally qualified individuals who can make valuable contributions to their board. One might start by reducing the number of board meetings per year, or extending the duration of each individual meeting. Additional analytic support from dedicated staff, rather than the purely administrative support that is common today, would also help directors fulfill their commitments. Technology enablers like video-conferencing are also sure to play a role. More dramatic structural changes that redesign rather than simply accommodate existing processes also offer promise. For example, advisory committees or local boards are often used to gain an understanding of country-specific or regional issues. The Australian company BHP utilizes an advisory committee of senior executives to get a better handle on issues in the U.S. ABB sets up boards in major countries in which they are operating, with these country-specific boards providing expertise about individual countries.

A final issue that has always been important for boards to understand, yet is critical for the Centerless Corporation, is defining an appropriate "trigger point." That is, defining under what conditions the board should get involved with major decisions. Just as it is important for boards to do more than they have, it is as important that they don't attempt to do too much. The big challenge for boards is to walk the fine line between governing the corporation in the interest of shareholders and actually shadow-managing the business. At a minimum, the board should evaluate whether the CEO is building the company's franchise (market, people, and capabilities) and delivering long-term financial results and strength.

In the age of the hierarchical command-and-control corporation of the past, it was pretty much taken for granted that the board was there as a last resort. Because the Centerless Corporation demands a more proactive and empowered board, it is much more important that the board and the management understand and accept the trigger point. With additional pressure from institutional investors compelling corporate boards to become more critical of management performance, it behooves the senior management team and board to reach a joint agreement on their respective roles.

In the United States, Campbell Soup Company is highly regarded for its approach to corporate governance. The company includes an extensive description of its corporate governance standards and board evaluation processes in the proxy statement distributed to shareholders. Not only does Campbell formally evaluate its trigger point for "involvement in major business policies and decisions," but it has also developed a list of requirements of management and directors. This list is, essentially, a description of the responsibilities of each party to the other, and forms the basis of the new partnership between them. It was developed following a 1995 performance evaluation that the board did of itself. The board performed a frank evaluation of its own performance, highlighted its weaknesses, and detailed actions to be taken to improve its performance. The specific steps taken by Campbell to upgrade its board, and the processes it developed, clearly show that it is already making the types of changes required by the board of the Centerless Corporation. The following is an excerpt from Campbell's 1995 proxy statement:

> The Board identified the following areas as the most promising areas upon which to focus collective efforts for self-improvement:
>
> 1. Expanding the portion of Board time devoted to long-range strategic planning.
> 2. Broadening and diversifying the skills of directors.
> 3. Encouraging active participation in meetings by all directors.
> 4. Upgrading the quality of Committees' reports to the Board regarding their deliberations.
>
> In response, the following specific steps were taken in fiscal 1996:

1. The frequency and length of strategic business presentations were significantly increased.
2. Explicit "Director Requirements" were drafted, approved by the Board and distributed to shareowners in order to declare clear expectations regarding contributions of directors.
3. The Board began consciously employing developmental rotations of directors among the various Board Committees, without foregoing the necessary critical mass of skilled and experienced directors on any Committee. In-depth orientation sessions were provided for each new Committee member in order to increase understanding of the business and Board operations and policies.
4. Attention was focused on upgrading the quality and substance of reports by Committee Chairs to the Board.

## FUTURE DIRECTIONS IN CORPORATE GOVERNANCE

In the United States, the United Kingdom, and Australia, the topic of corporate governance has recently assumed a very high profile. Participants in this debate—institutional shareholders, professional associations, academics, the general public, as well as business practitioners and board members themselves—have been focusing on how to accomplish two main goals: (1) how to achieve greater independence, and (2) how to achieve greater accountability. That the debate has centered upon these issues is due, in large part, to the nature of the governance systems operating in these three countries, particularly the fact that the owners of capital have become separated from those who manage it. Although the same issues are less relevant in the tightly interwoven system of Japan, or even Germany, they are likely to become more important as capital markets continue to grow throughout the world. It is therefore worth looking at the results and implications of the current debate in these three countries in more detail.

The debate has produced, in effect, an emerging set of

boardroom best practices, standards, and safeguards ensuring that directors are more likely to fulfill their fiduciary responsibilities. To a large extent, the best practices have revolved around issues of structure and composition, e.g., the separation of the roles of Chairman and CEO, the merits of having a "lead director," the role of committees, what proportion of independent directors to include, and what exactly constitutes an independent director. The list goes on. Over one-third of the large companies now have a lead director.

As the debate has continued, however, attention has also been focused upon the fundamental processes by which the business of the board is carried out—how the agenda is set, the quality and timeliness of board materials, and recruitment and evaluation processes. In addition, the issue of compensation, for both managers and directors, has taken on a high profile. By rewarding both parties largely in stock, rather than cash, it is hoped that a greater degree of accountability can be built into the system. In some respects, this is an effort to reconnect the owners of capital with those who make decisions on how to spend it.

The fact that this debate is still in full force today is, we believe, a sign of how slowly change in the boardroom takes place, rather than a sign of what corporations must do to prepare for the future. That is not to say that we would trivialize this debate. Quite the opposite. The resolution of these issues is a vital precursor to the Age of Reconstruction. The emerging solutions will form the foundation for the new era of proactive and strategically oriented boards. Leaping forward into the new age without a board that is truly independent and accountable to its shareholders would be to add a layer of stupidity onto a layer of folly.

Another reason why we believe the current debate to be so important is that many of the issues that will be relevant in the new age overlap with those of the past. For example, the issues of information flow, director qualifications, recruitment, selection, and evaluation that are all part of the current debate are also vital to the Centerless Corporation. Although the current interest in these issues has been to ensure a greater degree of independence and accountability, in the future interest will be focused upon developing a proactive and strategic orientation, developing and transferring knowledge and leadership, and creating linkages to the external enterprise.

Yet, at the same time, there are also conflicts between the present debate and the demands of the future. For example, the emerging strict standards for director independence raise the issue of whether it will be possible to build a board that is suitably knowledgeable about the operations of a company to offer the type of guidance and advice required in the new age. Furthermore, the demands on a director's time, already becoming prohibitive, raise questions about the availability of suitable director candidates in the new age. The answer, we believe, is in redefining the partnerships within the extended enterprise. Employees, managers, directors, shareholders (not to mention customers, suppliers, competitors) must recognize and understand their interdependence.

The board of directors, therefore, is one of the critical linkages that create coherence in the Centerless Corporation. It is a dynamic, not a static, structure. It is proactive and strategically oriented. It provides leadership. It is not simply reactive, nor is it simply a control valve. It is outwardly oriented, as well as inwardly focused. It considers both performance and conformance. It develops and brokers knowledge.

Much of the work we do for our clients today at the board level is to build the type of strong foundation of independence and accountability that is needed to prepare for the future. Examples of companies that are moving to the next stage are rare indeed. But by reconstructing their boards, it is precisely these companies that stand to gain the most from the dawning of the new age in global competition.

To sum up, the Centerless Corporation requires governance to go beyond current recommendations for best practices. Boards must be tailored to meet a company's strategic imperatives. Thus board composition must become more flexible to obtain those skills it needs. It must be able to adapt as fast as the corporation evolves, which is very fast indeed.

# CHAPTER NINE

# THE SHARING OF SERVICES

**THE** corporation never sleeps. The churn of commerce never stops. There are a tremendous amount of repetitive but necessary things that must get carried out in any company—pay taxes, hire and fire people, buy supplies, conduct a payroll, defend and instigate lawsuits. These must get done in Minnesota and in Chile, day after day, week after week. The basic support services of big business.

In Chapter Two, we discussed the natural evolution of systems from simple to complex. The literature abounds with how this evolution is inexorable in both physical and biological systems. To some extent, the complexity is created by the necessary integration of increasingly specialized parts. Remember, what distinguishes humans from the rest of the animal kingdom is the development of a very specialized organ called the brain.

As they find it necessary to integrate larger numbers of specialized parts, businesses are becoming far more complex. Among these parts are the different businesses within the firm as well as the external relationships with suppliers, alliance partners, and customers. Within the corporation, we see a greater need for sophistication in areas like production techniques, information technology, marketing, and research, among others.

It is clear that both services and Business Units are becoming more specialized. Increasingly, by separating the two, one fosters greater advantage from specialization. To fully realize this advantage, however, it is necessary to develop new forms to link the two.

Businesses are specialized in the sense that they focus on what they do to create value—develop, make, and sell products. They do not create value by performing and delivering services to themselves, especially when there are viable alternatives. Services are specialized in that they perform specific functions like payroll, accounts payable, benefits administration, and data processing. Many of these tasks could be done outside the firm. They do not constitute important parts of the value creation process. They consume management time and energy that could more effectively be applied to the value creation engine.

Unfortunately, the market for these services is often neither developed nor efficient. In other words, the prices are too high and the service levels too low. Over time, however, we expect continued development of these outsourcing businesses.

Despite the limited external markets for services, companies can still benefit enormously from specialization and achieve lower costs and higher service levels. How? The solution is to create a market within the corporation by establishing a separate unit to supply these services and forcing it to be market-efficient. This is the notion of Shared Services.

By embracing this concept, services take on a breathtaking new life in the Centerless Corporation. All of the commodity support activities of the company are stripped from the Global Core and from within the Business Units and assigned to a new Shared Services organization that must compete vigorously with the market to offer its menu of tasks to the Business Units. Scooped into this organization are both transaction-oriented activities to capture scale, and business and consultative activities to achieve shared expertise. Forced to live or die by the dictates of the market, this new entity has to collect, analyze, and disseminate best practices based on both internal and external benchmarks. The business units then have three choices: to purchase a service from the services unit, do it itself, or outsource it. Whatever makes the most sense. In this way, the Shared Services organization offers cost-effective and client-driven services.

Set up in this manner, the Shared Services unit has no choice but to be price-competitive. And that's the way it should be. This much-needed competitive posture for services compels a corporation to determine what the demand for the different services is and what the appropriate price for each of them is. In a sense, the Shared Services entity becomes a shadow business unit.

Remember, one of the five key missions of the Core is to share capabilities. When there is the opportunity to share commodity services, the Core should do just that. It is the path to less cost and greater effectiveness. And once the Core shares those capabilities, corporate should refrain from taking any active role in managing the services. It should wash its hands of them, other than to make sure that the Shared Services unit holds its own.

The idea of sharing services is a potent one. If done correctly, it can play a critical role in boosting shareholder value. Quite simply, this approach allows the Business Units to focus on the things that are really critical to inventing, making, and selling products. They need to do nothing but that if they propose to succeed in the new world. What is more, the Shared Services provide valuable linkages in a corporation that must become reliant on each and every one of its pieces.

How does this happen? A Shared Services unit can create shareholder value by lowering cost, which it does by capturing economies of scale, reducing layers, and erasing redundancies. The organization provides improved service levels specifically tailored to meet the actual needs of the Business Units. And there is a natural balance between the supply and demand of support service activities, which eliminates that dreaded and familiar "staff work created by staff."

The use of Shared Services liberates the Business Units to focus on inventing, making, and selling products by shuttling the non-core support functions to a separate service organization. Shared Services groups can manage outsourcing arrangements and free up the Business Units to do what they do best.

Shared Services also supply key linkages in the Centerless Corporation, by sharing expertise across businesses, hooking up to the knowledge structure of the firm, and in some cases even allowing for open-market people strategies. Taken together, these enticing possibilities make an especially persuasive case for the power of Shared Services.

## SHARED SERVICES CHANGES ROLES

It should be evident that Shared Services represent a fundamental change in the structure of the established roles of support services and Business Units.

In our new model, the appropriate way to think of the Business Units is as customers of the Shared Services unit. We are talking about customers in the full sense of the word, with the power to buy or shop elsewhere. What occurs during these dealings are arm's length transactions between the units and the services business, in which they mutually agree on cost, quantity, and service levels. Businesses are responsible for managing demand. Competitive costs and performance levels are ensured through external market comparisons. This gives rise to a natural buyer-seller tension within the company that eliminates any nonvalue-added work. And, importantly, the services unit provides service supply from a broad and appealing mix of internal and external resources, including joint ventures and outsourcing.

This arrangement works equally well with both transaction and consultative services. By transaction-oriented activities, we mean those characterized by high volume, sensitivity to scale, routine or repetitive tasks, common requirements across the businesses, and uniform demand. Examples are facilities and services, accounts receivable, data center processing, payroll, and benefits administration.

On the other hand, consultative activities tend to have low to medium volumes, requirements for specialized or technical knowledge, some degree of customization required by the businesses, and variable or project-oriented demand. What are some examples? Tax, government affairs, procurement, law, environment, health and safety, compensation and benefits design, and labor relations.

## SHARED SERVICES IN ACTION

In recent times, a number of enlightened companies have tested the waters of Shared Services and found them to their liking. At Mobil Corporation, for instance, transactional services like controllers, human resources, procurement, aircraft, and security, as well as expertise-driven activities like research, environmental health safety, legal, tax, treasury, real estate, public affairs, and medical, are all provided as part of regional or global service organizations. They were set up in 1996, and the expectation is that they will achieve a stunning 30 to 50 percent reduction in the cost of carrying out these tasks. Another oil company, Amoco, was one of the early adopters of Shared Services. For its part, it has realized more than a 25 percent reduction in the cost of its support services since 1994.

Monsanto has been another pioneer. Led by Bob Shapiro, Monsanto's CEO, the company decided that certain problems sorely needed to be corrected:

- Multiple layers and duplications of services
- Lack of clear delineation of responsibilities between corporate and business group service staffs
- Excessive internal reviews and delays
- Staff being created by other staff
- Overstaffing in excess of costs

Cognizant of these foibles, Monsanto conducted a staff alliance study which showed that its total staff costs had come to exceed the world-class cost performance of 150 benchmark corporations by a whopping 60 percent. To say the least, that was humbling information. "Simply put, staff support for Monsanto businesses provided too little value at too great a cost," said Nick Reding, the company's vice chairman. "Our staff structure had become a competitive problem. We realized that if we fixed the structure of the work of our staff people, we would have a significant competitive advantage."

A year later, Monsanto announced a new organizational model called Monsanto Business Services, which was to provide a broad range of staff support to the Business Units. It was designed to deliver high-quality service more efficiently and at less cost. Most important, the MBS structure shifted staff perspectives from an internal functional focus to an external client focus. The staff mix changed from 35 percent corporate and 65 percent business groups to 7 percent corporate, 29 percent business groups, and 64 percent MBS. The logistics groups found that there were nine different contracts with the same airfreight supplier. By renegotiating the nine contracts and turning them into one, a million dollars in annual savings was quickly realized. Monsanto is now moving toward a second generation of services.

George White, the director of customer service and communications at Allied Signal Business Services, explained in a Conference Board presentation in late 1995 that Allied Signal heard several key expectations for business services when they designed a new organization:

- Improved customer satisfaction
  Continuously improved service
  Consumer metrics
  Rapid problem solutions
- Cost effectiveness
  Value pricing
  Lower costs
  Cost containment
- Productivity improvement
  Reengineering
  Cycle time reduction
  Simpler, more responsive organization
- Free Business Units of transactional businesses
- Innovative service—move beyond today

Allied Signal Business Services' vision is to "deliver superior customer service at a competitive cost advantage through empowered teams, world-class processes, and innovative technologies." Their mission is to partner with their customers to promote a one-company perspective, implement best practices, and provide high-volume expert services.

A good person to listen to in this area is Thomas Dille, the head of Rhone-Poulenc. In 1995, he said that the principles he follows in his company's use of Shared Services are:

- Focus on servicing the needs of the enterprises and no more than that.
- Develop long-term service agreements with enterprises, competitive with outside services.
- Outsource nonstrategic services whenever it is more cost/value effective.
- Provide economy of scale by aggregating services that are quantity-sensitive, including negotiating leverage with vendors.
- Measure and benchmark against best practices.
- Remain committed to continuous improvement, in keeping with the principles of total quality management.

As Rhone-Poulenc implemented Shared Services, its corporate staff was reduced from almost 300 people to just 35.

## CREATING A PARTNERSHIP BETWEEN LINE AND STAFF SERVICES

The objective of Shared Services is a simple one: to create a market-based partnership between line and staff services. But for this to happen, a whole array of new staff behaviors must come into being. Staff must be customer-focused and market-oriented toward "comparative cost." They must share, borrow, and adopt best practices. They must become accountable for delivery against a partnership agreement with the Business Units. Needless to say, this is a fundamental shift in the nature of staff behavior in most corporations.

Line behavior must also change. The people in the Business Units must be aware of the cost/value trade-offs. They must learn to be rigorously selective in shopping for the best sources of supply for the services. They must accept flexible, sharing arrangements, and be responsible for outperforming the market once these services have been provided to them.

Under the partnership arrangement, the mind-set for transaction services must be, "No one does it for less." The service organizations must be able to consistently beat the benchmarks. In the expertise arena, it must be, "I help you find the best way." This means a clear understanding of the strategic needs, what is necessary and competitive, coupled with an ability to leverage knowledge and the internal knowledge network. The services must be fast, flexible, and responsive.

Beyond this, you need to understand that an assortment of new management processes underpin the market relationship between services and the line. These processes include:

- Understanding the customer's needs and alternatives by analyzing demand forecast, revealing external benchmarks, and reviewing past performance in order to determine service requirements.
- Developing a shared-service proposal and negotiating agreements, developing service menu options, agreeing on service levels and costs, rebalancing resources, and estimating charge outs. This leads to service agreements.
- Publishing a plan for transition in a scorecard format by prioritization of key objectives, selecting measures, and milestones, and resulting in a transition plan and scorecard.
- Measuring results by finalizing the budget, tracking actuals, executing charge-outs, and producing reports.

New organizational approaches are needed to provide a more disciplined bit of services sourcing practices. In the old model, performance measurement was usually nonexistent except for activities performed by outside vendors and was often internally focused. In the new model, key performance indicators are identified, tracked, and communicated. External and internal benchmarks and best practices are monitored routinely. In the old model, standard cost-accounting systems are employed, and allocations to Business Units are based on traditional drivers. The mentality is, "It all goes to the bottom line anyway." In the new model, it is activity-based costing that allows for customer billing on the basis of usage. Business lines compete or bid for internal resources, ensuring that the resources go where they can generate the most value. In the old model, outsourcing is virtually nonexistent. In the new model, there are routine periodic outsourcing reviews, and vendor management assurance is part of the responsibility of the Shared Services organization.

## THE STRUCTURED DECISION TREE APPROACH

We define the delivery model for staff services by using the structured decision tree approach shown in Exhibit 1.

As this exhibit demonstrates, various key questions need to be asked in order to determine whether the shared service in the Global Core is embedded in the position, eliminated, outsourced, or set up in some other arrangement. These questions include understanding whether an activity is part of the five key missions, whether it is a critical capability, whether Business Unit customers need this service, whether it provides a competitive advantage, whether someone else provides the same service cheaper or better, and whether it demonstrates economies of scale across business groups or across Business Units.

Once you've gotten the hang of it, you will find that Shared Services can improve efficiency, effectiveness, and accountability by capturing economies of scale, leveraging expertise across businesses, establishing customer/market based relationships, and enhancing adaptive capabilities of the organization. We have seen a number of companies realize startling efficiency gains over their competition in this way.

# EXHIBIT 1: SERVICES DECISION TREE

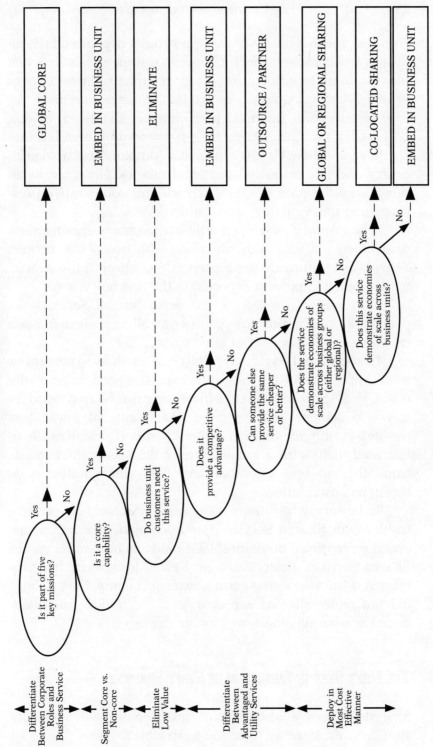

However, the magnitude of the opportunity depends on the industry and company-specific factors. Company factors often play the more prominent role—namely, things like number of product volumes, diversity of product volumes, company history, culture, and financial performance. Overhead, SG&A, cost analysis is a useful way for a firm to attain high-level insights. In addition, the dynamics of a company's particular industry and market are also crucial factors. Here, we mean things like the pace of change, price and comparative pressures, and the regulatory environment.

When Amoco developed a Shared Services organization, it included fourteen staff functions with over 7,000 people. There was an immediate 15 percent reduction in the people, with another 15 percent expected in the first few years.

How well a company succeeds in Shared Services depends a lot on the Business Units controlling their own costs rather than being dealt cost allocations.

Transactional services typically can result in 30 percent or more improvement in cost, while expertise services normally result in a 15 to 25 percent efficiency gain. Shared Services can also achieve better service and quality at lower cost through pooling demand and spreading best practices. As illustrated in Exhibit 2 a call center help desk gains benefits from sharing best practices and from the gaining scale through consolidation.

To be sure, while many companies have had very positive results with Shared Services, some companies have experienced more mixed outcomes. IBM made its human resources Shared Services group into a profit and loss center but prohibited it from servicing certain external clients. Cost savings did not materialize as expected, and the notion was abandoned as a strong long-term plan or strategy.

## THE NEXT STEP IN EVOLUTION OF STAFF SERVICES

Shared Services is an important next step in the evolution of staff services. Here we refer you to Exhibit 3.

## EXHIBIT 2: CALL CENTER/HELP DESK SERVICES

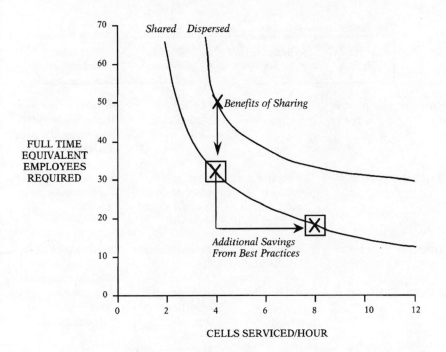

As you can see, services have evolved from Corporate Services to Business Unit Services to Shared Services, and next will evolve to an extended enterprise. As Shared Services evolve, new management processes are needed for people development and outside vendor management. Staff services that do not provide competitive advantage should be considered for possible outsourcing.

Shared Services leaders are the ones who become responsible for identifying, developing, and managing outsourcing opportunities. Over time, they will become resource managers. In the extended enterprise relationship, the Shared Services unit is responsible for outsourcing strategy, performance standards, and results. Thus it must build outsourcing management skills and establish formal management structures to oversee these relationships.

As a result, new strategies for Shared Services people development are required. Service staff must acquire skills that

## EXHIBIT 3: SERVICES EVOLUTION

| | 1970s<br>Corporate Sevices | 1980s<br>Business Unit Sevices | 1990s<br>Shared Sevices | 2000s<br>Extended Enterprise |
|---|---|---|---|---|
| **PROBLEM FACED** | Command and control | Inefficient processes | Duplication Business unit silos | Demand management Market pricing Differentiated service requirements |
| **SOLUTION** | Decentralize service | Reengineering business process with business units | Reorganize processes into internal shared services | Network of internal and external service providers |
| **SCOPE** | Corporate | Individual business units | Enterprise-wide | Industry-wide |
| **RESULTS** | Greater alignment through business unit services | Improved efficiency within business units | 30% cost reduction through elimination of redundancy and sharing of best practices | 20% cost reduction via capturing industry-wide scale efficiencies |

Note: The extended enterprise business model will extend to some,
      but not all shared service organizations.

hold intrinsic value. Compensation should be linked to business performance that is compared with external service providers. And benefit plans will have to apply across companies. Companies that execute the transformation of staff services successfully achieve dramatic results in shareholder value. When Mobil Oil announced its phase one results, it had created over $3.5 billion in incremental shareholder wealth.

## DESIGNING SHARED SERVICES

Evolving to Shared Services takes some calculated planning. The successful Shared Services transformation must occur within the three key dimensions of any transformation: content, process, and people.

The critical management decision is defining the scope of change and sequencing process redesign and organization restructuring.

It is our feeling that the process of designing Shared Services must address three key points:

- How big is the cost gap and the opportunity for improvement?
- What should be done to identify low-value and discretionary activities versus high-level processes that need to be redesigned?
- How do we implement it?

In bringing this off, many questions will have to be answered. The following are some of the ones we would pose:

- Where should activities be performed?
- What are the Shared Services organizations and Business Unit accountable for, and how will they work together?
- Where will the services be physically located?
- What are the outsourcing and insourcing policies?
- How will the activities and staff be organized?
- How will the management counsel work?
- How will buyers' committees work?
- How will performers of the Shared Services organization be tracked?
- How will external performance and best practices be monitored?
- How will service costs be tracked and charged?
- How will conflicts be resolved?
- How will staff be selected?
- How will Shared Services staff be motivated and compensated?
- What are the desired characteristics of the new culture that results?

As the Shared Services organization is designed, there is a need for an "owner's manual" for the new organization to address concerns that will surely surface during the organization's transition. This handbook should address the following questions:

- What is the purpose of the service?
- Why was the Shared Services organization created?
- Where did the service come from?
- Who are the key clients of the service?
- How is the service organized?
- What are the important changes in this area?
- What key business processes is the service involved in?
- How will the service be aligned with the businesses?

The transition to Shared Services requires leadership commitment and participation from all levels of the enterprise. All successful organizational changes involve an executive management team that champions the vision, makes the business care, sets defined implementation targets, and holds the organization accountable. The Business Unit management must manage the service demand, develop partnerships with services via buyers' committees, and dedicate line resources to implementing process change. And the service provider management must develop and foster a client service mentality, manage the transition to new processes, reduce service costs to target levels, and deliver improvements in effectiveness.

The implementation involves considerable activity. It includes staffing, process changes, defining roles and responsibilities, managing the project time line, identifying the work illuminated from process changes, ensuring the transition of remaining works through "desktop transfer" to new owners, phasing out transition resources in line and Shared Services, developing and executing a training program, and devising detailed budgets.

## LESSONS FROM THE TRENCHES

Having been intimately acquainted with the efforts of some leading companies to push toward a Shared Services approach, we've been able to assemble a number of lessons about adopting this philosophy that may be useful to ponder. These include:

- Set the bar high (the CEO should articulate the mission and set the target).
- Build the case for change up front with external benchmarks and internal surveys.
- The bigger the scope the better.
- Engage the line organization from the start.
- Select leaders early and get them involved.
- Move quickly.
- Change processes, as well as structure, set client service expectations, and track/measure progress to the baseline.
- Demonstrate the Shared Services organization's contribution to corporate performance.
- Reward and recognize project team members.
- Communicate, communicate, communicate.

As the Shared Services organization is designed and becomes operational, it behooves a company to staff the organization with many of its best and brightest, especially in senior management. Remember, this is an essential element in the workings of the new model. The services unit must demand major improvements through goals that are stretch but achievable. It must maintain a focus on the external marketplace. It must explain the price and quality trade-offs to the Business Units. It must understand controllable versus uncontrollable factors. It must keep it simple. It must establish a charge-out system to bill actual costs. It must establish credible options for outsourcing. And it must provide a governance structure which represents the organization as a whole.

Do all these things and you will see a corporation that really hums, a corporation that is integrated and yet entrepreneurial, a company that is large but swift, a company that is no less than a vigorous factory of value.

# Chapter Ten

# LEADING THE CENTERLESS CORPORATION

**ONE** useful way of thinking about the Centerless Corporation is as a pair of familiar shoes with new feet in them. While it embodies the same elements of the business model that we have long become accustomed to, it has assigned radically new roles to them. And so, just as those new feet can make those old shoes perform steps not seen before, the Centerless Corporation can accomplish unimagined goals. But it doesn't happen without appropriate leadership.

At a meeting not long ago with a group of successful CEOs, a well-respected management guru posed the following pithy question: "What business problem keeps you awake at night?" Among the answers volunteered were:

- "We are not getting the growth I believe our company is capable of achieving."
- "To be an effective player, my corporation needs to get innovation percolating at all levels."
- "We have to learn how to truly think and act as a global corporation."
- "Our environment continues to become more competitive, but the culture in the company is not reacting with a sufficient sense of urgency."

- "Over the past few years, we focused so much attention on cost cutting processes that we now have to learn how to be a growing, high-performance company."
- "We've defined a vision, but it is not being implemented effectively throughout the company."

A common theme dominated the concerns of these CEOs: a felt need for greater executive clout to ensure that all managers and employees down the line act in ways necessary for corporate success. While the top executives felt that they had the power to set strategy, to hire and fire, and to make performance commitments to shareholders, they also recognized the sobering reality that executing even their best-laid plans depended on the initiatives of thousands of employees spread across vast geographic distances. In making necessary changes and regulating how these far-flung legions behave with suppliers and other outsiders, as well as among themselves, even the most self-confident CEOs admit privately that the desired outcome is not fully under their control.

Unfortunately, executives in many companies have not found effective help in transforming organizational behavior, because this critical task has been defined as change management. Most change management efforts, however, fail to bring about the results that executives expect. The reason is that change management is often predicated on misperceptions that there is a simple formula to the problem of change, or that by applying a formula peoples' behavior can be managed, or that a good change management process is sufficient to achieve the desired results.

In an organization with new roles and priorities, and with a fresh way of approaching business opportunities, the CEO and top management must themselves take on new responsibilities and tackle them in a different way. The Centerless Corporation recognizes that a business is a complex system and that it is at the system level, rather than at the individual piece level, that the corporation creates value. What, then, are the leadership requirements? How does one lead amid all the complexity of the modern corporation?

## THE LEADER VERSUS THE MANAGER

First, let's explore the differences between leadership and management. Management is appreciably more bounded than leadership. After all, a manager usually has something quite specific to manage. In the business world, this could be a sales force, a gas station, or a corporation. The focus of management is to achieve certain prescribed results. The considerable segmentation of the modern business into boxes at the end of lines has very much gone hand in hand with the development of management as we know it.

Managers work at the tasks at hand. They are highly focused on a relatively narrow set of objectives and accountabilities. This oversimplification was a tremendous advantage when a corporation was able to function as a motley collection of independent parts. It is the reason why many corporations today complain about not getting a total company point of view out of its managers.

Leaders, by definition, have a more system-wide point of view. They worry less about specific parts and more about the whole. While some leaders may prove to be poor managers, great ones achieve both, though they may not do both themselves.

We can learn a lot from many of the great leaders of the past. A list of some of the more recent political and religious ones would include Gandhi, Roosevelt, Churchill, Pope John XXIII, DeGaulle, and Monnet. We also could look at recent business leaders like Bob Galvin, Bill Gates, or Andy Grove. What they have in common is that they have had a major impact on their worlds and have done so through an institution. They were not the mad inventors. Rather, they were leaders of others, of disciples, who helped them carry out a shared vision.

If leaders operate at the system level, what are the key elements of leadership? Here we see a link to the three key enablers we have discussed. Leaders need followers, who could be other leaders as well. They need a vision and they need a way of communicating and demonstrating progress toward their goals. Let's look again at the enablers. Coherence—leaders create a vision, a strategy for achieving that vision, and a set of shared values. People—leaders need followers and disciples. These are people who buy into the vision, strategy, and values. Great leaders motivate others to work toward a common goal. Knowledge—leaders create processes and methods, and have a know-how to deliver results.

One might say that a leader in the Centerless Corporation must continue to do some of the time-honored things that any current leader does, and to a certain extent that is true. But we feel that there are some specific assignments that are peculiar and of greatest importance in a corporation structured as we believe it must be. In fact, it could be said that some leaders of today cannot flourish in the remarkably changed environs of a Centerless Corporation, and especially inflexible individuals may well find that to be the case. We are reminded of what Kevin McGrath, the president of Hughes Communications, said: "It strikes me that leaders are like trees. You can plant them in some places and they won't grow well, but in other places they will. Some people with strong leadership traits don't go anywhere because they are in the wrong place at the wrong time."

One of the interesting things about McGrath is that he belonged to a team that helped transform Hughes' satellite communications division from a hierarchical organization to a circular organization composed of process- and product-related business units interacting with the office of the president at the center. From his experience, leaders still bubble to the surface despite an organization designed to level hierarchies and permit greater numbers of employees to demonstrate leadership.

It is clear to us that, in this model of ours an abundance of control is like a straitjacket, and any leader must temper the degree of control that he or anyone in management exerts on the rest of the corporation.

In the Centerless Corporation, there is no room for management styles that intimidate and inhibit. There is no room for leaders who frighten and overwhelm. There is no room for leaders with fists of iron and lungs of bombast. Everything about this new model is rooted in trust and teamwork and common belief. And if that doesn't radiate from the top, then all the other work of putting the model in place will ultimately be futile. The Booz•Allen leadership diagnostics have uncovered what seem to be the characteristics of successful leadership models, and these results form the basis for this chapter.

In companies that continually renew themselves, leaders act in ways that directly affect the behavior of employees throughout the organization. The key question often asked is what do they do?

- What does Lew Platt, the CEO of Hewlett-Packard, actually *do* as a leader that causes lower-level divisional managers regularly to create new products and work processes that continually best their competitors?
- What do Zurich-based Percy Barnevik and Goran Lindahl, the chairman and CEO of ABB, actually *do* that encourages their country managers in Canada to develop significant new business entrepreneurially?
- What does Herb Kelleher, the CEO of Southwest Airlines, actually *do* that motivates his front-line employees to "make flying fun" for all customers?
- What do the leaders of Toyota actually *do* in Tokyo that motivates hourly workers in the United States to take the initiative to stop the car assembly line to fix quality problems?

Leaders have to be concerned about four key things:

- The company's identity and values
- Architecture and business model
- Business performance
- Strategic innovation

## IDENTITY AND VALUES

What, then, should the leaders of tomorrow care about? It makes intuitive sense that the CEO and the top management team must set the moral tone for the corporation. They need to define what the company stands for. They need to establish a vision. They need to communicate relentlessly and talk the talk in the organization. And they need to resolve conflicts.

Identity and values are critical to the new model. A good example of what we mean is the tone set by Paul O'Neill when he became the chairman and CEO of Alcoa in November of 1987. O'Neill quickly realized that Alcoa needed a couple of linchpins that could define its identity and values. Thus he decided that Alcoa would be more than a compliance company. In his view, it had the wherewithal and capabilities to set the standards in regulatory compliance rather than simply reacting to external events.

O'Neill also felt that he needed one paramount issue with which he could connect the very top of the organization to the workers on the factory floors all over the world, the type of issue that would get people excited. Even though Alcoa was already a leader in safety, he chose to make safety his standard bearer. He committed the company to closing the gap between current practice and world benchmarks by a minimum of 80 percent in two years, and used safety as a tool to discuss with his leadership team and to bring up at every one of his plant visits.

Lew Platt of Hewlett-Packard has continued to foster the "HP way" embodied by the company's founders. In addition, he has stated that in virtually every case the company has reviewed, when HP does good things in the community, it helps the company. This sense of social responsibility is well understood inside HP.

## ARCHITECTURE AND BUSINESS MODEL

In the Centerless Corporation, one of the primary requirements of a leader is to form and unform teams. Teams are the
basis for getting work done in the Centerless Corporation,
since hierarchy largely disappears. With so much less of a corporate structure, the top management team needs to find
ways to topple barriers and get the best capabilities working
on the most important problems.

The leadership must also foster an inviting atmosphere
for learning. Jack Welch of General Electric says that in the
1980s GE began a relentless search for best practices anywhere and everywhere it could find them. He cites examples
of learning that it got from customers, competitors, suppliers,
and those who had a reputation for being good at sourcing or
getting products to market.

In GE's 1996 annual shareholder letter, its management
declared:

> The sweetest fruit of boundaryless behavior has been
> the demise of "not invented here" and its utter disap-
> pearance from our company. We quickly began to
> learn from each other: productivity solutions from
> Lighting; quick response asset management from
> Appliances; transaction effectiveness from GE Capital;
> the application of bullet train cost reduction tech-
> niques from Aircraft Engines; and global account
> management from Plastics.
>
> At the same time we embarked on an endless
> search for ideas from the great companies of the
> world. Wal-Mart taught us the direct customer feed-
> back technique we call Quick Market Intelligence.
> We learned new product introduction methods from
> Toshiba, Chrysler and Hewlett-Packard, and ad-
> vanced manufacturing techniques from American
> Standard, Toyota, and Yokogawa. Allied Signal, Ford,
> and Xerox shared their insights into launching a

quality initiative. Motorola, which created a dramatically successful quality-focused culture over the period of a decade, has been more than generous in sharing its experiences with us.

To ensure that learning occurs, companies must permanently break down the not-invented-here barriers. They must invest in human capital and knowledge systems. Keep in mind that the organizational structure within the Centerless Corporation is merely the wiring diagram that puts it all together. The organization needs to be fluid and evaluated on a regular basis.

One of the more important aspects of leadership is the need to manage transformation processes proactively. Many companies today have hundreds, if not thousands, of change programs humming along. In our work with one process industry client, we found over 700 change programs that were in progress in the early part of a major transformation effort. These programs were uncoordinated and often overlapping, and they were consuming an enormous pool of resources. It behooves leaders to get their arms around change processes and make sure that they are integrated.

Moreover, leaders must distribute responsibilities and risks within the company's portfolio, and it is imperative that they make sure that someone is always being held accountable.

In the Centerless Corporation, management hierarchy is replaced by flexible and fluid leadership teams. The traditional pyramid is turned upside down—the "boss" serves the enterprise and employees. Responsibility is transferred to people who are interacting with customers, and "we" replaces "I" in the contribution to the success of the enterprise. Peter Senge says that a healthy leadership ecology has local line leaders, internal networkers, and executive leaders who are leaders of clarification rather than exploration.

Leaders must set and enforce limits, recognize and reward, listen and support, empathize and celebrate, coach and empower, show persistence in vision, flexibility in tactics, fight complacency, stay focused, engage in symbolic acts, push change and authority further down into the organization, provide resources, create conditions under which others can succeed, and communicate (over and over) vision and values.

## BUSINESS RESULTS

Contained within the ivory towers and glass walls of many corporate headquarters of twenty years ago were an enormous number of measures of performance. As companies moved through the 1980s, they found that there were few key drivers that really made a difference in the results of the business. In the Centerless Corporation, we feel that leaders have to winnow out the ineffective drivers with a cool precision and really focus their attention on the few key drivers that truly impact the business.

Some of these drivers may be quantitative and financial in nature, but others may be qualitative. For instance, the ability to attract and develop world-class capabilities is an important qualitative measure that affects the long-term health of the business. On the quantitative side, companies must focus on drivers of performance in addition to indicators of performance.

There is no question that leaders must also set the bar higher and higher. When Hewlett-Packard decided to reduce product development time by approximately 75 percent and Motorola cut defects from 6,000 defects per million to 60 defects per million on its way to the goal of 4 defects per million, they demonstrated the enormous power of "stretch" goals. In his book, *Only the Paranoid Survive*, Intel's Andy Grove talks about the need to continue pushing for stretch goals even when your company has overwhelming market share. "The more successful you are, the more people want a chunk of your business and then another chunk and then another until there is nothing left," he says. "I believe that the prime responsibility of a manager is to guard against other people's attacks and to inculcate this guardian attitude in the people under his or her management."

In their book, *Built to Last,* James Collins and Jerry Porras talk about "big hairy audacious goals" (BHAGs) as a particularly powerful mechanism to stimulate progress. They found that all visionary companies use BHAGs extensively to engage people and get their juices flowing. As they put it, a BHAG "reaches out and grabs them in the gut. It is tangible, energizing, highly focused. People 'get it' right away; it takes little or no explanation."

The contrast between GE and Westinghouse in the late 1980s is particularly startling. GE's goals were to "become number one or number two in every market we serve and revolutionize this company to have the speed and agility of a small enterprise." Westinghouse's vision statement talked about things like total quality, market leadership, technology-driven, global, focused growth, and being diversified.

As Collins and Porras point out, Henry Ford stimulated his company in 1907 within an astounding BHAG "to democratize the automobile, to build a motorcar for the great multitude."

The other key leadership responsibility in business results is to stay close to the key performance measures. All companies have certain measures that will tell them whether they are getting into trouble or doing very well. In the semiconductor industry, to take one example, it may be orders for PCs or book-to-bill ratios. In the personal computer manufacturing industry, it might be reducing time to market or the number of products that are shipped dead on arrival. One prominent company in Silicon Valley has had a full 25 percent of a particular product's deliveries dead on arrival; one of its competitor's rate is less than 5 percent. In a recent client engagement, Booz•Allen found that each week's delay in introducing a new product cost a Silicon Valley company almost $2 million in profits. Whatever these barometers may be, the important thing is that the leaders keep an eye trained on them.

## STRATEGIC INNOVATION

As companies engaged in business process reengineering and downsizing, most were looking actively at how to grow the business. While strategy and portfolio management play a vital role in achieving growth, we find that the most important aspect of growth is creating a growth culture.

This means that leaders must force encounters with growth opportunities among their executive team. They need to create a business model that allows ideas for tomorrow's growth businesses to be nurtured and encouraged. Our research shows that in most companies that achieve long-term growth, there are no more than a few businesses that fuel that growth. But these growth engines establish an environment for growth that is contagious.

By now, companies have reengineered business processes, and they are currently in the process of reengineering for growth. This requires a similar commitment to reengineering, but with a focus on building capabilities, behavior, and business processes for growth.

An often overlooked role of a leader is to carry the company's flag in new growth areas. Particularly in emerging nations, the CEO and top management team are critical to demonstrating commitment to a country or a particular project.

## SIX PRIORITIES FOR THE FUTURE

As you can see in Exhibit 1, we believe that the task of leadership involves engaging followers; enabling the development of vision, value, strategy; and leadership processes.

Interestingly, the relative weighting of content, engaging followers, and process differ depending on a company's particular situation. At a company fighting for survival (e.g., Apple Computer or ValuJet), most of the effort should be directed at the process dimension (how to get it done). During a

## EXHIBIT 1: THE ELEMENTS OF LEADERSHIP

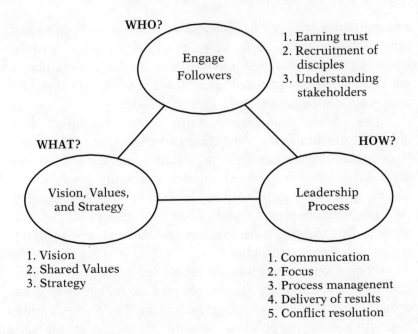

WHO?

Engage
Followers

1. Earning trust
2. Recruitment of
   disciples
3. Understanding
   stakeholders

WHAT?

Vision, Values,
and Strategy

HOW?

Leadership
Process

1. Vision
2. Shared Values
3. Strategy

1. Communication
2. Focus
3. Process managenent
4. Delivery of results
5. Conflict resolution

time of renewal, which pretty much is where most companies
are (ABB being a prime example), the content (what) of vision,
shared values, and strategy is most important. And in a learning organization (Motorola, Intel, or Toyota), there is more
balance among the three elements of the triangle.

As we set priorities for the Centerless Corporation, we feel
that six elements out of this leadership triangle stand out as
being the most important and deserving of the bulk of top
management's time. These elements are key responsibilities of
the Global Core. Let's take a look at each of them:

1. Vision
2. Shared values
3. Strategy
4. Earning trust
5. Recruitment of disciples
6. Communications

# VISION

A vision allows top management to communicate leadership and drive the organization. In a sense, vision is the starting point for everything that an organization does and how it should do it. At a minimum, it must achieve several things:

- Orient the company toward its customers and look to the future with a clear sense of purpose—that is, paint a picture of the future.
- Work toward the long-term development and stewardship of the company's brands.
- Define the value-added of the company.
- Set a framework for making strategic decisions and allocation choices.
- Allow flexibility and reward risk taking.
- Capture the aspirations and goals of the organization and provide a motivation to reach them.

Vision also guides critical strategic decisions like whether and how the company will change its portfolio, what choices need to be made, what capabilities will be needed to drive the company's success, what is the importance of innovation, cost management, customer insight, and so forth, what is the organizational philosophy, style, and model that the company wants to develop, and what should be the allocation of investments.

There seem to be two circumstances during which defining a new vision is particularly useful. The first is when the new leader takes over the organization. By defining a vision right away, the new leader is able to assert his or her leadership philosophy and direction. And that vision can then be cascaded through the organization to provide an effective catalyst for change.

The other circumstance is when an organization is in need of major change. What's called for here is the so-called burning platform. It creates the opportunity for a vision to do things like turn the company around, move it into new areas, and reduce costs.

Setting out a personal strategic vision is a primary area of action for new CEOs. In our interviews with almost a hundred CEOs, we repeatedly found that the process of creating a vision and establishing an agenda was one of the first things they concentrated on after they completed the transition to becoming a CEO. This entails setting the strategic vision and direction (establishing stretch objectives and creating momentum to go after them), assessing the company's competitive position and capabilities, choosing the team, and communicating clearly to stakeholders.

Accomplishing this marks a new era for the organization, for it unites the corporation and sets it toward a common goal. It creates a dynamic climate of change, offers a golden opportunity to build a team through the vision development process itself, and communicates the particular style of the new leader at an early stage.

Successful visions become catalysts by communicating clear and ambitious goals for the organization. In our view, the hallmarks of successful change include ambitious goals, consistency and continuity in building capabilities over time, a ferment of new ideas, the will to change, recognition and balancing of stakeholders' interests, leadership, and a bias for action.

The principal obstacles to change are usually people. One has to surmount such familiar hurdles as parochial thinking, the not-invented-here syndrome, lack of communication, mixed signals, and history.

Bob Galvin, the chairman emeritus of Motorola, is one of those visionary CEOs who has a clear view of how to march into the future. Listen to him and you hear him talk about the need for a company to outline a dream of what the world will be like in fifty years and what the company's position will be in that world. Then he says you have to sketch out what actions the company can take today to make that dream a reality. An essential principle of his is to write the rules of the game to achieve these dreams. In Motorola's case, the rules could be technical standards, business regulations for a new country, or tax regulation. In China, for example, Motorola believed that it could alter the rules by allowing people in the country to share in the dream for the business.

Many companies have used visions to mobilize their organizations. Procter & Gamble changed its internal focus from brand categories to increase its market responsiveness while reducing costs and raising the value proposition to consumers. Its vision statement was "to be the market leader in all product categories we compete in by understanding consumer needs, developing breakthrough products, creating loyalty from the start, and building loyalty with advertising and customer relations."

Merck likes to declare, "We are in the business of preserving human life. All our actions must be measured by our success in achieving this." Indeed, some of Merck's actions in making investments in orphan drugs have proven critical to attracting the best talent to the company.

Mars, the big candy company, expresses its five principles by saying:

> We at Mars share special beliefs about our business and the way it should be run. These beliefs—our five principles—set us apart from others, demanding that we think and act differently toward our associates, our products, and our business. These principles are not easy to fulfill, but they cannot be ignored.
>
> The five principles are quality, responsibility (as individuals we demand total responsibility from ourselves and as associates we support the responsibilities of others), mutuality (a mutual benefit is a shared benefit, a shared benefit will endure), efficiency (we use resources to the fullest, waste nothing, and only do what we can do best), and freedom (we need freedom to shape our future, we need profit to remain free).

To see how essential a role vision can play, one need look no further than Coca-Cola. Not long ago, the soft-drink giant faced a bruising cola war within its maturing U.S. market, and a new CEO saw the opportunity to become a more global company. And so the company adopted a new vision "to make Coca-Cola and our other products available, affordable, and acceptable to consumers, quenching their thirst and providing them with a perfect moment of relaxation. If we make it impossible for consumers to escape Coca-Cola, then we assure our future success for many years and we can reach our goal: creating value for our shareowners."

In pursuing this goal, Coca-Cola divested virtually all of its nonrelated businesses and set out the elements of its new vision by relying on four core capabilities:

- Consumer marketing. From global television advertising to simple sign posting, it would build affinity with consumers through every available means. The company launched new aggressive campaigns, first "Coke Is It," and then "Always Coca-Cola," global themes reinforcing that Coke is the "real" thing. At the same time, it felt a need to understand what the customer wants because people change continually.
- Infrastructure. It would work with business partners who offer the production and distribution systems that deliver the highest quality products at the lowest possible costs. It would ensure the aggressiveness of franchisees and make its own investments if this is not achievable.
- Product packaging, meaning creating a quality product with distinctive attributes and delivering it in a desirable package at an attractive price.
- Customer marketing to help customers create value by providing coolers, promotions, vending machines, and other tools that allow the customers to convert demand into actual purchases.

For almost a week, the CEO guided debate over the points of this new vision. Everybody had to question his or her own goals and assumptions. Management felt that they learned a lesson—namely, that they had to foster a new culture that is not afraid of intelligent risk-taking, a culture that didn't heed the experts but trusted its own analysis and made sure it understood the customer. It may lead to failures like New Coke, but also to great successes like Diet Coke.

Even St. Paul's Cathedral has a well-articulated vision: "To proclaim the Christian gospel according to the practices and traditions of the Church of England and, in an environment of excellence and beauty, to uplift the minds of men, women, and children to things of the spirit." It has nimbly translated this purpose into strategy, which includes daily worship service, pastoral care, serving the Crown, nation, and city, serving dioceses, fulfilling stewardship of the St. Paul's heritage, all the while maintaining an environment of excellence and beauty, attracting as many tourists as possible, uplifting minds, and earning as much money as possible for the cathedral.

St. Paul's has also added a values statement that says that the clergy and lay staff must act consistently with integrity, respect for individuals and the Christian community, open communications, respect for aesthetics, good discipline and order, and respect for imperatives of the religious arrangements.

There are, of course, many ways to develop a vision, and what works best depends on individual company situations. But whatever the circumstances, the most important element is to involve as many people, both managers and rank-and-file, as is possible with efficiency. Team-based processes seem to work best in reaching this kind of buy-in and acceptance of a vision.

But teams are not enough. Companies that go through this process successfully invariably identify transformational leaders who can get the job done and who will relish the challenge. One of our clients categorizes his top fifty executives along certain dimensions: do they understand the vision and the direction of the company; are they committed to it; can they successfully execute the changes that are necessary; and do they have the potential to be a CEO of a major business sector or the company?

## SHARED VALUES

Shared values are what engender trust. And these values must be stated as both corporate objectives and individual values.

Bob Shapiro of Monsanto says it right when he states that "core values are what link us together." From his perspective, there are three important core values:

1. To be an organization that is fanatically dedicated to customers, to anticipating customers' needs in a changing marketplace. This causes us to always attack the status quo by doing something superior to what's out there today.

2. An openness to newness and diversity. In a world that's changing, you don't want an attitude that says, "I don't like change much, how do we stop it?" When something new comes along, you want to react by saying, "How do we make use of it? How do we get out ahead of it?" We need to have people who recognize that success and survival are based on anticipation, not on hanging on to the past. That are linked as a matter of psychological habit to acceptance of diversity. Hanging on to the status quo as a mind-set is a real impediment in many companies.

3. The third major value has to do with the environment. Monsanto people developed a special commitment to environmental protection, to sustainability. They have had to deal with environmental issues because of the nature of the businesses they historically were in.

Every company and every leader will have a different set of values that are appropriate to its business situation. Values are also the identity by which a company is known throughout its business areas. In some companies, the firm operates through a series of brands, names, and images that may be unrelated to each other or to the corporation (e.g., Procter & Gamble, Unilever, Rubbermaid). Other companies use one name, image, and a common set of values throughout the organization (e.g., Shell, IBM, BMW, Sony, Mitsubishi). In some companies, the individual parts of the corporation can be readily identified and have their own name, image, or set of values, but are also seen as part of the larger whole. United Technologies is this way with its Otis elevator, Pratt & Whitney aircraft engines, Sikorsky helicopters, and Carrier air conditioners. The same is true of GE or General Motors.

The relevant type of identity for a company depends on the firm's strategy and competitive position. Companies like Shell or Mitsubishi, which use one name or image, communicate a single message that can be expressed to their different audiences. They usually have an implicit quality and performance promise in the delivery of any products or services throughout the firm. They convey a strong sense of cohesiveness and coherence both inside and outside the corporation. They also emphasize the total size, strength, and uniformity of the company. This allows them to facilitate the use of significant economies of scale when communicating the firm's identity. The extreme, branded identities (such as Procter & Gamble or Unilever) separate the idea of the company from the products, which can result in products that have a life of their own. This enables individual businesses to adjust their own identities independently to create or change markets. It provides the flexibility to expand the firm into other businesses and markets with limited regard for other parts of the company and insulates different businesses from each other during identity crises.

A company like GM, GE, or UTC that is a blend between a monolithic identity and a branded identity is attempting to have each business contribute to the strength of the whole while reinforcing its own position. It provides each individual business with a semiflexible identity that can be tailored to specific market segments. It allows the firm to retain the goodwill of acquired companies while superimposing their relationship to the whole. It emphasizes the total strength and size of the firm but does not demand strict consistency in performance, quality, or service across the corporation.

What is crucial to understand is that identity is a CEO and top management issue. As Shell found out when it did not intervene in an execution in Nigeria or when it dealt with disposal of offshore oil platforms in the North Sea, actions in one part of the world or in one Business Unit can affect units that are in another.

## STRATEGY

Put simply, the leader of the Centerless Corporation must have clear and well-articulated strategies. Whether it is Intel's strategy to be the dominant player in the world in chip production or Boeing's strategy to use investment and alliances to maintain or grow its market share in aircraft and airframes, strategies are essential for leadership to succeed. In the political arena, Gandhi's strategy in India was instrumental in his success.

In 1937, David Packard said, "We decided right from the beginning that we would be an innovative firm and would direct all our efforts toward making important technical contributions to the advance of science, industry, and human welfare." For sixty years, HP has followed this strategy. It has organized, measured, and planned for innovation.

## EARNING TRUST

Unlike some of the other areas, the process of earning trust cannot be prescribed or diagrammed in any explicit fashion. Trust results from a combination of actions, commitments, behaviors, values, competency, experience, and legitimacy. A corporate culture of openness and respect must be lived by all the top executives and communicated accordingly.

Great leaders do amazing things to earn trust. Perhaps one of the most interesting stories about trust concerns Hewlett-Packard. Bill Hewlett and David Packard established a whole system of values and behaviors that became known as the HP way. The essence of the HP way was stated about fifty years ago, and it has taken the company through many cycles in their business. It also set their strategy.

Colin Marshall of British Airways recognized the need to change the company to the "World's Favourite Airline." He felt that a key priority was creating trust throughout the organization.

Vaclav Havel, the leader of the Czech Republic after its independence in 1993, was in no way an experienced political manager. Through trust in his basic values and his moral integrity, however, he was able to help the Czech Republic make the transformation from Communist rule to a democratic nation.

## RECRUITMENT OF DISCIPLES

All great leaders have followers. This simple truism pervades business, government, religion, and other institutions. Just think of the great leaders of the past: the Gandhis, the Roosevelts, the Churchills. All of them were able to attract others.

It might be interesting to look at the characteristics of Gandhi as a leader, for they can be directly applied to the corporate environment. Among the things often said about Gandhi were that he understood himself, he was a man of action, he had a high aim, he took risks, he was focused, he had a vision that he was able to execute, he had real goals and hopes, he was highly principled, he had a great deal of self-confidence and ambition, and he was prepared to sacrifice for results. His symbolic acts of fasting, going to jail, and staging the salt march were all ways in which he created the trust that built the disciples. Ultimately, moral authority creates power and attracts disciples.

Max De Pree of Herman Miller, Inc., explains, "The signs of outstanding leadership appear primarily among the followers. Are the followers reaching their potential? Are they teaming? Serving? Do they achieve the desired results? Do they change with grace? Manage conflict? If so, Jim O'Toole, managing director of Booz•Allen & Hamilton's leadership center, says that then the company has a strong leader of leaders."

## COMMUNICATIONS

Great ideas, high purpose, and discipline don't build a group of disciples or create results, unless there is clear and relentless communication. In our consulting business, time and time again we see many companies in which the top management feels that it has a unified purpose, a vision, and a clear strategy, and yet many of the workers in the company are reluctant to come on board. They ask why aren't people listening, why don't they understand, why don't they follow our guidance?

The answer is that very few companies have disciplined and consistent communications programs. The first element of communications is a communications strategy. This boils down to: what is the message and content you want to get out, what priorities are you planning to set, what is the target audience, what are the channels, frequency, and delivery methods? Communications strategy must be supplemented by processes both internally and externally that get the message out consistently. Most companies spend more time on external communications than they do on making sure that the messages are clear inside the firm.

The very best communications programs are rigorous and consistent. They involve regular face-to-face and written communications starting at the highest level and working their way through the organization in a rapid and disciplined manner. And the messages are part of orientation programs, training curricula, and senior management needs.

At Intel, the company's results and important messages are transmitted by electronic means on a quarterly basis. Results are explained, reasons for performance are identified, and other highlights are reported. Andy Grove and his management team also make it a point to attend every major training session. As another means to get the message out in a more personal approach, videos are distributed widely throughout the company.

In his early days at SAS, Jan Carlzon spent most of his time in meetings communicating live messages. He talked about moments of truth, symbolic acts, and other aspects of leadership communications.

## LEADERS COME IN MANY FLAVORS

Ultimately, no one leadership style works for every company or leader. We have seen great leaders who are eloquent and others who are not. We have seen leaders who are tough and others who are softer. We have seen leaders who are ruthless with performance numbers and others who lead by vision.

We have developed some key leadership tenets. They are as follows: leadership is not just the CEO's responsibility, it must exist at every level; leadership is a requirement to institutionalize behavioral change; leadership cannot be separated from vision and architecture; strategic leadership goes beyond attributes to activities that are determined appropriate to the organization's situation; similarly, leadership is separate from style; successful managers create leaders instead of replicating their style; the role of senior leaders is to create leaders throughout the organization; the role of junior leaders is the actual implementation of change; the best way to build leadership is to create the conditions under which others are empowered to lead; and leadership is defined by actions—what leaders do, *not* who they are.

As shown in Exhibit 2, leaders create disciples who achieve continual renewal. They foster an environment to achieve changes, they lead rather than manage, and leadership cascades throughout the organization.

At the very foundation of leadership, however, is purpose, what the company stands for, what its vision is, what identity and values it wishes to impart to its employees and other stakeholders.

## EXHIBIT 2: WHAT LEADERS DO

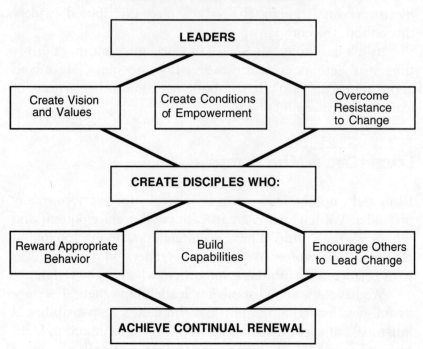

There is little doubt that value-oriented leadership is a must in flat organizations characterized by transparency and the easy availability of information. As Steve Jobs, the co-founder of Apple Computer, put it, "The only thing that works is management by values. Find people who are competent and really bright, but more importantly, people who care exactly about the same things you care about."

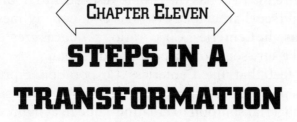

# Chapter Eleven

# STEPS IN A TRANSFORMATION

**NOW** that we have examined the various elements of the Centerless Corporation, it is worth considering the whole and how it ticks. In short, it has us cast aside standard theories of business organization, asks us to renounce the familiar and replace it with a thoroughly fresh view of business behavior. There is a parsimonious elegance to its principles. It moves the corporation away from needless complexities to a sublime simplicity by sensibly focusing on the levers of value creation and eliminating activities that fail to generate value. This exquisite simplicity equips the corporation to function in a more turbulent and baffling environment by endowing it with nimbleness and flexibility.

If you step back and consider this new business model as one might a new car model, you should see flatter and more nonlinear structures (hierarchy is too slow). You should see a Global Core focused on its five key missions, much smaller and less elaborate than its historical predecessor, but adding appreciably more value. It doesn't rest in Nashville or Chicago but is distributed geographically. You should see Business Units creating system value with rare gumption, by sharing knowledge and ideas, with a greater sense of purpose in creating value regardless of organizational lines. You should see people programs that ensure the firm has the people resources to flourish. And you should see sharper focus. No matter how many lines of business it has, the Centerless Corporation produces greater coherence and a sure sense of purpose and direction.

We feel that the Centerless Corporation represents a major step in the evolution of big business. It is the structural and managerial solution to creating value in a highly complex environment by dealing with the system-level issues of complexity. It is the vehicle to halt the unfortunate downsizing and minimization of the corporation that we see as companies strip down their businesses to cope with the escalating confusion of the environment. In our view, creating the Centerless Corporation is a necessary step to reach the next plateau of size for a business.

As we hope we have conveyed, leading a $500 billion or a $1 trillion enterprise requires a new set of principles if one is to navigate the twenty-first century. And as more and more companies adopt these principles, even smaller firms will have to adjust to meet competitive pressures.

## CHECK YOUR IMPERATIVES

Evolution often happens in bursts. The same is true for the nature of businesses. Thus the speed of the changes required to get from here to the Centerless Corporation is rapid. Many of the changes can be designed and implemented in a year or less. Others, like those more dependent on behavioral adaptation, require a longer time for effective results, and they demand constant attention to guarantee that people are responding.

To actually put in place the elements of the Centerless Corporation requires two broad steps. The first is to decide what are the right set of characteristics, the desired group of attributes and behaviors consistent with where the firm is headed. Some of the elements may have to be put in just to answer the question of where to direct the business. The second key step is to come up with a way to make the changes. For many firms, some of these changes constitute significant transformations from where they are today.

To gauge how much a company must change to adopt the principles of the Centerless Corporation, we have developed a "Business Imperative Checklist" (Exhibit 1). This quick checklist is based on the traits we believe are essential for any corporation to be successful. See how many you satisfy. If you find yourself marking few, if any, checks as you run down the list, then you better get moving. We should stress that this is a generic list and that each firm will also have its own company-specific issues to weigh. A corporation should make sure that it has chosen the right model, the right form of the Centerless Corporation, to meet these minimum criteria.

---

**EXHIBIT 1: Business Imperative Checklist**

- Generating and exploiting sufficient value-creating opportunities

- Developing strong awareness of emerging market trends coupled with a clear customer focus

- Establishing a continuous transformation process

- Tailoring a geographic reach (global, multinational, regional, local) to match evolving business

- Developing and transferring knowledge across the firm

- Improving quality and cost-effectiveness

- Providing an environment to attract and retain the best people

- Developing leaders

- Encouraging prudent risk-taking and managing risks actively

- Working seamlessly across the organization to maximize shareholder value

With each of the items on this checklist, one needs to ask certain diagnostic questions. Here are a few worthwhile ones in each area of concern:

- Generating and exploiting sufficient opportunities: Is our rate of new product introduction increasing? Are we entering new markets successfully? Do we have enough growth potential in our investment pipeline?
- Developing awareness of market trends and customer focus: Are we considered a leader in our markets?
- Establishing continuous transformation: When was the last time we tried to do things differently? Does every change we make seem to be a crisis?
- Tailoring geographic reach: Has our business model changed to reflect any geographic expansion?
- Developing and transferring knowledge: Do we seem to be "reinventing the wheel" a lot? Does each part of the organization know what the other parts are doing?
- Improving quality and cost-effectiveness: Are our defect rates and unit production costs falling? Are our customer satisfaction numbers improving?
- Attracting and retaining the best people: Is employee turnover falling? Are we able to hire the candidates we most want?
- Developing leaders: Are we able to identify many qualified replacements for executives? Are our key leaders in demand by other companies?
- Encouraging risk-taking and managing risks: How many innovative ideas do our employees develop and bring to the table each year?
- Working seamlessly to maximize shareholder value: Is our shareholders' return higher than that of the market as a whole? Do we spend enough time creating cross-business advantages and little time on "turf" issues?

To arrive at the company-specific list of business imperatives, we have developed a technique called "divergent/convergent scenario" (see Exhibit 2). In this approach, both the

**EXHIBIT 2: DIVERGENT/CONVERGENT ANALYSIS**

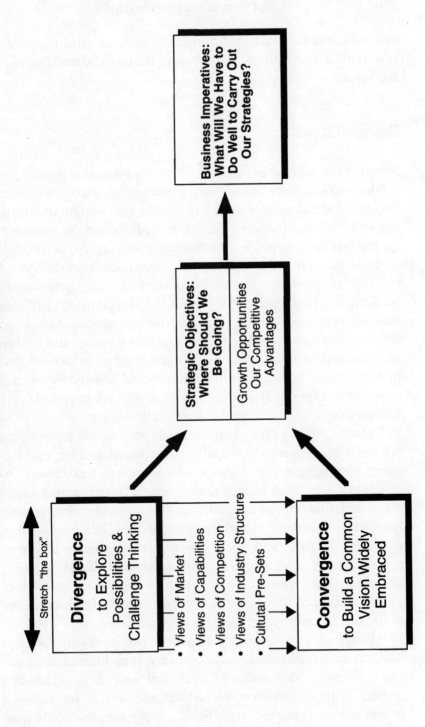

external and internal environments and conditions are assessed vis-à-vis what the corporation needs to be successful in the future.

## BRINGING CHANGE

Now for the second broad step. How do you actually shuck a model that you have been accustomed to and convert to something so radically different, all the while that you are continuing to conduct business? To begin with, a certain gestation period has to be expected, no matter how adaptive your organization is, for moving to a new business model very much represents a full-fledged transformation of the corporation. Nothing will be untouched by it. It is not all that much different than if one were to gather up the members of a large family, amply endowed with siblings and cousins and grandparents, and announce that everyone was going to be deployed in a new role. This pronouncement would ultimately impact every type of family dynamic, from how to curry parental favor to how to secure a raise in the weekly allowance.

Managing any type of change is a formidable undertaking not for the squeamish and easily discouraged, but large, infrequent changes are particularly treacherous to lead. Every individual needs to be taught a new way of thinking and a new set of activities (this is a significant step beyond reengineering business processes). Teaching people new behaviors takes considerable time and effort. Indeed, programs resulting in significant behavioral change that is fully embedded in the organization can consume many years—depending on factors like the extent of the crisis the company faces, the dimensions of the organization, and the previous culture.

For change to take hold, pressure must be continually applied to each individual—with constant repetition of the message, sanctions for noncompliance, and rewards for achieving results. Without question, some staff will need to be removed from their current responsibilities, simply because some people cannot (or will not) change their thought processes and

behavior. Some are unwilling to adapt to a new set of values
and behavioral norms. Left in place, these dissenters will have
an adverse influence on peers and subordinates, and they
must be removed to minimize their negative impact on the
change program.

Many companies fail to bring about significant changes in
behavior, which may be worse than doing nothing. Most change
programs do not achieve their full objectives, and failed change
programs can be very damaging. They result in employees
learning to ignore management. Time and resources spent on
failed implementation are wasted. Costs creep back up after restructuring. And there is a failure to take advantage of an opportunity or avoid danger to the organization.

As we argued in the first chapter, the standard business
model is dead. Successful firms will be the ones that can
evolve to the new business model. For most companies, this
requires a big change, and a big change needs a well-thought-
out transformation program.

The transformation to the Centerless Corporation can
proceed in parts. Creating the Global Core and Services unit
often go together. Downsizing the corporate center is a common occurrence in the corporate world. While that satisfies
part of the equation, it is putting in place the capabilities for
the five key missions of the Global Core that will enhance the
corporation's ability to grow.

A Global Core is necessary to make the new generation
Business Unit work. The Core will provide the corporation
with the ability to manage a more networked enterprise, thus
freeing the businesses to do more networking to gain access to
customers, capabilities, and geographies.

The new governance model can go in independently. The
challenge is to accelerate a very slow change process which is
too often tied to attrition.

While these structural and role changes are being put in
place, a superstructure of the three key enablers—People,
Knowledge, and Coherence—has to be developed. These three
enablers should span the entire corporation. Remember, they
will be the glue and the levers for performance.

## THE MEANS OF TRANSFORMATION

Although we cannot find a true Centerless Corporation—they are still evolving—we can find ample examples of large-scale transformations. We have studied many of the recent ones and have extracted lessons and best practices that are worth pondering as you try to move your own corporation to a centerless state. The process consists of four essential elements (as shown in Exhibit 3):

- Facilitate development of a shared vision
- Change the content of the work
- Build the processes to institutionalize the changes
- Help people adapt to the work

It is by integrating these four elements that one achieves true change.

### EXHIBIT 3: TRANSFORMATION PROCESS

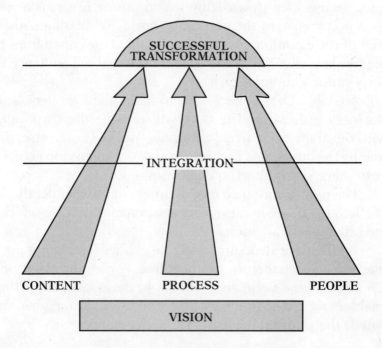

To illustrate the process, it is worth looking at some of the recent successful transformations (see Exhibit 4). Each of these firms faced a crucial turning point, and each identified a brash new course. In some cases, part of that new course required putting in place a significant piece of the Centerless Corporation. We use these to illustrate the change process, not the creation of the Centerless Corporation.

Now let us take you through the four elements of transformation.

FACILITATE DEVELOPMENT OF A SHARED VISION. In order for significant change to be accepted by the organization without great fuss and resistance, there ought to be a shared vision of why the change is necessary and what is the direction that the company is moving in. There are four discernible benefits to a shared vision:

- Creates a common agenda for the senior executives
- Creates a common language and set of objectives for the organization
- Unifies and inspires the organization
- Embodies the core values of the organization

Building the shared vision involves four steps.

1. Make a clear case for change. This could involve such staples as a "burning platform," imminent gloom and doom, far greener pastures, or great wealth. Keep in mind, there is always a lot of inertia to change. The bigger the reason, the greater the movement.

   British Airways used a "burning platform"—namely, recent poor financial results and the dire prospect of privatization—to get the rapt attention of its senior managers. It then defined its vision of competing through service to become "the world's favourite airline." New types of desired behavior were also described—caring, openness, clarity, performance, and responsibility.

## Exhibit 4: Successful Transformation

| Company | Description | Leader | Imperative for Change |
|---|---|---|---|
| ABB | Engineering and construction concern | Percy Barnevik | • Capture value from merger of Asea and Brown Boveri |
| British Airways | Worldwide carrier | Colin Marshall Lord King | • Become profitable<br>• Prepare for privatization |
| British Petroleum | Oil, exploration, and chemical firm | David Simon John Browne | • Grow market value and increase speed of decision-making |
| General Electric | Diversified | Jack Welch | • Increase revenue and income ahead of GNP and increase market value |
| National Semiconductor | Manufactures semiconductors | Gil Amelio | • Turn around decline in revenue, income, and market value |
| Norwest | Banking | Richard Kovacevich | • Underperforming loans and unclear strategy |

*Source: BA&H Transformation database*

| Key Model Attributes | Results |
|---|---|
| • Three global businesses split into 40 global business areas<br>• Experts deployed to self-contained operating units<br>• Integrative mechanisms used to capture and transfer learning | • Market capitalization grew nearly 5-fold from 1987–95<br>• Respected worldwide as a "multidomestic" global company |
| • Customer information system<br>• Knowledge sharing | • Losses of £520 million from 1977–83 were turned into profits of £1,059 million from 1984–89<br>• Consistently one of the most profitable airlines in the world |
| • Business units consolidated and management layers reduced<br>• Global Core distributed to three regional "alter egos"<br>• Team-based decision-making begun at lower levels | • Market capitalization doubled from 1992–95<br>• Reduced bureaucracy and hierarchy |
| • Hierarchy dismantled<br>• Management process adopted to make company fast and flexible<br>• Training center teaches 10,000 managers a year | • Market capitalization grew by more than $100 billion from 1981–95<br>• Leading shares in nearly every market |
| • Decentralized into two groups<br>• Quarterly executive off-site forums begun<br>• Network of mechanisms created to coordinate the transformation<br>• Founded National Semiconductor University | • Market capitalization grew 4-fold from 1991–95<br>• Asset and staff utilization at industry norms |
| • More authority to the field<br>• New people strategies | • Strong growth in operating profit and return to shareholders<br>• Clear and focused strategy |

2. Build an executive team that will serve as the "disciples of change" and fully support the vision. Change cannot be done alone. The executive team must be ardent and enthusiastic supporters of change. Often resistance requires altering the composition of the team.

   In the wake of poor financial performance, National Semiconductor defined a tough objective—to increase shareholder value. To lead the way, the top thirty executives participated in a workshop to further refine the objective, and together they defined five critical business issues. They also clarified the nature of their relationship with employees, customers, shareholders, and the community. They then spread the message to the rest of the corporation. British Airways went so far as to categorize the "conversion" of managers into four classifications that summed up their adoption of the new values: "apostles," "Peters," "Thomases," and "pork barrelers." They used high potentials to help articulate their personal view of the vision.

3. Provide a compelling description of the future of the company. Go beyond the need for change and establish a sense of the final destination. What will the company be like and what will it stand for when it gets there?

   ABB described a future as a "multidomestic" company—in other words, a company with many home countries. Local managers are hired to inject a strong local flavor, but they are rotated through international assignments and trained in the ABB philosophy. The overriding objective in all markets is to decentralize and streamline to compete on costs. British Airways' vision was to be "the world's favourite airline," while Motorola focused on a tenfold increase in quality.

4. Set objectives and targets that are a stretch, but attainable. The end-game must go beyond the verbal description. It must include how well the company should perform, and it must establish how much more shareholder value gets created and how fast the firm will grow. These targets have to be both tangible and measurable.

Motorola's "Six Sigma" quality program was so radical that it forced managers to think about the businesses differently. As a result, they smashed the old inspection paradigm.

Achieving a shared vision is not an easy undertaking and involves several common pitfalls, as illustrated in Exhibit 5 below.

CHANGE THE CONTENT OF THE WORK. You must make the change real. To accomplish this, it is necessary to incorporate the change in the fabric of how people contribute to the new vision. This has six advantages:

- Recruits the middle managers and front-line employees into the change program
- Aligns the business processes with the corporate vision, objectives, and targets
- Builds an organization structure that supports the business processes
- Defines the activities and the performance expectations for all staff
- Highlights for all how their activities directly support the corporate vision
- Provides feedback on performance versus targets for front-line employees and management

Again we can break the process down into four steps:

1. *Recruit middle managers as champions of change.*
   It is important to broaden the support for change, and this is often best accomplished by making people part of the process. British Petroleum brought huge change to its organizational structure, simplifying the reporting relationships and transforming the 11 x 70 matrix into a 4 x 3 one, in other words four business streams and three regions. The multitude of committees at the head office was slashed, and responsibility

# EXHIBIT 5: REQUIREMENTS FOR FACILITATING THE DEVELOPMENT OF A SHARED VISION

| Requirements | Common Pitfalls |
|---|---|
| 1. Make a clear case for change | • The benefits that the organization could capture are not rigorously defined or explained<br>— How bad the results could be if action is not taken to resolve the "burning platform"<br>— How great the company could be if the path is not followed to "greener pastures"<br>• Senior management underestimates the resistance of middle managers in "Job for Life" cultures. These middle managers have rarely made changes to survive and therefore are strongly attached to the status quo |
| 2. Build an executive team to serve as "disciples of change" and fully support the vision | • The senior executives were not involved in developing the vision, therefore they do not have ownership for the vision and the change program<br>• Failing to quickly replace senior executives that ignore or even undermine the change program and the vision |
| 3. Provide a compelling description of the future of the company | • The vision does not contain a simple articulation of<br>— The businesses and geographies that the organization will be operating in<br>— The capabilities that the organization will use and develop<br>— The financial results that are desired (and expected)<br>— The organizational behaviors that will achieve these objectives<br>• The vision is not clear, simple, and easy to communicate |
| 4. Set objectives and targets that are a stretch—but attainable | • Without objectives and targets it is unclear whether success has been achieved<br>• If targets are not a stretch then the organization does not see the need to significantly change their behavior and the way that they work<br>• Stretch targets are viewed as unattainable because they are not based on the realities of the organization's current capabilities and market position |

was pushed down to the lowest level possible in the organization. Employees were empowered to make decisions on the front line.

2. *Link operational, behavioral, and financial targets to the corporate vision.*

   Siemens-Nixdorf developed a set of scorecards of drivers to financial performance. These were cascaded down into each business unit.

3. *Launch initiatives to redesign the business processes and the organizational structure to help the company meet objectives and targets.*

   Here we cite Hewlett-Packard. Thirty-eight separate committees were dissolved by management, and employees were required to work in small teams. From the very beginning of each project, cross-functional teams are now involved. Plans are no longer shuffled from one department to the next. This new way of working not only decreases product development times, but unleashes the potential for learning, as employees throughout the organization transfer skills and knowledge rapidly between departments and management layers.

4. *Embed performance measurement systems into the organization. It is important to hard-wire the changes and have a way to test what has been achieved.*

   Motorola is a good illustration here. Every department in the company, from production to sales, coalesced around a single quality metric: defects per unit of work. This was chosen because it most closely defined customer satisfaction, and therefore was also the main driver of financial success. The metric also provided a common language for people from all parts of the company to communicate and transfer learning.

HELP PEOPLE ADAPT TO THE CHANGES. It is important to remember that any organizational change is really a change in the behavior of people. Many change programs fail because people don't change other behavior. Why? There are a number of reasons: they do not understand what they are being asked to do; they perceive the change as being inconsistent with the culture; they don't see their bosses supporting it; they have too many change initiatives on their plates; there is a track record of failure in change programs; or they feel a lack of accountability or control for implementation. Focusing on the people aspect has distinct advantages:

- Prepares the organization for change and keeps everyone informed of progress by providing information and answering questions
- Lowers the risk of panic in the organization by limiting the volume of incorrect information spread through the grapevine
- Gives senior executives, middle managers, and frontline staff the support and confidence they need to make the necessary changes in characteristics and activities
- Creates support for the change program by introducing incentives for supporters and sanctions for resisters

The four steps:
1. *Build a two-way communication channel with the organization.*

   The CEO of Siemens-Nixdorf developed and structured a "cascade of communications." He recruited the company's top thirty thought leaders to help define the communication messages. Then he implemented one- and two-day forums with 300 opinion leaders from all levels of the organization to spread the messages. Having seeded the company with these disciples, he also communicated directly with nearly 10,000 employees to explain his vision for the company.
2. *Train the organization in new concepts, ideas, and tools necessary for new activities and behaviors.*

   Jack Welch tutored GE in how the work of employees must change by identifying the "3 S's": speed, simplicity, and self-confidence. He said the key to achieving his vision would be Speed. To develop speed, employees at all levels in the company would have to Simplify complicated processes. And to simplify what had traditionally been very complicated and time-consuming processes, employees would have to develop Self-confidence. Perhaps nothing earth-shattering there, but a very effective means to buoy employees to direct themselves to adapt to something new.

3. *Provide time and resources to make the changes.*

Here, full-fledged in-house colleges and sophisticated training programs are the way to go. At Motorola, for instance, Motorola University has taken on a primary role by providing a forum for senior managers to debate and identify new strategies and emerging issues. Its Senior Executive Program has developed from a platform for the CEO to introduce important issues to a forum in which managers on their own regularly identify and begin important new change initiatives.

4. *Offer incentives for successful changes and sanctions for failure, and adapt and align human resource systems to support all changes.*

British Airways introduced a bonus system for middle managers and front-line staff that explicitly reflected the new behaviors that were desired. Under the plan, 60 percent of the bonus was for attaining targets, and 40 percent was for displaying the hoped-for behavior.

Ultimately, there is no such thing as organizational change; there is only individual change. Change is driven by leadership which ushers desired behaviors throughout the company. Thus, it requires building leadership skills at all levels of the organization and providing change management tools.

BUILD THE PROCESSES TO INSTITUTIONALIZE THE CHANGES. Making changes a reality means institutionalizing them, so that they become a familiar part of day-to-day existence. We find that working the process for change as a distinct activity will yield significant benefits:

- Provides a description of what the organization is doing to achieve the shared vision
- Creates rigorous decision-making standards that require all projects to link to and support strategic objectives
- Identifies the key tasks, milestones, timing, and responsibilities for each initiative
- Arms senior management with a tracking tool to monitor progress against corporate plans and initiatives
- Allows senior management to make timely interventions to remove blockages and manage risks

The four steps:

1. *Make the plans to coordinate the change.*

    National Semiconductor created an interrelated group of councils for feedback and coordination of the change effort. The linkages were from top to bottom and across the whole organization. Ultimate responsibility for the coordination of plans rested with a council at the corporate level. Employees were regularly surveyed to provide an additional feedback loop and to adjust initiatives in midcourse.

2. *Track progress against your plans, and address any potential blockages or risks.*

    To track progress toward becoming "world class," Motorola undertook an extensive worldwide benchmarking study. Much to its surprise, management discovered that its milestones and targets were far behind where they needed to be. The goals were adjusted to reach "Six Sigma" within six years by meeting ever-tougher standards each two years.

3. *Maintain consistent message from senior management.*

General Electric introduced "Work-out" to resolve blockages quickly as they arose during the huge changes at the company. New England-style town meetings are used throughout the organization to allow managers and workers to interact directly, and managers have to give immediate answers to every question. Everyone is invited, from senior executives to middle managers, front-line employees, customers, and suppliers.

4. *Celebrate progress toward vision.*

Norwest's philosophy is that if someone is doing a great job, tell him. The company has numerous employee recognition programs in all of its departments to celebrate progress against "profit models."

These change programs were designed to address very-company-specific issues. Yet several of the programs moved toward the principles of the Centerless Corporation. For example, ABB reduced its corporate center to a bare minimum. British Petroleum distributed part of its Global Core to three regions. British Airways built strong linkages with CARESS, which shared customer information throughout the company and facilitated decision-making. Hewlett-Packard flattened the organization and took advantage of more cross-functional teams. Norwest put a renewed focus on its people.

ABB's change program, which initially sprang from the merger of Asea and Brown Boveri, is illustrated in Exhibit 6, and it involves a well thought-out philosophy and set of activities.

## Into the Future

The assumptions necessary to achieve real change are a vision, an architecture (business model) consistent with achieving the vision, and great leaders who set the tone and energize their followers.

**EXHIBIT 6: ABB's CHANGE PROGRAM**

| Setting | Constraints | Barnevik's Philosophy | Leader Activities |
|---|---|---|---|
| • Merger of Asea and Brown Boveri (with Westinghouse and Vasa) | • Different cultures<br>• Component companies were not all industry leaders<br>• Owners looking for short-term savings and long-term industry leadership<br>• Managerial resistance<br>• Need to keep the old profitable while building the new | • "Baking the cake" rather than "mixing a salad"<br>• Strategic leadership, not change management<br>• Opportunity for greatness<br>• Cascading leadership ("Virtual Percys")<br>• Goal is self-renewing organization | • Assemble team<br>• Create vision/strategy<br>• Outline structure<br>• Establish metrics<br>• Initiative process<br>• Communicate<br>• Educate/mentor top management<br>• Train down the line<br>• Form implementation teams<br>• Push leadership down<br>• Reward appropriate behavior |

It is essential that leading corporations manage these three elements of vision, architecture, and leadership coherently and completely (see Exhibit 7). Two out of three won't do. For example, a strong vision and architecture without a good leadership model does not bring change and performance to all levels. If the company is missing the vision and strategy but has the architecture and leadership in place, there is no focus and the company stumbles from one initiative to another without a clear direction. A company with a good vision and leadership model but an incoherent business model or architecture has no process for implementation. And, clearly, if you have only one of these three elements you're looking at either academic exercises, bureaucracy, or empty charisma.

By looking at any large-scale change programs, we see how much effort and how much time they take. We would be

## EXHIBIT 7: FRAMEWORK FOR ACHIEVING BUSINESS PERFORMANCE IMPROVEMENTS

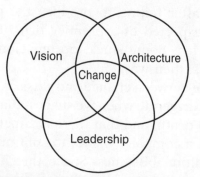

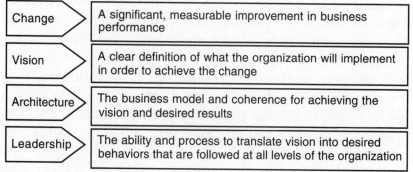

| Change | A significant, measurable improvement in business performance |
| Vision | A clear definition of what the organization will implement in order to achieve the change |
| Architecture | The business model and coherence for achieving the vision and desired results |
| Leadership | The ability and process to translate vision into desired behaviors that are followed at all levels of the organization |

foolish not to acknowledge that it will take a good deal of time and concerted effort to shift a large corporation from the musty and antiquated model that has been its home for so long. It will not be easy or entirely painless. There will be some hard-edged resistance. No one likes to leave the familiar, even if the aging porch is sagging and the ceiling has begun to sprout leaks.

Throughout this book we have given evidence of companies that have implemented portions of the Centerless Corporation. Those that have adopted significant elements of the model have achieved superior performance along those particular dimensions. They have risen to their challenges with more gusto. There is a zip to them. They have achieved speed despite great size. And they have catapulted into leadership positions, both within their industry and in the global business community.

It is our view that change toward this model is inevitable. Companies that do not evolve are doomed. The list of former Fortune 100 companies is replete with the once mighty that melted away after failing to produce the growth in shareholder value expected of a premier firm. Their faults were many and varied. Some stuck too tenaciously to the status quo. Others lost their way.

The choice between change and stasis is a crucial one. We don't feel we exaggerate when we suggest that it is a choice between life and death, and that there is a meter-is-running nature to this. If a company wishes to continue to create value and to win additional Business Space, then it is not a matter of whether to change, but of how fast and how often to do so. And companies that develop the capability to change are able to accomplish it on a less disruptive basis, not while fighting for their lives.

By traveling through the maze of a well-crafted transformation plan, we allow that it will be far less treacherous adopting the Centerless Corporation than one might imagine. The signal benefits, we are confident, will come swiftly and more than justify the effort.

Be mindful of the alternative. The evidence is all around

us that the current business model does not work anymore, and it hasn't a prayer of withstanding the brutal and unrelenting forces of change and unfettered competition that the future holds. With the new model we propose, we feel corporations will again have the ability to solve their real problems and realize their full potential. We should accept nothing less.

# NOTE ON SOURCES

**WE** relied extensively on Booz•Allen & Hamilton Intellectual Capital. That is the distilled and codified learnings from our various consulting engagements, interviews, surveys, and programs. These constitute the body of knowledge we try to grow and bring to our consulting work. In the development of this intellectual capital, we conducted over 100 interviews with top management of companies throughout the world. The key reports we used included: a summary of interviews from the New CEO Program; Final Report from the Global Core Task Force; papers from the Knowledge Symposium; CEO Agenda interview summaries; New People Partnership human resource interview summaries; Corporate Governance Best Practices; Shared Services Best Practices; and various cases from Booz•Allen & Hamilton's Strategic Leadership Center.

Most of the quantitative data cited were obtained from published sources such as the business press (*Wall Street Journal, Fortune,* etc.), company press releases, annual reports, and various Web sites.

# SELECTED REFERENCES

"A Merger Not to Be Ignored." *Petroleum Economist*. vol. 63, no. 4, April 1996.

"Broken Hill Proprietary: The Big Australian and the Tigers." *Economist*. vol. 366, no. 7922, July 8, 1995.

"Canadian Fireplace Co. Becomes North American Leader With Second Strategic Acquisition." *Business Wire*. March 7, 1996.

"CFM Majestic Inc. Announces Completion of the Acquisition of Vermont Castings." *Business Wire*. May 12, 1996.

"CKOs Are 'What People'—CIOs Who Want to Be Considered for Chief Knowledge Officer Positions Need to Combine Technical & Strategic Know-how." *PC Week*. August 5, 1996.

"Corporate Boards and Corporate Governance." *Conference Board Report*. No. 1036.

"Dismantling Daimler Benz." *The Economist*. November 18, 1995.

"Disney's Growing Empire: How the Entertainment Giants Measure Up." *The Wall Street Journal*. August 1, 1995.

"Enron Corporation Reports 15 Percent Increase in 1995 Earnings per Share, to $2.07 per Share; Expects to Achieve Doubling of Net Income, Exceeding $1 Billion, in Year 2000." *Business Wire*. January 24, 1996.

"Growth Factors." *Chief Executive (US)*. no. 105, July 17, 1995.

"Hewlett-Packard Wins $36M Contract to Supply Automotive Diagnostic Systems to Ford Motors." *Electronic Times*. March 1991.

"HR Executive Review: Competing as an Employer of Choice." *The Conference Board*. vol. 3, no. 4, 1996.

"Intel to Exit Dynamic RAM Chip Mart." *Computerworld*. October 14, 1985.

"International People: On the Move: Goeran Lindahl." *Financial Times*. International Edition, October 22, 1996.

"Intranet Impact: Post and Conquer: Lure of New Markets Beckons, Is Using Intranets to Generate New Business." *Communications Week*. July 29, 1996.

"Investors Flock to Monsanto." *Chemical Week*. March 27, 1996.

"Leadership in the 21st Century Enterprise." *SEI Center for Advanced Studies in Management.* The Wharton School. Philadelphia, PA: University of Pennsylvania, November 1994.

"Managing Risk: Spreadsheets v. The Black Box." *Institutional Investor.* vol. 28, no. 8, Aug 1994.

"Medicine, Management, and Mergers: an Interview with Merck's P. Roy Vagelos." *Harvard Business Review.* Nov/Dec 1994.

"Membership and Organization of Corporate Boards." *Conference Board Report.* no. 940.

"More Gas Reserves Will Be Focus of Sun E&P Company." *Oil & Gas Journal.* December 5, 1988.

"Motorola: Training for the Millennium." *Business Week.* March 28, 1994.

"Netscape Fosters Innovation and Streamlines Processes at Olivetti Research and Design Laboratories." Netscape Communications Corp. *PR Newswire.*

"Netscape Unveils Full-Service Intranet Plans. (Excerpt, Netscape white paper on company intranet strategy)." *Computer Reseller News.* no. 708, November 4, 1996.

"Penske to Acquire K-Mart Auto Service." *Discount Store News.* October 16, 1995.

"Rhone-Poulenc Reengineering Focuses on Work Process, Not Downsizing." *Chemical & Engineering News.* vol. 73, no. 22, May 29, 1995.

"Sears Shareholders Approve Allstate Spin-off." *Chicago Sun Times.* April 1, 1995.

"Step Technology Taps Industry Veterans to Form New Media Business Unit." *Business Wire.* September 1996.

"Sun Exits US Upstream in Restructuring Move." *Oil & Gas Journal.* July 18, 1988.

"The Best and Worst Boards." *Business Week.* November 25, 1996.

"The Corporate Board: A Growing Role in Strategic Assessment." *Conference Board Report.* No. 1152-96-RR, 1996.

"The Learning Organization." Anonymous. *Chief Executive.* no. 1, March 1995.

"The Very Model of Efficiency: Asea Leaves Mark on IBM Overhaul." *New York Times.* March 2, 1992.

"The Wirthlin Report: Current Trends in Public Opinion." *Wirthlin Worldwide.* vol. 6, no. 1, January 1996.

"Time Warner Entertainment and Hewlett-Packard Co. to Develop Interactive Printing for Full Service Networks." *Business Wire.* November 1993.

"U.S. First to Use New Global Manufacturing Technology." *Industrial Engineering.* vol. 25, no. 12, Dec 1993.

"Unisys to Break Up Operations Into Three Businesses." *Financial Times.* October 7, 1995.

"Using Derivatives: What Senior Managers Must Know." *Harvard Business Review.* Jan/Feb 1995.

"What the New SEC Rules Do for Activism." *Institutional Investor.* April 1993.

"Where Employee Ownership Is Taking Us." *Destinations.* United Airlines, 1994.

"Why General Electric and Asia Are Good for Each Other; Power in Asia." *Financial Times Business Information Ltd.* Sep 27, 1993.

Aeppel, Timothy. "Whether Jordan Has Saved the Industrial Business Remains Undetermined." *The Wall Street Journal.* November 13, 1996.

Bartlett, Christopher A., and Sumantra Ghosal. "Changing the Role of Top Management." *Harvard Business Review.* May/June 1995.

Barton, Crockett. "Banc One Aims to Cut Costs Largely Without Layoffs." *American Banker.* vol. 159, no. 89, May 10, 1994.

Belsky, Gary. "Why Dean Witter Will Expand by Buyouts." *Crains New York Business.* vol. 4, no. 47, November 12, 1988.

Benson, Tracy E. "Paul O'Neill: True Innovation, True Values, True Leadership." *Industry Week.* vol. 242, no. 8, April 19, 1993.

Black, B. S. "The Value of Institutional Monitoring: The Empirical Evidence." *UCLA Law Review.* vol. 39, no. 4, April 1992.

Bray, John, Kathleen Brooke, and George Litwin. *Mobilizing the Organization.* Englewood Cliffs, NJ: Prentice Hall, 1996.

Brecka, Jon, and Laura Rubach. "Corporate Quality Training Facilities." *Quality Progress.* vol. 28, no. 1, January 1995.

Browder, Seanna, Alice Cuneo, Ann Therese Palmer, and Catherine Yang. "Low Wage Lessons." *Business Week.* November 11, 1996.

Carnicelli, Jeff. "Mobil Center Achieves Best Practice in Shared Service." *Corporate Finance.* no. 140, July 1996.

Chakravarty, Subrata, N. "Back in Focus." *Forbes.* June 6, 1994.

Chandler, Alfred D., Jr. *Strategy and Structure: Chapters in the History of the American Industrial Enterprise."* The MIT Press. Cambridge, MA, November 1978.

Chandler, Jr., Alfred D., Thomas K. McCraw, and Richard S. Tedlow. *Management Past and Present.* Cincinnati: South-Western College Publishing, 1996.

Collins, James C., and Jerry I. Porras. *Built to Last.* 1st ed. (paperback). New York: HarperCollins Publishers, 1997.

*Communications Industry Forecast,* Interactive Digital Media. Veronis, Suhler & Associates. August 1996.

Culbertson, Katherine, and MacSearraigh, Stephen. "Shell Give In, Scraps Plan to Dump Brent Spar Offshore." *Oil Daily.* vol. 45, no. 118, June 21, 1995.

Elliot, Mick. "Going Global (Electronics Distribution)." *Electronics Weekly.* no. 1685, Jun 15, 1994.

Fritsch, Peter. "Enron's President, Kinder, Will Leave at End of the Year." *The Wall Street Journal.* November 27, 1996.

Galambos, Louis, and Joseph Pratt. *The Rise of the Corporate Commonwealth: United States Business and Public Policy in the 20th Century.* New York: HarperCollins, 1988.

Galvin, Robert W. "Knowledge Makes the Difference at Motorola." *Strategy & Leadership.* vol. 24, no. 2, March/April 1996.

Gill, Mark Stuart. "Stalking Sig Sigma." *Business Month.* vol. 135, no. 1, Jan 1990.

Grant, Linda. "A School for Success: Motorola's Ambitious Job-Training Program Generates Smart Profits." *US News & World Report.* vol. 118, no. 20, May 22, 1995.

Grove, Andrew S. *Only the Paranoid Survive,* 1st ed. New York: Bantam Doubleday Dell Publishing, Inc., 1996.

Hemphill, Thomas A. "Penalties for Polluters: Finding a Fair Formula." *Business and Society Review.* no. 87, fall 1993.

Henkoff, Ronald. "Companies That Train Best." *Fortune.* vol. 127, no. 6, March 22, 1993.

Henry, Brian. "Monsanto Confirms Plan to Float or Sell Chemicals." *Chemical Marketing Reporter.* vol. 250, no. 16, October 14, 1996.

Holland, Kelley, Linda Himelstein, and Zachary Schiller. "The Bankers." *Business Week.* October 16, 1995.

Johnson, Ken. "Rising From the Ashes." *Lawrence Eagle-Tribune* (North Andover, MA). December 8, 1996.

Kaplan, Daniel. "In the Year of the Big Deal Aggregate Value Tripled." *Mergerstat Review.* Merrill Lynch, 1992, 1993. SNL. *American Banker M&A Yearbook.*

Kerwin, Christine, ed. *1996 Directory of Corporate Affiliations—US Public Companies.* Reed Reference Publishing. vol. 3, 1996.

Knott, David. "Shell: The Target After Nigerian Executions." *Oil & Gas Journal.* vol. 93, no. 47, November 20, 1995.

Kolesar, Peter J. "Vision, Values, Milestones: Paul O'Neill Starts Total Quality at Alcoa." *California Management Review.* vol. 35, no. 3, spring 1993.

Kovacevich, Richard M. "Sharing the Vision, Living the Values." Norwest Corporation. October 1995.

Kumar, Nirmalya. "The Power of Trust in Manufacturer-Retailer

Relationships." *Harvard Business Review.* November/December 1996.

Kuprianov, Anatoli. "Derivatives Debacles." *Economic Quarterly.* Federal Reserve Bank of Richmond. vol. 81, fall 1995.

Lancaster, Hal. "Managing Your Career." *The Wall Street Journal.* November 15, 1994.

Leonard-Barton, Dorothy. "The Factory as a Learning Laboratory." *Sloan Management Review.* vol. 34, no. 1, 1992.

Lewent, Judy. "Palisade Corporation; Risk Analysis at Merck." *Harvard Business Review.* Jan/Feb 1994.

Lipin, Steven, and Dave Kansas. "SBC to Buy PacTel; Trading Is Delayed Nearly Three Hours." *The Wall Street Journal.* April 2, 1996.

Loeb, Marshall. "Getting Hired by Getting Wired." *Fortune.* vol. 132, no. 10, November 13, 1995.

Loeb, Marshall. "How to Grow a New Product Everyday." *Fortune.* vol. 130, no. 10, November 14, 1994.

Lorsch, Jay. *Harvard Business Review.* Jan-Feb 1995.

Louth, Nick. "Focus-Lucent Starts a New Life After IPO." Reuters Limited. *Reuters News Service.* April 1996.

Magill, Frank N., ed. *The Great Scientists.* Danbury, Connecticut: Grolier Educational Corp., 1989.

Maglitta, Joseph. "Smarten Up!" *Computerworld.* vol. 29, no. 23, June 5, 1995.

Marino, Kenneth E. "Developing Consensus on Firm Competencies and Capabilities." *Academy of Management Executive.* vol. 10, no. 3, Aug 1996.

Markels, Alex. "How One Hotel Manages Diversity." *The Wall Street Journal.* Nov 20, 1996.

Marks, Anita. "Sale of Woodstove Maker Warms PacifiCorp Portfolio." *Business Journal–Portland.* vol. 11, no. 28, September 9, 1994.

McWilliams, Brian S. "Have You Considered Insourcing?" *Across the Board.* November 1996.

Meister, Jeanne C. "Training Workers in the Three Cs." *Nation's Business.* vol. 82, no. 9, September 1994.

Meyer, Marc H., and James M. Utterback. "The Product Family and the Dynamics of Core Capability." *Sloan Management Review.* vol. 34, no. 3, spring 1993.

Miraglia, Joseph P. "An Evolutionary Approach to Revolutionary Change." *Human Resource Planning.* vol. 17, no. 2, 1994.

Moltzen, Edward F. "After Sale of Prodigy, Is Public Offering in the Offing?" *Computer Reseller News.* no. 686, June 3, 1996.

Monks, Robert A. G., and Minnow, Nell. "Corporate Governance." *Blackwell.* 1995.

Moody, John, ed. *Moody's Manual of Industrial and Miscellaneous Securities.* vol. 1. New York: The O. C. Lewis Company, 1900.

Morain, Dan. "Deregulation Bill Signed by Wilson." *Los Angeles Times.* September 24, 1996.

Morgan, Kenneth O., ed. *The Oxford History of Britain.* New York: Oxford University Press, 1993.

Motorola: "Training for the Millennium." *Business Week.* March 28, 1994.

Nonaka, Ikujiro, and Hirotaka Takeuchi. *The Knowledge Creating Company,* 1st ed. New York: Oxford University Press, Inc., 1995.

Oloroso, Arsenio Jr. "About That Spinoff, Vern." *Crains Chicago Business.* vol. 20, no. 3, Jan 20, 1997.

O'Reilly, Charles, and Jeffrey Pfeffer. "Southwest Airlines (A)." *Stanford University Graduate School of Business.* HR-1A.

Oslund, John J. "3M Co. Spinoff Is Given Name Imation Corp." *Star Tribune-Minneapolis.* Apr 17, 1996.

O'Toole, James. *Leading Change: Overcoming the Ideology of Comfort and the Tyranny of Custom.* San Francisco: Jossey-Bass, 1995.

Packard, David, *The HP Way.* New York: HarperCollins, 1995.

Rogers, C. Gregory, and Dr. Michael Beer. "Human Resources at Hewlett-Packard." *Harvard Business School.* no. N9-495-051, April 14, 1995.

Sheridan, John H. "Lew Platt: Creating a Culture for Innovation." *Industry Week.* vol. 243, no. 23, December 19, 1994.

Simmons, Robert, and Christopher Bartlett. "Asea Brown Boveri." *Harvard Business School.* May 19, 1992.

Sloan, Allan, et al. "Corporate Killers." *Newsweek.* February 26, 1996.

Spain, Patrick J., and James R. Talbot, eds. *Hoover's Handbook of American Business: Companies M-Z, vol. 2.* 1996.

Spindler, Konrad. *The Man in the Ice.* London: Weidenfeld and Nicolson.

Stewart, Thomas. "Welch Is Rewriting It—to Tap Employees' Brainpower." *Fortune.* vol. 124, no. 4, August 12, 1991.

Stewart, Thomas A. "Your Company's Most Valuable Asset: Intellectual Capital." *Fortune.* vol. 130, no. 7, Oct 3, 1994.

Stewart, Thomas A., Rosalind K. Berlin, Jacqueline M. Graves, et al. "THE KING IS DEAD. Booted Bosses, Ornery Owners, and Beefed-Up Boards Reflect a Historic Shift in Corporate Power. The Imperial CEO Has Had His Day—Long Live the Shareholders." *Fortune.* January 11, 1993.

Stuller, Jay. "Why Not 'Inplacement'?" *Training.* vol. 30, no. 6, June 1993.

Templin, Neal. "Strange Bedfellows: More and More Firms Enter

Joint Ventures with Big Competitors." *The Wall Street Journal.* November 1, 1995.

Tichy, Noel, and Sherman, Stratford. *Control Your Destiny or Someone Else Will.* New York: HarperCollins, 1994.

Ubois, Jeffrey. "Spinning the Corporate Web: Inexpensive and Easy to Build, Intranets Are Transforming the Way Companies Operate." *CFO: The Magazine for Senior Financial Executives.* vol. 12, no. 9, September 1996.

Van, Jon. "Training Enables Motorola to Cut Defects to 60 per Million, From 6,000." *Chicago Tribune.* November 5, 1991.

Vlahos, Kiriakos. "Taking the Risk Out of Uncertainty." *Financial Post.* Nov 9, 1996.

Walker, Tony. "Companies & Markets: ABB Lukewarm on China Infrastructure Projects." *Financial Times.* January 6, 1997.

Warner, Malcolm, ed. *International. Encyclopedia of Business and Management.* Cornwall, England: Routledge, 1996.

Waterman, Robert H., Judith A. Waterman, and Betsy A. Collard. "Toward a Career Resilient Workforce." *Harvard Business Review.* July-Aug 1994.

Weber, Joseph. "A Big Company That Works: J&J's Ralph Larsen Gives His Units a Lot of Latitude—And They Produce." *Business Week.* May 4, 1992.

Westervelt, Robert. "Olin: Change for the Better." *Chemical Week.* vol. 158, no. 5, February 7, 1996.

*World Almanac and Book of Facts.* 1995.

Yoffie, DB, M. Aoki, K. Debari. "World VCR Industry." *HBS Case Study.* January 5, 1987.

# INDEX

# ABOUT THE AUTHORS

**BRUCE** Pasternack and Albert Viscio are the founding partners of Booz•Allen & Hamilton's Strategic Leadership Practice, which focuses on serving top management of the world's corporations in areas of organization, leadership, transformation, and corporate renewal. They have over thirty years of combined experience with this prestigious global management and technology consulting firm and have published extensively in the areas of growth, globalization, people strategy, and leadership.